Peasant Life
in the Medieval West

D0871731

Peasant Life
in the Medieval West

Robert Fossier

Translated by Juliet Vale

Basil Blackwell

Copyright © Basil Blackwell Ltd., 1988
French edition © PUF, 1984

First published in English 1988

Basil Blackwell Ltd
108 Cowley Road, Oxford OX4 1JF, UK

Basil Blackwell Inc.
432 Park Avenue South, Suite 1503,
New York, NY 10016, USA

British Library Cataloguing in Publication Data

Fossier, Robert
   Peasant life in the medieval west.
   1. Western Europe. Peasants. Social
   conditions, ca 900–1400
   I. Title
   305.5'63

   ISBN 0–631–14363–7

Library of Congress Cataloguing in Publication Data

Fossier, Robert.
   [Paysans d'Occident, English]
   Peasant life in the medieval West / Robert Fossier; translated by
   Juliet Vale.
       p.   cm.
   Translation of: Paysans d'Occident.
   Bibliography: p.
   Includes index.
   ISBN 0–631–14363–7
   1. Peasantry – Europe – History.   2. Middle Ages.   3. Europe –
Social conditions – To 1942.   I. Title.
   HD1531.5.F6713 1988   305.5'63–dc19   88–5094
                                                CIP

Typeset in 11 on 13pt Plantin
by Opus, Oxford
Printed in Great Britain by
T. J. Press Ltd, Padstow, Cornwall

Contents

Translator's Note

For this English-language edition the bibliography has been revised and amended in consultation with the author; it does not aim to be comprehensive. A glossary of technical terms has been provided; many terms, however, are explained in the text. For advice on specific points I am indebted to David Mabberley, Nicholas Purcell and Malcolm Vale, but they are not responsible for any errors that remain.

Juliet Vale

Abbreviations

Ann.	Annales (Economies, Sociétés, Civilisations)
BEC	Bibliothèque de l'Ecole des Chartes
BPH	Bulletin philologique et historique (jusqu'à 1610) of the Comité des travaux historiques et scientifiques
Econ. H.R.	Economic History Review
Et. rurales	Etudes rurales
PP	Past and Present
RBPH	Revue belge de Philologie et d'Histoire
RH	Revue historique
RHDFE	Revue historique du droit français et étranger
RHES	Revue d'histoire économique et sociale
RSJB	Recueils de la Société Jean Bodin pour l'histoire comparative des institutions
Spec.	Speculum
TR	Tijdschrift voor Rechtsgeschiednis

Introduction

'Not another book on medieval peasants', many readers will groan! Their reaction is in many ways justified, and I must explain why I have written one. It is true that during the past 20 years at least much has been written on rural Europe in the Middle Ages; in the 20 years, that is, since Georges Duby wrote *Rural economy and country life in the Medieval West*, a synthesis that is still extremely valuable (Bibliography, p. 196). The Middle Ages were duly considered in the recenly published *Histoire de la France rurale* (Bibliography, p.198) and there have been any number of the regional monographs so popular in France, many covering long-neglected regions. Areas with abundant statistics naturally provide the foundation for the most illuminating studies: this high level of documentation is not found until just after the end of my period, but at least it provides a profile. What is more, since the principle of in-depth regional studies has proved successful in France, French historians have been able to contribute to the study of the countryside, especially in southern Europe, an area which Duby was forced to ignore because so little evidence was then available. Of course it is imperative that we should avoid academic chauvinism in any guise, for that would soon lead to the total collapse of the subject, but at a period when all the talk is of team research programmes and projects it is worth acknowledging the contribution of individual historical research in France. Moreover, every country has made its own distinctive mark on the subject: theory and reality of social hierarchy in Germany, the economy in Italy, the changing face of the countryside in Belgium, public and private institutions in Spain and changes in administration and human relationships in England, while even the theoretical observations of Soviet or Japanese historians on very familiar topics offer new insights and interpretations. Today we have a much better understanding of living conditions, the state of the land and of agricultural methods and the market economy. We should make use of all this information about the Christian West to extend, amplify and, where necessary, correct Duby's study of 1962. It is obvious that this is quite beyond the scope of this small book, whose aims are much more limited. I should merely like to weave the most important new strands into the web of what is already known in order to deepen our understanding of the issues involved. This is why the book lays such emphasis on material culture (the fabric of daily life), relationships within the family and between individuals, and even, perhaps rashly, the world of their imagination (realms where, just for once, feudal lords and the nobility do not predominate). Of course I realize that other issues are important too, but assarting, enclosure and serfdom are familiar topics and any reader who wants to know more about them can easily find books on these subjects. This conception of my subject lies behind the limits I have set and the scheme I have followed. First of all, I must explain the reasons for my choice.

The last 20 years have been very fruitful ones for historical research, but some areas have yielded more than others; almost all of them impinging on the anthropological approach which, as Jacques Le Goff has emphasized, has made an important contribution to our understanding of the Middle Ages. We now have a deeper understanding of vocabulary that was already familiar and can attempt to elicit the hidden meaning – an approach that has been successful in the study of many epics and courtly romances, employing the techniques of sociological enquiry and the comparative approach of the ethnologist: gesture, rite, symbol and taboo all emerge from anecdote and biography. There is material for the study of the peasantry here (although they were by no means a central concern for writer or audience) and evidence is also to be found in *exempla*, sermons and short lyrical or satirical pieces. Folklore, which was for so long ridiculously undervalued, has become a rich source for the historian. Archaeology is also an important new source for the medievalist, no longer the exclusive domain of the prehistoric specialist or the ancient historian in a field without written evidence: peat bogs, palaeobotany, underground water levels, plough marks, the reconstruction of field boundaries and, of course, the excavation of settlements have naturally shed light on peasant history. Today no-one could attempt a serious study of the agrarian economy, equipment, the environment or levels of wealth and sources of power, without referring to building structures, the extent of land under plough, glacial movements or fluctuations in the area of beech woods. These tangible realities finally cut through the formal structures in which legal historians had sought to envelop the realities of daily life. But there are many areas in which it is to be hoped that progress will be made in the future: great strides have been made in the analysis of bone remains which should eventually permit the construction of a theory as to the distribution of human types in medieval Europe, their dietary requirements or susceptibility to particular diseases; it is not a question of unfocused curiosity, which would provide no solutions at all. So our knowledge of the medieval period is continually improving: it can certainly not be described as a limited field of blinkered specialists unaware of the latest methods and unresponsive to them. The fabric of peasant life is a vital, tangible reality, still often surviving in part and accessible to anyone with the least interest in his own roots.

What is the best approach? One of our prime aims must be at least a relatively consistent treatment across the period and covering the whole geographical area. Marked regional variations and quite individually distinct cases are of course peculiarly typical of the Middle Ages, but there is a danger of becoming swamped in detail, even though specialized local historians will find such a general approach irritating. We must discuss the issues in the broadest terms to minimize the risk of inaccuracy. The years AD 400–900 which are sometimes called 'medieval' will be omitted from the discussion for a number of reasons – not least because in terms of the system of production, family structure, and even living conditions, they are not medieval – indeed, to my mind, they have more in common with classical than with medieval Europe. Moreover the sources for this period are poor, the subject of continuing debate and open to widely differing interpretations, with some historians valuing them highly and others casting grave doubts on their accuracy; great stress is also laid on local variations. It makes more sense to begin in about 900 or 950 at the start of what was clearly a new era. At the other end of our period, equally, it is prudent to end our study before the great changes of the late fourteenth and fifteenth centuries, although they are closely linked with the earlier period and indeed resulted from it. But the more work is done on this period – when the historian is suddenly overwhelmed with statistics where previously there were none – the clearer it becomes that the inquiry should be pushed much further forward right into the sixteenth century. I have left this two-fold task for other historians.

So we shall focus on the four centuries which witnessed the great economic and social changes of the Christian West. We should be quite mistaken, of course, to think of them as homogeneous in any way: we have only to contrast light soils with poor vegetation, a high degree of urbanization, familiarity with a written culture and a host of other typically Mediterranean characteristics with retentive alluvial soils, fertile woodlands, compactly grouped villages or the warfaring existence of Nordic society to find one level of contrasts, to say nothing of the differences revealed by archaeologists, osteologists or by those who have made a specialist study of diet, technological development or collective attitudes. But even these differences cannot obscure the great watersheds that characterize this stage of human development: firstly, the constantly fluctuating balance between cultivated land and wilderness (*saltus* and *ager*), between woodland and open countryside (*bosc* and *plain*), between unworked and tilled land – the ecological balance which was responsible for the supply of foodstuffs to all sectors of the population, for all processes affecting primary materials, like wood, textiles, metals, the harnessing of water-power and livestock to the productive process; followed then by the slow establishment of a system of production (scarcely perceptible but long-lasting for all that), which enabled the peasant to keep for himself the bare minimum required for his survival (or *necessitas*) and granting the individual or institution in authority such services and revenues as would enable him to maintain control and live on a grand scale, rewarding his followers and living in the noble style expected of him. This was also the time when the towns became less important, even in areas where their age and prestige is not open to doubt, or rather their dependence on the surrounding countryside and its inhabitants, indeed on the natural cycle itself, was greatly increased. Finally, there were tightly knit communities with their own structures, where men gathered together in the circle of home (*domus*) and household, with ties of blood, clientage and neighbourliness, shared interests, a collective responsibility and barely Christian religious practices. This equilibrium was naturally disturbed by the hermit in the forest or the Jewish pedlar, just as moral conformity was affected by the more or less important role played by special interests and taboos; but they had no fundamental impact.

It would be natural to envisage a concentration of modern research upon this 'classical age' above all. But, paradoxically, this has not been the case: sometimes historians obsessed by the quantitative approach and the construction of theoretical models have turned their attention to the foundations of modern statistics and examined prices and structures; sometimes they have placed the very few, over-familiar texts dating from before 900 in a new psychological or linguistic context. Between these two approaches – where even the archaeologists make a poor showing – there is a great lack of monographs and thematic studies, especially in France. It is therefore essential to clarify areas of ignorance and so I have decided to concentrate upon five approaches which are all in need of additional research.

First of all we shall look at the structure of peasant society and the units within which they lived. These lay at the root of both the production and the consumption of foodstuffs and we must establish whether they were compact or loosely structured groups, entirely inward-looking or open to external influences and whether there were opportunities for division of labour, specialization or wage payment. At this level especially there are very few sources for the peasant family. We know if anything even less about the way in which they lived – and what is the point of holding forth about their rights and obligations if we know nothing of the houses in which they dwelt, the food they ate, their taboos and customs? That is a purely formal exercise for legalistic minds without any practical value. Even less is known of my third topic: the equipment the peasants used, how they used it, and the results obtained – an area so devoid of contemporary evidence and definite facts that everything to do with working the soil, the nature of the plot and the countryside itself remains confused and open to a wide range of interpretations. For the later period things are somewhat clearer, but by no means cut and dried: a picture of the lord emerges (ecclesiastical or secular) because documents are essentially concerned with him, but it is less easy to discern what motivated or modified his rights and demands. There is evidence about production itself and the profit derived from the sale of produce in markets, in towns and villages but there are other aspects, such as debt, the minimum subsistence level and the importance of game, wild plants, fruits and fungi in the diet, which are either impossible to assess or on which there has been little research. Finally I shall come to the peasant group: some communities were more or less firmly entrenched in their fiscal privileges and established customs; we do not know how many others were untouched by these benefits, how many were well-off and how many struggling to keep body and soul together.

This list of factual deficiencies is not intended to discourage readers; on the contrary, it is to make them realize that despite constant progress in medieval history, numerous areas still await investigation. It is most definitely not a case of repeating incontrovertible truths in the temple of medieval scholarship. On the contrary, few areas of anthropological research are as open to new techniques or as new and lively. Although adults continue to describe as 'medieval' everything that is awkward, stupid, violent or inequitable, in France many schoolchildren are realizing that their roots lie here rather than in the classical period or the revolutionary upheavals of more recent times. The Middle Ages often follow the prehistoric period in popularity amongst schoolchildren and although aspects of a traditional and narrowly classical education persist, the medieval period is not generally considered the dreary dead end of civilization that it was a generation ago.

1

Individuals First and Foremost

It has become traditional (especially in France since the work of Marc Bloch) to assert that the discovery of man himself is the historian's highest goal and to begin any study with a social dimension from this angle. For once I see no reason not to follow the well-trodden path and even without this distinguished tradition two facts would prompt me to adopt this approach. For anyone who adopts a bird's-eye view of the Middle Ages is struck by an amorphous mass of seething individuals rather than by the institutions, legalities or the 'great men' of other centuries: instead he sees peasants, clerics, warriors and artisans in continual motion and (to all appearances) lacking any cohesion whatsoever – not being engulfed in this crowd of people is an achievement in itself. Less direct and more compelling, the other reason appeals to common sense in any discussion of the peasantry: nine men out of ten belonged to this group and it is impossible to examine their rights or their tools, their duties or their work, without knowing how many of them there were.

How many peasants?

This is not the place for a long dissertation on the difficulties or even the pitfalls of medieval demography: plenty of articles and entire books have been dedicated to the subject. Without believing in the absolute precision of statistics, it must be agreed that some light is now being shed on this area which for so long has been one of subjective impressions. Much research is now in progress on the numbers of witnesses, copyholders and tenants in thousands of documents, such as the hearth-tax returns (*cherches de feux*) and the fore-runners of the *catasto* (an Italian property tax) which bring us to the dawn of historical statistics. By this I mean the French *état des feux* (survey of hearths) of 1328, the English subsidy returns of the mid-fourteenth century, the returns of the Provençal *cadastres* and similar records from Hainault and Piedmont at the very beginning of the fifteenth century; all these documents, which would infuriate a modern historian with their gaps, their inexactitudes and their contradictions, constitute a thoroughly creditable source: like many others I have worked on them and found them sound. It is well known that before 1330 or 1350 there is only one surviving document that covers a large area, the vast and diffuse Domesday Book which William the Conqueror had drawn up in 1086 for all of England that fell under his jurisdiction – an invaluable source, but unique of its kind. That does not matter: piercing the darkness from the eleventh to the thirteenth century in places as disparate as Fulda, Gorze, Evesham, Tillenay, Urgel, Bath, Farfa, Braga, Saint-Maurice-en-Valais and a score of other places, lights of knowledge sparkle, illuminating our ignorance.

Population increase

The clearest demographic trend in this period is the marked increase in the European population. All that I shall have to say about the reclamation of wasteland, the extension of cultivable soil, the settlement of virgin ground, soon followed by the subdivision of houses and the appearance of new social categories within the peasant class, bears striking witness to this characteristic. Here I can do no more than mention the rise in the urban population or the conquest of distant lands. There is little uncertainty about the first phases of this movement: it occurred in the middle of the tenth century, in about 920–30 in the Mediterranean area, in central Italy, the Po valley and Catalonia, slightly later in Provence and along the Atlantic seaboard; then after 1010 or 1030 along the valleys of the Loire, the Sâone and the Meuse, 20 years later in northern France and the Rhineland, not until 1100 in England and central Germany, later still in more easterly areas. This preliminary sketch raises many problems. Firstly, the sources are perhaps deceptive and increasingly insubstantial towards the north and the east: it is impossible to be absolutely certain, but nevertheless the pattern of later increase in France, the more accessible English case and the evidence of archaeological excavations at rural German sites seem to endorse this chronological sequence. However, there is another problem: the areas where this expansion first occurred, the southern end of the Continent, were often subject to severe attacks by the Muslims and indeed, surprisingly enough, by the Hungarians; the trend is similarly evident in Atlantic and Channel coastal regions at an earlier date than in the continental areas spared by the Vikings. In cold logic this should lead one to see the Norman and Muslim invasions as a positive dynamic force in the European population explosion. In these conditions – which I accept – the problem of a possible burgeoning of the countryside in the ninth century at the time of the so-called Carolingian Renaissance would be settled once and for all with a decided negative. Judging by the evidence of the fragile Austrasian attempt there could only have been a few flickers of the seventh-century classical revival which followed the 'Justinian plague'. The population was small, possibly decreasing, between 900 and 950.

This thesis does nothing at all to answer the crucial question, 'Why?', on which all others depend. Why did the population expand between 950 and 1050, later in some places? The ebb of the invasions, says Duby – but the movement began before the end of these upheavals; the demand of the East for western iron and slaves, proposes R.S. Lopez, but this is scarcely credible for deepest Brittany; as a reaction against victorious Islam was Pirenne's theory long ago – but if so it was a very tardy reaction, at least two centuries after the arrival of the Arabs; the influx of Muslim gold, affirmed M. Lombard – but one looks in vain for hidden treasure; Lefebvre-Desnouettes' solution was the appearance of technical inventions from Asia and is followed today by Lynn White Jr., but we know nothing at all about them before the twelfth century. Where does this leave us? Was it a process that was activated by the gradual release into circulation of the profits of war in the Carolingian period, which in time became the creative forces for productivity and also the basis of feudalism? I have my doubts, because the increase most definitely did not begin between the Seine and the Weser, the heartland of Carolingian warriors. Two explanations remain and I shall let the reader choose between them: that divine will inspired God's ministers and his newly-chosen people with material vigour and moral power, thus sustaining an expansion at once Christian and material; or the onset in western Europe of a climate that was very favourable for the animals and plants on which man depended for his food and indeed for his own genetic and physical development.

Without being irrelevant to the point of our inquiry, these arguments certainly draw us into the realm of hypothesis. Where possible, let us try instead to calculate the population level, leaving the broad outline for a generalized approach. Here and there (in England, in the Laonnais region and Provence, near Namur and round Chieri) a happy chance has left us figures for the heads of households in one or two villages at successive dates, largely, it is true, in the second half of the thirteenth century, showing increases from 300 to 650, 80 to 110, 180 to 290 and so on. These figures give no idea of total population, but there is at least some indication of an essential trend: with an average of four or five people to a household – a point to which I shall return shortly – these villages were enormous. Like some in Sicily and Hungary today they were virtually small towns and this was their primary characteristic. There is another, scarcely less important source in the excavated cemeteries of mid-twelfth-century Poland and thirteenth-century Sweden or Hungary. The proportion of infantile skeletons is horrifying, with 20 per cent under 5, 30 per cent under 8 and 43 per cent less than 14 years old. A frightening level of infant mortality, but one which implies a society positively teeming with children in order to explain the population increase which undoubtedly occurred. There are no examples from more westerly areas because medieval cemeteries are still in use and examination is consequently difficult. But there are no grounds to believe that the situation would be very different. Further evidence comes from the genealogies of important families and also from the groupings of families of humbler origin in witness lists, which both re-enforce this impression of superfluity. After much detailed research on many similar cases the following sequence of the number of children per fertile household can be postulated: 4 in the tenth century, 4 or 5.3 and then between 5 and 5.7 in the first and second halves of the eleventh century, between 6 and 7.3 from 1100 to 1150, between 5 and 6.5 until the end of the twelfth century; the thirteenth century seems initially to have been a demographically stable period, but a decrease is evident after 1250. The annual rate of growth estimated by various researchers is shown (in percentages) in table 1.1.

Table 1.1

1000–50 (%)	1050–1100 (%)	1100–50 (%)	1150–1200 (%)	1200–50 (%)	1250–1300 (%)
0.5	0.38	0.55	0.45	0.35	0.18

Presented with the relatively credible figures of table 1.1, the reader familiar with twentieth-century demography will not fail to be struck by their small size, even bearing in mind the death in infancy of one child in three when very young. The rate of increase was much lower than that of numerous countries today, some of which easily attain an annual increase of 3 or 5 per cent, the high price of medical progress. On the other hand, it is evident that this annual average of 0.4 per cent was spread out over nearly three centuries, implying a doubling of the workforce and of their food consumption over this period.

Finally, there is one other approach, but the least reliable: what was the total population at any one given time? Only in England is there comprehensive data: there were nearly 1,300,000 men within its strict geographical limits at the time of the compilation of the Domesday Book in the late eleventh century; when a poll tax was levied just before the Black Death in 1348 there were 3,800,000, a 300 per cent increase in 250 years, credible figures in such a sparsely populated country. The rate of increase might have been less than this, however. Without dismissing all global estimates as 'ridiculous' (as M. Bloch did), the figures calculated by such German, Italian and American scholars as Russell, Bennett, Cipolla or Abel, can only be put forward with the most extreme caution. According to their theories the area covered by modern France would have reached a population level of 6,200,000 in about 1100 and over 9 million in 1200, while F. Lot put it at 22 million in 1328, the year of the *état des feux*. Italy, on the other hand, experienced an estimated increase from 5 to only 8 million in two centuries and the German Empire from 4 to 9 million. These are very tentative conclusions and those of the studies which supposedly estimate the entire European population even more so and I shall not cite them for that reason. Nevertheless, these hypotheses are instructive on two counts: because they show, firstly, a smaller increase in the older countries, Italy and France and, secondly, the remarkable, even astonishing, numerical superiority of the latter, whose population comprised between a third and a half of the western European total. Perhaps this in itself was sufficient reason for the importance of Capetian France in the thirteenth and fourteenth centuries.

But, it may be argued, even if one accepts these figures, they make no distinction between town and countryside – and this is a valid criticism. Nevertheless, the many urban studies, which Léopold Genicot has brought together in his study of the later thirteenth century (*Mélanges . . . Perroy*, Paris, 1973), show the relatively low level of town populations at this period: in 1300 there were 6 to 7 towns with over 50,000 inhabitants, over 30 with 20,000 to 50,000, at least 40 with 10,000 to 20,000 and – if indeed they can be called 'towns' – 100 with a population between 5,000 and 10,000. The total gives a round two and a half million, a very small figure for the area concerned and one which leaves a good 90 per cent of the population in the open countryside. This characteristic is well known and of great significance, but it is important to take account of regional variations, for the number of rural inhabitants can be reduced at least to 75 per cent in Italy, where between 30 and 75 towns had populations of over 10,000, while perhaps 80 per cent of the French and 85 per cent of the Spanish and Portuguese populations lived in the country; in England and the Rhineland, however, the rural figure was well above the European average, while in more northerly regions virtually the entire population lived off the land.

This rural population, very considerable by any standards, and vast in relation to the towns which in practice it dominated throughout our period, also displayed such scattered and unpredictable settlement patterns that it is extremely risky to put forward any theoretical figures of population density. In theory it should be possible to divide the estimated surface area by the likely number of inhabitants to obtain 'average' figures. For the beginning of the fourteenth century this method results in some 20 inhabitants per square kilometre in France or Italy, 12 to 15 in England and Alsace-Lorraine, fewer still in Spain and the Empire, hardly 8 in central Europe and 5 in Scandinavia. However, the minimal practical value of this method is demonstrated by the discrepancies between such putative figures and the details of settlement in a specific area occasionally revealed by contemporary documentation. This characteristic is still more striking before the period with which we are concerned: Carolingian documents from Saint-Bertin or Saint-Germain-des-Près attest population densities of forty to sixty per square kilometre, here and there sometimes even higher than today. For there were in fact – even in those areas where the barriers between settlements were gradually being demolished – dense patches of habitation separated by vast uninhabited areas. As late as 1328 the *état des feux* reveals surprising inequalities of population density: in the Paris region, for example, there were only 6 hearths per square kilometre in the Hurepoix, but the Beauce and Gonesse reached 18 hearths. Similar calculations have been made for England in the period of the Domesday survey, where there is a marked contrast between the northern regions with 4 to 7 families over 50 hectares and the southern counties, where the figure is 15 to 30. South of Florence in about 1300 population densities of over 60 inhabitants per square kilometre have been calculated in areas beside steep mountain slopes covered with scrub (the impenetrable *mescla* of contemporary texts) or the boggy lands of the river valleys.

It must have been every medieval historian's dream to reconstruct a map of rural population density for the period before the returns of the *cadastres*. With this end in view there have been some recent French studies based at least on the apparently justifiable assumption that present-day variations in population density reflect the settlement patterns of the original parishes. It is tempting to see the parishes as primary indicators of rural population density, at least after 1000 when the parish network was established: far-reaching conclusions could be drawn from the combined study of land typology and parish boundaries, if the facts were only more certain than they are at present. The damp and wooded Puisaye region with its large parishes of 30 to 50 square kilometres could be contrasted with lower Burgundy where, with a comparable population, they seldom exceeded 15 square kilometres. In this way the outlines of thinly settled areas would emerge – in mountainous regions, of course, but also in Brittany, the Limousin and the Cevennes and Provence – and there would be others that were positively crowded, like the valleys of the Sâone and the Loire, the plains of the Ile-de-France and the Toulousain and the limestone plateaux of northern and eastern France. It is obvious, however, that this approach could not be taken much further because throughout the Middle Ages there was a continual process of adjustment in the balance between attractive and unattractive regions, familiar to Roger Dion 50 years ago: thus, for example, it is demonstrable for England that in 300 years there was a barely perceptible increase in the population in some southern counties already densely settled at the outset, whilst in some northern areas there was a 750 per cent increase over the corresponding period – and that in areas where only a third of the ground was cultivable. As one might imagine, the nature of the land prevented this counterbalance from operating to its full extent and hence the variations in settlement patterns. Nevertheless, a determined effort to settle the wastelands is undoubtedly characteristic of this period.

There is one other largely neglected line of inquiry open to the historian attempting a more precise delineation of settlement patterns and that is to calculate the areas that remained uncultivated – the *saltus* of classical writers, *bosc* of the medieval Frenchman. As the reclamation of this virgin soil is one of the peasant activities that I shall examine below it will only be considered in the most general terms here. Even understood in the medieval sense of the term it is extremely difficult to assess: firstly, because unoccupied ground (the *riés* and *larris* of northern France, the *garrigues* of the south and the *brosses* and *gastes* of the central region – to confine ourselves to France alone) are only mentioned by chance as a result of breaches of grazing or hunting rights or in accounts of military activity; conversely, the word 'forest' could, as in England, refer to all land reserved to the king (even when disafforested) – this approach would undoubtedly also be fraught with imprecision.

A world 'full' of people?

'Full' is a key word in historical demography, deemed suitable for many situations. We must examine both technical capacity and contemporary needs in each case. Thus for the first half of the fourteenth century (the first or perhaps even the second stage of demographic shift, when there was a decrease after the steady level maintained from the mid-thirteenth century) we must remember that many communities in Normandy, Picardy, Comminges, the Oisans, Wessex and the Tirol were more densely settled, if not than today, then at least than they were in 1900, the apogee of rural Europe. That is to say that they were over-populated in relation to the available means of production and the levels of consumption: one has only to recall that regions such as Middlesex, Walloon Flanders or the Rhine Palatinate were considered over-populated with 50 inhabitants per square kilometre (less than a third of today's levels).

As far as one can see – and making allowance for the fact that this statement is less true as one goes towards central or northern Europe – the peasant population reached its highest levels in the reign of Louis IX (1226–70). There is tangible evidence of this in the plains where little satellite hamlets sprang up and in the *censes* and *mas* which were separate from the large fortified settlements previously the rule. Hillside villages either crept down the slope, or, more frequently, there was a double settlement with a high and a low village. It is also reflected in the fragmentation of field plans into tiny portions that were probably insufficient to feed all the family crammed under one roof. Finally, in 1232, 1240 and 1254 there are records of famine once more, still very localized and forgotten a century later.

Even at this stage in the inquiry it is clear that there was a decline in the population level: in Picardy the rate of growth seems in fact to level out at the maintenance of existing population levels; in England the difference between estimates for the late thirteenth century and the tax returns of 1340 suggest a drop of as much as 400,000. It has been justly observed that the growing incidence of remarriage amongst widows reflects not only a higher male mortality rate, but also ultimately a fall in the birth rate, because of the reduced fertility and shorter duration of these marriages. It should be noted that all of these warning signs occur long before the great upheaval of the so-called 'crises of the fourteenth century'. Clearly one must also take account of the migration from the countryside into the towns that was a very marked characteristic of the period. The urban population expanded as a result and this undoubtedly explains the contemporary failure to recognize the overall downward trend.

I explained earlier why this account stops before the demographic crisis of the mid-fourteenth century intervened. But the causes – or what we believe we know of them – of this decline in population still have to be set out, just as they have been for the period of growth. This is admittedly conjecture, although further research may yield a more concrete explanation. At this later date there were external factors, notably plague, famine and flood. Astronomical observations, pollen analysis of peat bogs, examination of the datable levels of glacial movements and other facts occasionally noted by a more than usually perceptive observer all lend credence to the probability that this period witnessed a sharp deterioration in climate, characterized by heavy rainfall, unpredictable temperatures and a succession of bad harvests. The manorial accounts of Winchester and Ramsey both record abrupt falls in production levels which undoubtedly contributed to the long and very widespread famine of 1315–17. Then again studies of wills in Forez and the Lyonnais show a steady increase in the mortality rate after 1340, which is also reflected in the famous parish register of Givry in Burgundy, the only one to survive in France before the series dating from the fifteenth century. Now, while a sudden change in external factors produces an abrupt rise in the level of mortality, gradually increasing mortality rates reflect an organic tendency which can only be attributed to malnutrition and the loss of resistance to disease which is one of the consequences of a poorly regulated diet. The records of baptism at Givry and references in wills elsewhere show a drop in the number of children, but a more detailed study of the history of contraception is required to determine whether the whittling away of inheritances by the practice of equal division amongst all heirs (in countries where there was no primogeniture) resulted in some kind of voluntary birth control.

All these theories impinge on man's bodily state, which is why I refer to them here. But the very structure of society, as well as the inadequacy of modes of production beyond a certain level of technical expertise must be considered quite as important as other causes, and they will be discussed at length in the appropriate place.

Hearts and minds

Throughout this chapter I have referred continually to 'man' and 'men' as if the population consisted solely of one confused mass or, worse still, of a single sex; but I trust my meaning is clear despite this stylistic device. But now we must look into the seething mass that confronts the medievalist and examine the individual grains of sand. It is couples that then immediately stand out on this broader canvas of individual particles; and I have no hesitation whatsoever in stating that this pattern is clearer in the cottage than the castle and in the country rather than the town.

Hearth and home

This is the case primarily because the relevant sources refer more frequently than others to the union of the two sexes, whether in property documents, conciliar canons or *fabliaux*. Here male superiority – so distinct in the military and political spheres – appears blurred, and is certainly challenged by woman's control of household management and of food supplies. The castle resounds with the cries of men, the clash of arms and the thud of horses' hooves; in the town the artisan is prominent, merchants and civic officials dominate the stage; in the village the man is in the fields or the woods: everything else is in the woman's hands and it is impossible to ignore this fact. One has only to read the *exempla*, collections of model sermons written in the thirteenth century for the use of preachers short of inspiration and the speciality of Dominicans like Etienne de Bourbon: women easily occupy first place, as they do too in *fabliaux*, lyric poetry or *chansons de toile*. The superhuman exploits of Roland or Lancelot appealed only to a tiny masculine audience. And there is an overwhelming preponderance of objects of female use amongst archaeological finds from rural sites. As I have said, it is not until the end of the thirteenth century that our texts provide adequate statistical information and officials or notaries used the terms 'hearth' or 'household' as if the grouping round the hearth or in the house was the primary unit. These terms have been the subject of heated debate for far too long, with some historians insisting that the domanial or financial official saw individuals only in terms of small household units of certain size. They have advanced theories as to their possible size – all with excellent and incontrovertible supporting evidence but at odds with that provided by other researchers – which has been estimated variously at 3, 3.5, conceivably 4, or (at the other extreme) as much as 6 or 7.

It is inevitable that differences of period, place and social class, and even the context of research, will result in variations and make it futile to search for a universally applicable solution. It is not a case of 'asking the wrong question' – the easy way of dropping a tedious subject – but a genuinely insoluble problem. I shall only add one observation (and that a very tentative one) to the general disagreement, that since a number of cases in the thirteenth century suggest that between 25 and 30 per cent of households and individuals were without surviving issue, at least three children were generally required to maintain the population level, in which case the 'hearth' of a married couple would consist of at least five individuals – a figure which I hasten to stress is purely hypothetical.

On the other hand, I think it is much more interesting that the official's knowledge went no further than the average unit, although there might have been an elderly widow living alone in one household and a couple with eight children in another. For him, as it should be for us, the primary unit of productivity consisted of those who lived together under one roof (*à feu et à pot*, sharing the same fire and food, as the later saying went) and, if they were man and wife, in *mesnie* or *ménage* (household). Thus it was that the sixteenth century formulated the legal tag, '*manger et dormir ensemble, c'est mariage, ce me semble* (eating and sleeping together constitutes marriage)'. We are now very familiar with this definition of marriage, whether defined by the Church at the end of a long period of evolution, or stemming from the accumulation of rites and formulae connected with earlier societies and constituting the *mos patriae*, common practice, which scarcely impinged on the Christian world.

Let us concentrate on essentials. Amongst the aristocracy and the urban patriciate endogamous marriage was necessary to preserve the family's high connections and to keep the estate intact. This was an in-bred union after negotiations of an almost commercial character between the two fathers, to which the children's agreement and mutual affection (*dilectio*) were entirely irrelevant. This concept hardly impinged on the great majority of peasants, who were unaffected both by the young people's feelings and by any fear of incest. (In the period before 1215 the Church had gone so far as to forbid unions of the seventh degree, that is between the descendants of four successive generations.) It was in fact precisely in rural society that endogamy (marriage within the confines of the extended family), with its attendant risks of illegal incest, was most likely to occur: the serfs did not have the resources to pay a tax for the privilege of finding a wife outside their lord's domain (a practice known as *formariage*) and the isolated populations of mountains, islands or newly reclaimed regions undoubtedly resorted to marrying their cousins. In about 1170 Pope Alexander III realized that these prohibitions were in fact encouraging concubinage and adultery; his successors at the Fourth Lateran Council agreed to annul them. Again, it might sometimes be in the interests of two well-off peasant families to conclude a formal alliance by means of a marriage of convenience, decided upon by its older and wiser members; the brilliance of peasant weddings has not yet been completely dulled and these occasions are perhaps a mute echo of the celebrations open to all-comers at which each family tried to outdo the other in munificence.

Nevertheless, I believe that in the great majority of cases, rural marriage was a much simpler affair: mutual attraction, with close relations doubtless keeping an eye on the courtship to ensure there was no disaster in material or moral terms. In other words both *dilectio* and *consensus* (affection and consent) were present. The ceremony itself required witnesses, possibly a notary in the south, the exchange of promises, followed by the exchange of rings and gifts – a relic of the protohistoric custom of mutual gift-giving. The intervention of a priest (which seems to have become standard after 1275 or 1300) made no real difference, for the Church admitted that it was the exchange of promises and not the blessing by the priest which constituted the sacrament accepted by the two spouses. This kind of union was generally accompanied by village festivities – a meal, dancing and bawdy entertainments, even true *saturnalia* in the form of the *charivari*, when the local youth disapproved of the match. But the material aspect should not be neglected, for the countrydwellers did not need to realize that they were following the precepts of Justinian's *Novella* (of which they had never heard) in order to appreciate the contractual aspect of the *mise en ménage* (setting up home), a term still sometimes used in French. In the ordinary course of events marriage was preceded by *sponsalia*, incorrectly rendered *épousailles* (espousal) in modern French, whereas this was in fact a formal agreement which involved the reciprocal settlement of revenue, the dowry brought by the girl on the one hand and the gift on the occasion of the wedding which the husband agreed his wife should have from his goods on the other. This was called the *donatio propter nuptias*, *sponsalium* or *maritagium* and might vary from a third to a tenth of their total value. This *douaire* (dower), as it was later called, was essentially a guarantee of income for the woman in the event of widowhood, while the dowry, or what remained of it, returned to the wife's family should she die before her husband.

The 'Joys of Marriage'

Legal terminology still held sway even when the parties present understood no Latin at all and it brings us face-to-face with peasant life for a married couple. We should be sceptical – as those rural households undoubtedly were – of homilies exhorting chastity, continence and moderation, not to mention virginity. Sexual relations, the *copula carnalis* of the lawyers, were the inevitable corollary of cohabitation. Nevertheless, before attempting any scrutiny of an essentially private subject, a few preliminary remarks about differences from twentieth-century practices are in order.

First of all, it would only be at a fairly late date, in my estimation, that the couple would have a room of their own inside a peasant house and that the matrimonial bed replaced collective sleeping arrangements. In other words (and without dwelling on the temptations and satisfactions which are the same whatever the period and whose details are irrelevant to our present subject) the intimacy between man and wife bore no resemblance to that of our own time. But more than the practical arrangements of married life, the moral climate differed from our own. Perhaps less forcibly than the artisan living in the town, where everything was expensive, or the noble who had to wait for his inheritance before he might seek a wife, the peasant had nevertheless to experience the same enforced delay in marriage whose causes and effects were both of fundamental importance. When the girl was of marriageable age, perhaps about 15 years old, she was put on the marriage market, while a boy had to wait, employed as his older brother's stable-hand until he had an 'estate', that is the wherewithal to provide a dower for the girl he wanted to marry; he could of course look for a rich widow, but at the risk of a *charivari* that would ridicule and humiliate him; or he could borrow or hire himself out. The man was generally at least 25 or 27 years old when he took to wife a girl of 16. During the period before his marriage it is unlikely that he paid much attention to clerical exhortations and probably sought sexual satisfaction either in ancillary concubinage, which is well documented, or in prostitution, of which by contrast virtually nothing is known in the countryside apart from the reference of St Bernard in the mid-twelfth century to the 'women of ill repute' offering their services to young men waiting their turn outside the miller's door, which suggests a traditional commerce that was inevitably tolerated.

The essential problem, but one so distant and so elusive, is that of emotional attachment. What did this man in his thirties, labouring in the fields, expect on his return from a 20-year old wife, almost constantly pregnant, whose place was at home with the children she had borne? His authority was inevitably brutal because it could be exerted only occasionally; he was happy that they no longer lived *sub iugo patris*, that is in the house of an older relative and under his sway. There has been much interest in the role played from the twelfth century onwards by wet nurses, women whose still-born children left them with milk with which they could suckle others'. Historians have detected in this practice a conscious wish to increase the birth-rate, since, as the paid wet nurse suckled the baby, the mother's own lactation soon ceased and she could become pregnant again more quickly. Whatever the case, there is little evidence of such practices in the country: all the iconographical evidence tends to show the peasant woman with a child at her breast. But in terms of the effect on society, the result was identical: by very lengthy breast-feeding (18 months, or even 22 for boys) the woman was able to space out her pregnancies, but they continued without a break, nonetheless, binding her to motherhood throughout most of her young life. When the surplus of women in the population after 1160 or 1170 caused the Church to look more favourably on second marriages, with the supposed aim of protecting the attractive young widow from the lust of young men in search of adventure, even this condition no longer procured her freedom.

What conclusions should we draw? That deprived of the distractions of the courtly life and knowing nothing of the contraceptives of which a townswoman might avail herself, the peasant woman was bound to a considerably older spouse, constantly preoccupied with the provision of food for husband and children and could not have experienced any of the 'fifteen joys' of marriage listed in the fourteenth-century satire? How are we to pierce the thick veil of fabliaux, where the husband is held up to ridicule, and reconcile sermons, in which the wife is all but a martyr, with legal texts multiplying her legal rights with remarkable emphasis? Perhaps simply by drawing attention to various scattered observations, which underline the same trend: the number of documents in which the husband who has had to make inroads into the woman's dower takes pains to re-endow her with lands elsewhere (in the presence of a notary in Italy), providing a good income and concerning which action is taken *similiter et insimul*, as equals and together; the cemeteries where, with none of the effigies of the noble classes, the bodies lie close together; and the terms of endearment which husbands lavish in wills upon their future widows. And even in our society, which is based upon an approximate equality of age between spouses, there are occasional marriages between a young girl and a man in his fifties whose feelings are sometimes more than usually passionate. Why then should we deny to these people the possibility of an intense love for one another even when the match was arranged by their fathers? It is easy to overlook the brief duration of the union which may have made the flame burn more brightly: their marriage would probably last between eight and, at the very most, 20 years, terminated by the premature death of the husband, or of the wife, worn out by difficult pregnancies.

Literary evidence for the life of a peasant couple is too often of urban origin to carry much weight. But there are *pastourelles*, short pieces written in the thirteenth century for singing and dancing, a form sometimes adopted by authors famous for other works such as the poet-minstrel from Arras Adam de la Halle (*fl.* 1250–87) or his prolific contemporary Rutebeuf. These were very traditional compositions generally intended for an exclusively noble audience in which a knight makes advances to a shepherdess, who either rejects or accepts them. But behind the very generalized canvas of so much of Adam de la Halle's *Robin et Marion* (composed for the soldiers of Count Robert II of Artois campaigning in southern Italy) a picture of love in the country does emerge – distorted, but familiar to the members of the lord's household, themselves countrydwellers, who might listen to the piece. Certain characteristics occur repeatedly and there is every probability that they are accurate: pre-occupation with custom and propriety; fear of the reproaches of their older relatives, the notion of a contract broken on peril of damnation; the many 'attentions' which the young people bestowed on one another – and if nobles laughed at the spectacle of Robin bringing Marion a cheese which she hid in her bodice, it should give historians food for thought. In the miniatures of country dances with which Books of Hours and moral treatises were decorated the couples form a continuous chain, hand in hand, defying all sexual discrimination.

Fathers and sons

The condition of children in the Middle Ages has been the subject of many studies and opinion has long been divided as to whether these unformed creatures, most of whom would meet an early death, were the object if not of scorn, at least of persistent adult indifference; or whether economic factors made it imperative that the parents should bring up an individual who would be self-supporting as soon as possible. Supporters of the first theory point to the representation of children in the visual arts, where there is no attempt to indicate age or sex, if indeed they are portrayed at all, while written sources are silent on the subject or, should they have to narrate the death of a child, do so with cool detachment. The other school emphasizes that from the moment of his birth until death was no longer a daily threat, the *puer* was educated by the example of his elders and, from six or seven years old, 'on the job', so that when he was 12 or 14 he could be an apprentice, squire or stable boy. Once again it is archaeology that has provided a fuller picture of the child in his home environment, justifying in the process individual features of both theories. Excavations of settlements from the Frankish and Saxon periods onwards have revealed fragments of little toys, miniature crockery, lead soldiers, wax dolls, knuckle bones, tops and dummies, demonstrating an interest in children's toys quite comparable to our own. No cradles or baby seats have survived (probably because they were made of wood and have consequently perished), but grooves close to the fireplace are evidence of the regular rocking of new-born babies. The discovery of skeletons of foetuses, or very small babies buried in the actual floor of the house bears witness to the peasant superstition that credited them with a special bond with the spirits of their ancestors.

Although visual representations are traditional and unconvincing, they provide a wealth of detail about the behaviour of the *infans*: Jesus is swaddled tightly in his crib and strapped to his bed to prevent him from falling out; scarcely able to move and grotesque in a miniature version of adult clothing, he plays on the ground in the middle of the shavings that have fallen from Joseph's work-bench; or Mary kisses his hand tenderly, or hugs him close to her. Portrayed like a little angel he plays with his mother's hair, as a peasant child she feeds him and spins at the same time; a little older he follows his mother about, clinging to her skirts. There is nothing exceptional in these timeless activities of a small child. Nor is there anything very revealing in the depictions of an angry father's blows, or the accompanying text. The father had authority over the child by law: in Sweden he could still put it up for sale or adoption in the twelfth century and markets for the sale of children are documented in Barcelona at a slightly earlier date.

So there are two contrasting faces in the short period between weaning at about 18 months and being put to work at 10 or 12 years: in the first (the 'night' which St Augustine said he did not wish to experience again for anything in the whole world) the mother undoubtedly played the principal role; the man (the *baron*, as men even of peasant status were called in Normandy after 1250) was master of the household, custodian and protector and dispenser of punishments. Now all child-specialists know that an individual's character is formed during this first phase, when the dominant influence in our period was entirely female. Apart from the signs of affection we have already noted there is virtually no evidence for relations between parents and children. E. Coleman recently suggested that small girls were more at risk than boys because they were more neglected and weaned relatively soon and that this explains the higher incidence of female mortality at this period, since the supposedly 'weaker' sex usually has greater resistance to disease. But during these early years young children played a role which seems incomprehensible today: they were the intermediaries between the other world and this: it was through their words and actions and in the guise of their desires that the dead were to be recognized and spoke to those who had outlived them. It was as if the child were the temple of memory and his (or her) innocence protected him from adult temptations. The importance of this role (above all in areas where it held a more prominent place in country superstition) explains both the protection which children undoubtedly enjoyed until they were eight or 10 years old and the *enfances* – stereotyped and somewhat improbable accounts of the childhood of an individual destined for an exceptionally saintly or heroic existence and whose first years were steeped in the supernatural.

When this stage of childhood had passed the father took over the child's education at the approach of adolescence; he set the boy to gleaning and the girl to look after his flock; he taught the tricks of his trade, the receipts and rules of life on the land; the mother had only hastily to teach the girls some needlework before they were married. However, it should not be forgotten that the basic precepts of social life, such as conviviality or thrift, were instilled at a much earlier stage, under the mother's influence. It may have been then, too, that the bond between maternal uncle and his nephews and nieces was established, the 'nepotism' well known in noble circles, when the difference in age between husband and wife would account for the presence of her younger brother, from whom the children grew to expect a more protective attitude than from a father whose presence was synonymous with instruction or punishment. Moreover the child would have had virtually no-one else to turn to: there were no grandparents who might intervene between father and son. Since life expectancy was relatively short (50 or 60 years, with rare exceptions) they were already dead before they could have any influence; or, alternatively, the new household that had stemmed from theirs was henceforth independent and its members led their own lives. At any rate the child would have known nothing of the buffer role which is so readily thrust upon older relatives today. Many a young man must have waited impatiently for his encumbrance of a father to die. For although he might legally lead an independent life at the age of 15 – witness Bracton in about 1270 and the *coutumiers* of Champagne and elsewhere – this was still too young an age to hope that the youth might have the wherewithal to live of his own.

The living dead

As a child, married or widowed, even alone in his house and without friends and relations, the peasant never escaped the company of the dead. This was perhaps the essential difference between the medieval peasant and even the most credulous twentieth-century villager. Until the very end of the Middle Ages, even beyond it, the age-old tyranny of the dead caused the living considerable suffering. It was not a question of fear conjuring up a picture of suffering and putrefaction: death was too familiar to these people surrounded by illness, hunger and violence; they spoke of it often and without emotion, in contrast to our silent fear. Simply because, whether they were truly Christians or simply deists without realizing it – the distinctions would have been lost on them – they saw death or 'passage', as they called it, as the entry into life itself, or rather the period of waiting for the judgement that would determine their destiny for ever. Perhaps the celebrations with music and feasting that accompanied a death were less a consolation for the survivors or a last present for the dead man or woman, than an outburst of unalloyed joy at the knowledge that one of their number had at last entered the final phase of existence. Even after 1350, when death's embrace became more intense and was represented in increasingly gruesome forms in both the visual arts, the written word and sermons, the living never conceived of death as a hopeless condition that was hideous and terrifying. Jacques Le Goff has recently shown how, in addition, the increasingly widespread belief in Purgatory after 1180 or 1200 (a middle way that offered hope) made the passage into the other world a simpler and perhaps a sweeter affair for even the worst of men.

For the living, the dead were interlocutors with the supernatural far more than the memory of what they had said or done whilst they were alive. Until the sound of the Last Trumpet they wandered without repose, asexual and joyless, where they had lived, round the church where they had been baptized and where (often in the bare earth) they had been buried. At night a lantern shone in the church tower to keep demons at bay and gather together the spirits of the dead; with the exception of the Jews (buried elsewhere) and the still-born buried in their homes they

were like a double village community. There they made
themselves known only to women, whilst in the daytime they
spoke through the mouths of children or idiots in their former
houses. Moreover, as in classical times, they had their altar close
by the fire which the women tended. They cast spells or foretold
the future; several times a year, the young girls, widows and
mothers all went in procession to asperge their tombs, burn an
offering of incense or corn, even to put lard by their tombs on the
eve of Lent. Can we report that the Church protested, threatened
and sermonized? It seems unlikely: from the councils of the fifth
century to the Dominicans in the thirteenth there is a continuous
series of complaints about female credulity, abuse by demons,
and the laxness of the men who allowed it to continue. These
protests were all to no avail.

What could be more desirable than intermediaries and
fortune-tellers in one's own home? When a member of the family
group died, the hair and nails continued to grow and were cut
and kept by his relatives, incontrovertible proof that death did
not mark the end either of the person who had died or their
family. And, as I said earlier, the corpse of a still-born child was
buried under the threshold, fixed to the ground by a stake so that
the devil could not remove the earthly remains of this creature
that had not become truly human. Unlike their master in his
castle peasants very rarely had the wherewithal to build a chapel
in which everyone was buried and the family clan preserved even
in death. This dynastic concern, what the Germans call
Sippenbewusstsein was the preserve of the nobles, who believed
(or wished to believe) in a descent that was of Carolingian, if not
of supernatural origin. In the peasant's cottage the dead man
lived on in a more modest form: his example was cited to the
children and embellished the tales told round the fire by the
diseur or story-teller, perhaps a cousin with a reputation for
conversing with the dead, or simply the father of the family.
These stories were not likely to be about exploits in battle or
prestigious duties in his master's service, but the purchase of a
rich meadow, the discovery of treasure or a surprising marriage.
Today these byways have been obliterated in an almost exclusive
concentration on the genealogy of noble families, and our only
access is by means of a surname or first name, acquired and then

transferred from generation to generation. It is striking that women as well as men could introduce an enduring name of this kind into the family group. Soubriquets of this kind first appear amongst men-at-arms between 1050 and 1100 and are found several generations later in lists of villagers witnessing a document or of tax-payers who have discharged their obligations. They sometimes recall the qualities attributed to a totem – wolf, bear, eagle, boar – but more frequently a physical characteristic, a trade or an exploit, such as *le fort* (the brave), *le fèvre* (the smith), *d'outremers* (from overseas). It is unclear whether these names were transmitted systematically before the thirteenth century; when this did occur, it was an indication that the family group had found an ancestor whose protection should be sought. It was at this juncture (1050–1100) that the nobility on the other hand opted for the name of a fief or their own land, that is the toponymic usage which until then had been more common amongst peasants. The same concern for links with the dead is reflected in the adoption of their name at baptism by peasants and nobles alike; fashion certainly played a part, witness the sudden eruption of Jean, Hans and John (according to geographical situation) after 1160 or 1170, but so did the practice of using more noble names, faithfully transmitted from generation to generation, above all royal names like Charles, Louis, Conrad, Heinrich and Edward, that had long been taboo. What peasant in his modest dwelling would not consider his life enhanced by such protection?

The family group

The growing body of historians of the family are well aware that this structure was the primary unit of production and mutual assistance. The salient characteristic of the medieval economy was its reliance on these individual constituents and it really does not matter whether we call the system 'feudalism' or 'seigneurial exploitation', or refer to it by any other term, medieval or modern, so long as the principle of working within the family unit is understood. The combined efforts of these productive individuals supported the system which, as is well known, involved a heavy and sometimes excessive tax on the goods produced or finished by the worker in the fields or in his workshop, indeed on all sorts of services, in return for the supposed exercise of justice and the protection of the individual which the state, the *Res publica* – regardless of the ruler – was in no position to provide. Our picture has to be fitted into this social structure, which was established in about 950 or 1000 and gradually declined in the period 1250–1300.

The indivisibility of work

The *ménage* (household) which I have just described, based on the couple and unmarried children living under the same roof, was of course the dynamic force behind production. As long as there were sufficient sons or daughters working at home (in the *domus*, or, in Languedoc, the *ostal*) the group clearly operated in an almost exclusively domestic context, without the option of seeking outside assistance, in contrast to the lord whose ample resources allowed him to do so. Seigneurial dues undoubtedly meant that the peasant had to work harder than if he had only to be self-sufficient. He did not have the means to do more than meet the immediate, practical needs of food, clothes and implements: the notion of accumulating capital with a view to profit or new investment was quite foreign to such a system. It was in fact the progressive introduction of precisely this concept which undermined the system. But initially peasant farming was simple and the peasant knew nothing of specialized labour with a specific end in mind, nor did he see the possible advantages of greater effort, since the general level of needs and expectations remained low. The limitations and weaknesses of such a system are very apparent: on the one hand, the greater the importance of the household group, the less stress was laid on individual effort – hence, no doubt, what to our eyes seem a surprising number of hours for rest, feast days and siestas which punctuated the working day. (It has been calculated that scarcely 250 days were worked in a year.) On the other hand the peremptory financial demands of the lord or a chance combination of circumstances, climatic or otherwise, destabilized a system that had no reserves to fall back upon and no contact with neighbouring areas. The consequences are more comprehensible in these circumstances, both the periods in which groups either grew closer together or, alternatively – but as a result of the same causes – the violent outbursts that occurred if it transpired that the crisis did not impinge equally on all sections of society.

This concept of the peasant as no more than a tiny grain of sand – the *paysan granulé* as E. Le Roy Ladurie has called him – explains a certain fragility in the social structure as a whole to which I shall return. First of all we must provide some details. As no-one could do anything until they had been shown how to do it by an older man, such as a father or older brother, there is a clear concentration of effort, not in respect of age (for children were soon assimilated into adult life in this scheme of things, even if it meant sparing them the heavier physical tasks) but in respect of sex. And here we are once more confronted with the problems posed by the rural female population.

I shall deliberately pass over the misogynist tirades of a supposedly 'popular' literary genre that is almost exclusively masculine and urban in origin, and which draws to the full on the reservoir of feminine faults and weaknesses. We clearly lack its counterpart on the egoism, vanity and idleness of men, whose damaging effect on rural production one would have no difficulty in documenting. On the other hand, I would emphasize in the strongest terms that it is a facile excuse for the twentieth-century historian to accuse his contemporaries or his predecessors of the last two centuries of a total failure to understand domestic tasks. I have already said how much archaeology has contributed in this area to the restoration of the image of the 'mistress' of the household. If one adds the exclusive care – and for very good reasons – of children under seven or eight, it must, I hope, be agreed that in a society founded on the triple pillars of subsistence, education and procreation, the women who ensured the provision of the labour force had a position of prime importance. The bourgeois spirit of the nineteenth century has been primarily responsible for grouping these duties with all that was demeaning in the life of a peasant couple and we must stop thinking of them as servile and degrading, especially in a rural context. Moreover, although contemporary literature (with a few honourable exceptions such as St Bernard, Rupert of Deutz and, later, Christine de Pisan or the Knight of La Tour-Landry) referred scornfully or with hypocritical pity to women at home, iconographical representations are clearer and more charitable. Women appear sporadically at first, then with increasing frequency in the course of the fourteenth century, in the calendar scenes in Books of Hours, but it is above all in illustrations from the Bible that women are shown distributing alms or food and as the source of good counsel.

That said, I must return to my earlier remarks, firstly about the unimportance of age and also the physical disadvantages of repeated pregnancies and subsequent breast-feeding which affected the wife and placed her in a state that was morally and physically inferior to that of her husband. Moreover, as a result, he would only carry more responsibility for work in the fields or the woods in preference to household tasks; and it was undoubtedly the husband who dug and tilled, sowed the seed, reaped, dressed the vines and performed the labour and carrying services demanded by the lord. The wife, if her physical state permitted, was responsible for haymaking, milking, sheep-shearing and sometimes the grape harvest. The tasteless country saying about this division of labour – the land to the man who fertilizes and the fruits to the fertile woman – has been quoted in this context, perhaps with some justification. It was even more true in the case of an old maid, for countrydwellers did not have the money to secure her a place in a convent and there was nothing for her to do but grow old and wizened before the fire, amongst her brothers and sisters-in-law, maid of all work, but good for nothing. But, even pregnant or fitting these tasks in between feeds, the woman was responsible for the provision of water – a worrying necessity we can hardly conceive of – for looking after the fire, preparing gruel, seeing to the milling of corn and the baking of bread if the lord had not made milling and baking at the communal mill and oven compulsory: even then it was often the woman who went there and although St Bernard railed against the loose women who tempted young men there, St Dominic advised his friars to go and preach there to the village gossips, who would be forced to listen or lose their place in the queue. Then we should also remember the opportunities to meet afforded by carrying laundry to the river, mutual delousing and the communal spreading of dung and household wastes on the kitchen-gardens which surrounded the village.

Historians have looked for signs of evolution in this conservative and unbalanced structure. These have been observed in the employment of domestic servants and the introduction of technical improvements and in both cases the remedy seems to have been worse than the original ill: servants were undoubtedly either members of the wage-earning class and thus a contributory factor in the deteriorating system of domestic labour, or they constituted part of an expensive system of subsidy if it was a case of a relative in need. As for the introduction of the spinning wheel into the cottage in the thirteenth century, it undoubtedly saved the women invaluable time, compared with spinning with a simple spindle, but the contraption also immobilized the woman in the home, for there was no means of taking it about with her to spin in the fields, an activity documented in twelfth-century iconography. The old maids were certainly bound to it for life; indeed the English word 'spinster' originally meant no more than 'one who spins'.

The division of wealth

Since wives and the young men of the family were literally in the fields, by the fire or at the mill (the daughters having been married off as quickly as possible), their contribution to any acquisitions the household might make cannot be doubted nor, therefore, their right to it should the father and head of the household (the *cap d'ostal*) die. Here the historian is almost overwhelmed by the great mass of inheritance customs formulated over the years between Ulpian and the lawyers of the thirteenth century. As Robert Boutruche observed, in this field more than any other the legal windmill turns in the empty air, for it is extremely difficult to unravel all the accumulated local practices and find those which impinged significantly on the peasant community, or determine the peasants' relationships with the letter of the law or the ritual of custom. There can be no question therefore of dissecting formal structure and labelling the constituents according to time and place. It is more helpful to take note of what was not known in particular areas than to emphasize nuances whose practical impact was minimal.

We turn first to that fundamental characteristic that at once separated the man in the village from one who lived in a castle: any wealth that the peasant acquired or inherited would be divided on his death. This was the law and it made no difference whether it was expressed in terms of Roman law or Germanic usage. Behind this may have lain the memory – and in some parts of northern France and of Germany the practice – of the old principle that the land was to be equally exploited by all free men – the *terra francorum* of the Mâconnais, the *communia* of Picardy, the *Allmende* of Germania, the relict of a vast allod in the classical past; or maybe the effects of the death of a head of household and the dispersal of his patrimony in Roman times were responsible for the continued survival of the typically rural notion that everyone should have portions of equal value. However, the opposite side of the coin remained very influential and was widely supported by the aristocracy whose power rested in the size of their lands, while the expectations of a peasant couple were minimal. What was the origin of this flaw? It is hard to detect it at this level of society, but the reasons must have been closely related to the reduction of available land and, consequently, throughout the period of demographic pressure (1150–1250), when a father died there were many claims on a relatively small amount of good land. Whatever the case the successive depletion of family landholdings was everywhere apparent.

Let us start with the widow: her dower could not be taken from her, for that was guarded by the Church. After many dubious transactions by the rest of the family in the course of which more than one dowager undoubtedly witnessed the plundering of her rents and capital, she was entitled to a third (the Italian *tercia*) of the deceased's inheritance, even if the dying man had attempted to dispossess her in his will. That was the law; as for reality, it continues to elude the historian. Then the lot of the daughters was arranged; old maids were sent to a convent, possibly regardless of the widow's attitude: it has been observed that in the west of France in the thirteenth century almost half the professed novices came from this group whose secular life had not been so very different from that of a member of an enclosed order. The other daughters – married, or marriageable – had their dowry and were consequently excluded from the remainder of the inheritance. This exclusion was an old Germanic practice, found in the eighth-century Laws of Chur (eastern Switzerland); it was admitted in Italy where there was nothing in the practices relating to dowries to justify such a development. The practice of exclusion of daughters in possession of a dowry is documented in northern France towards 1100, then in the south in about 1150 or 1155; it became general in Norman territories and at the beginning of the thirteenth century, whether they were sent to a convent, reduced to being their brothers' servants or married with a dowry, daughters disappeared completely from the ranks of their father's heirs.

The sons were left with possessions into which dower and dowries had made considerable inroads. The practice of partible inheritance – the *frérèche* of Poitou and Aquitaine, the *frairie* of the Lyonnais, the Catalan *hermandad* and the Italian *fraterna* – tempted many of the warfaring nobility to leave the fief or the honour intact and in the hands of one man (*una manu*). There is little evidence that countrydwellers were tempted by the practices of partible inheritance at the same time (between 1080 and 1150). The disadvantages a generation later are immediately obvious, with the problem of doing business with surviving uncles, rivalry between sisters-in-law, an excessive number of rival claimants. That is why there is every reason to believe that as far as rural possessions were concerned, and particularly where allods (*allodia*) were involved, the practice of inheritance by the eldest son, or primogeniture, gradually adopted by the nobility from the Loire Valley to the Holy Land between 1100 and 1180, became equally widespread amongst commoners. Moreover Roman law, based on the Code of Justinian, enjoyed renewed influence in the twelfth century in southern Europe from Bologna to Barcelona and did nothing to counteract the tendency to 'prim hereter' (primogeniture). Further north the concept of inheritance by the eldest son for which Ranulf Glanville (*fl.* 1180) claimed Saxon origin – a very questionable assertion – took root at a slightly later date. But other customs prevented its widespread adoption in the lower ranks of society where the pre-eminent requirements of feudal service and of maintaining the lordship had no currency. In other areas the idea was prevalent that, if the eldest, or at least one of the sons, was entitled to inherit the lands which the father had held in his own right (as Roman law dictated, *paterna paternis*), the younger sons, on the other hand, had a right to the possessions acquired subsequently by the parental household. Even the increasingly widespread use of the will in the thirteenth century did not enable an inheritance to be left either to a single individual or to people unrelated to the deceased; a third of the disposable portion of the estate was still automatically allocated to the widow and another third to the heirs by consanguinity, so that the testator could only exercise any degree of free will over the disposal of the remaining third. As for the division of acquisitions between younger children it is likely in a peasant milieu that the modest amount of goods to be shared between a vast number of relatives resulted either in the further fragmentation of the land into minute pieces, or the departure of younger offspring to seek their fortune in the towns or on the roads, swelling the ranks of those who eked out a marginal existence there.

And so the gradually established practice of peasant inheritance tended to encourage the great increase in property ownership or bequests of money. Tension increased as a result within the seigneurial unit with both a demand for more land and resistance to higher levels of taxation. These pressures played a considerable part in the breakdown of the seigneurial system, notably when only very small areas of cultivable virgin land remained that did not threaten the forests (that other pillar of the medieval economy) with excessive clearance, or when the nobility's increasing need for liquid capital led them to make more forceful financial demands.

If the practice of partible inheritance eventually proved disastrous, it served at least to demonstrate the extent to which the peasant couple remained aware of the memory and responsive to the attraction at least of the clan, if not of the tribe, in which their origins lay. However, there is no reflection at village level of the circumstances that made it imperative for the nobility to close ranks: for the peasantry the 'family' in the widest sense of the term (one, moreover, which we still use) was the natural framework of mutual aid and protection, the crucible of a shared folklore which they alone could transmit. Unfortunately, – and this situation possibly extends beyond the period with which we are concerned – the surviving evidence is of noble origin or from the vocabulary of erudite scribes, sparing of detail.

However, it looks very likely that the familiar pattern of development that has emerged from the continuing studies of German scholars like Munster, Tellenbach, Schmit and Werner, or Duby and his followers in France, is also characteristic of the peasantry. To rehearse some of its definite features: initially there were very large gatherings and clans remarkable for a distant totem of the type of the Roman *gens* or the German *Sippe*. At this numerically extended stage the only dominant group was one with supposedly greater 'magic' powers in which women were accorded a considerable role in Celtic and, later, Aquitanian areas. In my view the transition to a stage when the 'clan' was dominated either by a single man or all the males of one generation (these two structures had a parallel existence but the first was more characteristic of the south) took place during the early Middle Ages: by about 900 or 1050 at the latest it had occurred everywhere. Men who recognized mutual ties of blood, or indeed of marriage or friendship, grouped themselves around the prince or the simple head of the village. There is an immense vocabulary to describe such groupings: the *bandos* of Biscay, the *casaleres* of Béarn, the Italian *consorzio*, the *agermanent* of the Saxons, the Flemish *faides*, the Germanic *Geschlecht*, the Tuscan *fraterne*, the Polish *szlachtas*, the *hermandades* of the Iberian peninsula and the *parçonneries* of central France, not to mention Latin terms, such as *familiares, cognati, agregati, germani, proximi, parentes* and so on. It is the transition between the first and second stages which has made it difficult for genealogists of every period to establish a line of descent going back before 800–50. This 'familial' grouping survived unchanged in some areas, such as Frisia or the Celtic lands of Brittany, Scotland and Ireland. Elsewhere the dramatic development to the stage with which we are concerned took place, centred on a house (*maison, domus, Haus*) where there was a fixed settlement with a stable male population in control of the surrounding countryside and where the exigencies of an itinerant existence no longer had to be reckoned with.

Yet this picture would seriously underestimate the strength of bonds of mutual assistance that existed, especially in the villages, between nuclei that in theory were gradually becoming increasingly independent. Whether it was a question of the loan of tools or money, of food given to those less well-off in return for work in the home, of vengeance taken for a crime that dishonoured another group, or even a communal call to arms, there are hundreds of different examples and hundreds of ways of offering assistance. This is why an assessment of the continuing influence of the *familia* on the autonomy of the household has been an indispensable element in historical studies of the eleventh, twelfth and even the thirteenth centuries.

It is virtually impossible, outside the nobility, to assess the influence of a father in the choice of a wife, or of a father-in-law over a couple's behaviour. To make any calculations on the subject we are forced to return to the arid domain of property transactions, the only concrete details recorded in contemporary practice. Parental approval of every change in the disposition of the patrimony was by no means a custom exclusive to the nobility: it is to be found wherever there were owners of property and smallholders. This was the *laudatio parentum* of the lawyers, that was eventually to develop into the principle of retrocession, either to the group as a whole or to one of its members, of any property judged to have been wrongly ceded or sold – the *retrait lignager* of legal French, the *ritorn* or *tornaria* found in documents of the period, a practice in the south from 1070–1100, and established in northern Europe in the second half of the twelfth century. The calculations that have been based on these diverse practices show that the extended family interfered less and less in the affairs of a couple, but that there were revivals as a result of changes in social structure or in habitat and very considerable regional variations. The examples in table 1.2 below show the percentage of documents in which relatives intervened in the transaction, either spontaneously or after protest:

Table 1.2

	950–1000 (%)	1000–50 (%)	1050–1100 (%)	1100–1200 (%)
Catalonia	35	46	41	25
Mâconnais	55	38	49	70
Picardy	17	36	21	25

Such intervention declined further in the thirteenth century: in Picardy the rate fell to 15 per cent before 1250, 5 per cent after that date; in Flanders and Namur it was between 13 and 32 per cent about 1250.

The psychological inter-relations between households and their group interaction will inevitably largely escape us. This sensitive area is only revealed by a document as exceptional as the Register of the Inquisition at Montaillou, studied by Le Roy Ladurie. But there is one other course open to us, relating to England alone at this period, as manorial courts of justice recorded reasoned sentences. The evidence of this material from one study of five English counties between 1202 and 1276 is important, expecially in comparison with the town. It shows that if the average level of criminality appeared comparable to that of the eighteenth century, offences committed in the country generally elicited the intervention of the victim's relatives, women amongst them; that the perpetrators of these offences might, or might not, belong to the property-owning classes but responded much more readily to challenges to the honour of the group, or threats to the integrity of an inheritance, than in the town and as a result the proportion of pre-meditated crime was higher in rural areas. It would be pointless to attempt any further extrapolation, but it is worth noting that these trends do not contradict any of our earlier observations.

Knowledge and belief

This is an ambitious title to which we all know it is impossible to give a satisfactory answer. Even in the modern period any understanding of rural attitudes is hampered by irrelevant assumptions. These people could not write and speak to us only through clerics and nobles who presented them as absurd caricatures. Iconography continued, unperturbed, to reproduce the classical and Carolingian *topoi* of men working the land. As we shall see, it is only their fantasies which have reached us untouched, because the Church tracked them down in its fight against witchcraft and heresy and they are sometimes illuminated by accusations in trial proceedings. But for the anonymous poets of *Aucassin et Nicolette* and *Le Charroi de Nîmes* and for Chrétien de Troyes these deformed beings, dressed in rags with squashed features and filthy mops of hair, black hands and yellow teeth, verged on the bestial. Thought was beyond them!

Beliefs rather than a faith

All preachers were unanimous and all the conciliar canons in agreement on one issue: that peasant worship was irregular, their knowledge and understanding of dogma scanty in the extreme. St Bernard in the twelfth century and Jacques de Vitry 100 years later both deplored the misconceptions on which heresy thrived; Dominicans like Hugues de Romans or Etienne de Bourbon, prelates like Eudes Rigaut, archbishop of Rouen, who scoured their dioceses, documented poor attendance at mass, ignorance of the Creed and even the Lord's Prayer, the infrequent practice of confession and even more of communion; the men were in the tavern, the women doing their laundry together: behind the lord and his household at mass there was a handful of children, widows and spinsters. Moreover, they had no knowledge of Latin, an ignorance sometimes shared by their priest, and there was no question of learning to write. At first sight, although the church dominated the village with its sheer size and served as a meeting-place and defensive retreat, it was little more than a communal building whose bells marked the hours of work and rest. It made little difference if the fields and houses were owned by a monastery, or whether they were one of the restitutions of patronage usurped by the laity and very, very slowly surrendered to the monasteries between 1050 and 1225–50.

This miserable picture, a little brighter in the thirteenth than in the eleventh century, distressed Rome at the time and affects too many historians of the Church today. This is undoubtedly to misunderstand peasant spirituality; in our largely urban and mechanized world we take too little account of the effect on the peasant soul of the forest encircling the village, the heath or marsh covered by sudden mists, thunderstorms and capricious rains. Where were God and the Incarnation to be found in these experiences? This was why the practice of the Christian faith remained at the level of what was useful, visible and probable, mingling the Christian message with the phantasms of protohistory. Of the sacraments proclaimed by the hierarchy of the Church only baptism was universal, for that was a rite of passage, a ceremony of introduction to the world in which they were to find their place and there were difficulties in persuading the villagers to proceed with it at the earliest opportunity. In their eyes this rite should accompany the dawn of the child's full consciousness when he was six or seven years old. The Last Rites were also in demand, but bore a strange resemblance to the pagan departure for the other world. Moreover, well into the thirteenth century there are descriptions of strange ceremonies performed by women in which new-born children were exposed on the edge of the forest, immersed in water, passed nine times between the branches of a tree or lighted tapers: 'Puerile superstition!' exclaimed Etienne de Bourbon, who knew nothing of anthropology and had no comprehension of the rites of separation, purification and retrieval which freed the new-born child from the powers of evil and made him truly his mother's son. For supreme power was seen to reside in Nature who was to be flattered and entreated. This was why women were intermediaries with the irrational: preachers saw this as the consequence of the Fall from grace in Eden, also brought about by a woman, without realizing that Earth, Moon and Water were also female. Only women could avert or precipitate sterility by the enchantments they practised at night in the *escrennes* in the wood or the land round the hut where they spun and wove. Only they could concoct philtres of mandrake, deadly nightshade or mint which served as contraceptives or abortifacients; only they could turn into witches and fairies to mislead credulous males or spoil the crops. Think of Yvain, Perceval or Tristan, ridiculed by wandering Melusines, goddesses of death and misfortune. The forest remained the favoured place for manifestations of this kind and of beings, good or evil, like elves, or the werewolves that have since metamorphosed into the child-eating wolves of fairytales.

Throughout this period the Church did not attempt to forbid – although little inclined to indulgence, like St Bernard, many priests made a real effort to understand – but it did attempt to regain control of these agrarian, sexual or initiation rites. When fertile rains had to be induced in late spring, the village priest placed himself at the head of the Rogationtide procession (on the Sunday before Ascension Day) and sprinkled the fields with holy water; after the harvest, when the earth had set an example of fecundity, boys and girls danced or coupled on the threshing floor to beat the grain; afterwards purificatory fires were organized in the name of St John, who could do nothing whatever about it; similarly, in May, the priests led torch-lit processions to plant a new tree or decked the girls who were to be married with garlands. Lent, too, was happily placed at the moment when the granaries were empty, transforming grudging penury into voluntary sacrifice; there was the sacrificial Paschal lamb of the Bible from whose blood the God was reborn and also the sacrifice of the pig fattened during the autumn and killed at Christmas, not – as once upon a time – to celebrate the winter solstice, but the presumed birth of Jesus.

Our list will stop there. The 'conversion' of the European peasantry was not complete at the beginning of the fourteenth century; it could be maintained that the process was not finished until after the Council of Trent. But this distorted faith was based on essential beliefs rooted in centuries of agrarian life: the bonds between the living and the dead, the belief in salvation, the concept of good and evil and the certainty that there would be a Judgement when the indistinct Godhead who ruled the world willed it. This Godhead was so indistinct that the workers in the fields required an intermediary to make themselves understood: if men did not consult a wizard or a hermit in the forest, it would be the Virgin or a patron saint – a terribly human Virgin with a child in her arms, a saint still more so, because they kept a relic such as a piece of bone or clothing.

Overall during this period the peasant gave the Church all his not inconsiderable tokens of acceptance and obedience: the 'Hail Mary' was easily introduced and became widespread at the time when statues of the mother of God were also appearing in church portals; the priest was virtually everywhere and it was he, even more than the blacksmith, who went up to the castle and talked to the lord of the manor; the wealthier man was prepared to make a bequest to the neighbouring monastery on his deathbed; peasants were willing to fast and to receive the body and blood of Christ once a year. The peasant accepted the Christian faith because in it he found the roots of simple belief – rustic in the full sense of the word – which gave a regular pattern to his daily earthly life. As for the future of the world and eschatological hopes and fears, if he gave way to moments of exaltation and terror, it was always because an impassioned preacher had led him to join a wandering band searching for a better existence. There were feverish outbursts of milleniarism at intervals throughout this period: around the years 1000, 1033 (millenium of the passion of Christ), 1095 (when the fall of Jerusalem was believed to have defiled the city), but it also broke out around 1107 and 1120, then again in 1170–80, in the middle of the thirteenth century and at its close. But in each case religious desire for purification was mingled with a specific upheaval of a different kind – oppression by the lord, famine, the threat of an epidemic, a desire to re-establish peace or to save the king.

Concrete knowledge

The concept of mutual education has been held in high esteem even at periods when there were schools whose masters could make their views known. Peasant education, however, was only mutual. Many technical manuals in the vernacular have survived from the beginning of the thirteenth and above all the fourteenth century, such as English 'Books of Husbandry', or collections of receipts about plants and their particular qualities, compilations known as *chatonnets* in the north of France, because they were attributed to the classical Cato, as well as illustrated bestiaries and lapidiaries. Such volumes were to be found in monastic libraries and lords of an enquiring turn of mind would have passages read aloud to them. But should we seriously believe that this empiricism reached the peasant's cottage? And which peasant would have been able to read even these unpretentious volumes? And so it was from father to son, mother to daughter, that knowledge was handed down, enriched by unexpected successes or illuminating setbacks. Should this piece of land be marled? Is triple ploughing required for that? A horse would be better here, if we had one; the vine should be cut back hard there. It is impossible to make any judgements in the murky darkness of the history of techniques, methods and different stages of development: all we can say is that irregular progress undoubtedly occurred.

If the peasants were not even taught what was the essence of their daily work how could they have known about anything else, other than from a pedlar passing through, by cross-questioning a vagrant or by watching a wandering Jew administer a cure? Their lack of geographical knowledge is still evident at the close of the thirteenth century: departing pilgrims, especially those bound for the Holy Land, were completely ignorant of the distances involved, the countries they would pass through or the dangers they would encounter. On the other hand it is surprising to learn that, at least according to their priests, these men whose life was rooted in the soil were not only well informed about their legal rights (which can only reflect a body of inherited knowledge) but also had some concept of the great events that might affect them: when Suger in 1125 and Guillaume le Breton in 1214 describe rows of peasants cheering Louis the Great and Philip Augustus, the one leaving for, and the other returning from, campaigns against the Emperor, one has the impression that there is more than the taste for spectacle in these crowds. The king was only a vague entity: in the thirteenth century when it was known that St Louis had been captured by infidels, bands of peasants took up arms with the idea of going to free him.

But to my mind the most important aspect of these illiterates who had no time for formal education was the existence of an extremely active social conscience. Although this undoubtedly stemmed from the pressure exerted by the dominant social class, it was indisputably fostered by spontaneous personal reflection, for these movements were not influenced by any specific combination of circumstances, any known leader or doctrine and many historians (Fourquin, Morghen and Musy amongst them) have only been able to explain them as religious phenomena. In fact the situation is very different. The movements should be linked to the increasingly tight control exerted by the ecclesiastical and secular authorities at the end of the tenth century and until about 1075. In Champagne around 1025, in the area around the river Po in Italy between 1030 and 1050, in Catalonia from 1020 to 1060, in Normandy in the tenth century and possibly after the Norman Conquest in England, the aim of peasant uprisings was to halt the movement towards rigorous social control, accompanied by fiscal pressure. They refused to agree to new labour services, to accept taxes like the *exactio* or the *questa* (soon to be called the *taille*), slightly later they resisted the obligatory grinding of corn in the lord's mill (for which, moreover, they had to pay) and they upheld their rights of common (*usages*) – their right of free access to naturally fertile ground, to woods and to the edges of marshes and meadows. Moreover, it was at just this period that the Church, uncertain exactly which course to take, was promoting the development of institutions to foster peace and went so far as to include peasant militias as one of its means of action, as in Berry in 1038 and later in the Rouergue or Velay; with this encouragement armed peasants had no hesitation in proceeding behind their banners of the saints against the castles of those lords most resistant to the establishment of the 'Peace of God', even though they were despatched without much trouble and driven back to their villages with a sword through their innards.

It will be objected that these were only economic or religious reactions to innovation, something that was by definition evil in the Middle Ages. However, the *parlements* which the peasants held to agree their course of action and the oaths of mutual trust they swore have every appearance of the conscience of an oppressed class. When the twelfth-century poet Wace wrote his verse narrative account of the Norman uprising of 998 he gave this slogan to the villeins who rose against the nobles: 'We are men as they are'. Whether this concept dated from the original revolt or was an invention of Wace is irrelevant: what matters is that such sentiments could be attributed to peasants at the time when he wrote. Moreover, the rural areas were constantly in the throes of simmering unrest, although outbursts of direct force are rarely documented (such as occurred in Asturias (Spain) in 1120, Picardy in 1125–40, the Lyonnais in 1160, Velay in 1175); this is partly because this was a phase of adjustment in the relationship with the lord of the manor, based on compromise and bargaining over money payments and also because it is highly probable that the great majority of instances have not been recorded: the buffets inflicted on the village in the predictable forms of sabotage, inertia or theft. There are strong grounds for believing that this conscience was an important factor in the thirteenth century, notably in the most developed areas where population pressure, the development of agricultural techniques and release from feudal dues were most distinct. I am quite clear on this point, without which we could not understand the violent peasant movements of the fourteenth century, affecting the whole of the West between 1325 and 1385 and bringing the period with which we are concerned to a close. It is important to understand the so-called 'revolutionary mechanism' identified by Tocqueville long ago: burdens that have been alleviated in part seem much less bearable than those which remain unremittingly overwhelming. It was the hope of seeing even these remaining burdens disappear completely that inspired the *jacqueries*, violent uprisings of the relatively well-off. These were totally misunderstood both by contemporaries appalled at rebellion by the more privileged members of the lower classes and also by countless modern historians accustomed to seeing revolution as a reaction to desperate poverty or in terms of the frenzied outbursts of the slaves of antiquity. There were many such movements all over Europe in the mid-thirteenth century, in the south of England, Flanders, Picardy, Champagne, Swabia, Limagne, the Vivarais, the Toulousain, Catalonia and Tuscany – the *Pastoureaux*, the *Enfants*, the *Capuchonnés*, the *Statutarii* and many others centred upon a hermit, a crank or simply a mere village craftsman. One has only to note the welcome, certainly muted but in general sympathetic, which they received from many towns and even some lords to be convinced of their social character. The revolutionary characteristic of the movement lay in precisely this mixture of men from different orders of society with theoretically irreconcilable points of view, contrary to the opinions of those historians who see social conflict only in terms of the nineteenth-century struggle between workers and capitalists.

We must bring our assessment of the peasant to an end here, or rather of the role which the family group at least theoretically played in village life. The picture I have presented is not a static one. Many things changed between 1000 and 1300, and this trend will become clearer when we follow the worker to the fields or to market. But from now on it must be emphasized that the peasant group was in a state of perpetual flux and far from being the changeless social stratum which the rash eighteenth-century *philosophes* and the nineteenth-century positivists were so ready to portray. This was partly because the bonds surrounding them shifted and their tension varied with regard, for example, to marriage, the authority of the *familia* and the state of knowledge, but also because it was constantly subjected to two centres of attraction. One of these was centrifugal, tending to remove the marginal elements of the group that served as its antennae – younger sons who emigrated, children who went to live in another village, inheritances that fragmented the family's lands, relatives no longer consulted. The other force was centripetal, and re-enforced some of the features of the village grouping that were reflected in the notion of a common economic and social interest in their dealings with the lord of the manor, a growing body of local folklore, an increasing number of shared festivities and festive rendez-vous and the consolidation through common experience of a body of knowledge that could only be transmitted from one generation to the next. However, my treatment of the peasant family would not be complete if I did not add what we now know, as a result of recent research, about their immediate context – the peasant house.

2

Houses and Villages

For the last twenty years or so medieval historians (paying scant attention to the lessons of contemporary rural areas) have asserted that the village was a stable, tranquil and unchanging place, with traditional building techniques. In 1962 G. Duby wrote, 'In the ninth century western Europe was populated by a static peasant population, rooted in the soil. . . . We sense them well and truly established in their village'. The entire weight of the geographical traditions of the eighteenth and nineteenth centuries inclined towards this stable and unchanging picture, apparently also endorsed by common sense. In our own time, however, the unplanned or bureaucratic regrouping of farmland, the destruction of hedges (and with them the enclosed field system), the increasing number of second houses in the country and the growing uniformity of building materials, the continual movements of the rural population and the upheavals caused by changes in the road system which have all torn apart the fabric of rural life since 1950 at least, would have made it advisable to consider the possibility of parallel movements at an earlier date. Archaeology cut through these assumptions: the enthusiastic excavation of village sites, graveyards and refuse pits in Germany, Poland, the Low Countries and England, then, at a later date and on a more modest scale, in France, Spain and Italy, has destroyed the old positivist theory with concrete evidence to the contrary. Instead it transpired that the stereotyped 'peasant house' and the village established since time immemorial were in a state of continual change and development. The situation now seems so totally different from what was generally accepted five or ten years ago that we must consider it in greater detail.

The roots of the villagers

English and German historians of the early Middle Ages did not doubt the superficial and mobile character of ninth-century agriculture. They described a changing pattern of tillage, the expanses of moorland, marsh and scrub and the often enormous herds that wandered over them. In southern France and the romance-speaking borderlands of Europe in general, these historians claimed to see coherent land-use and an occupation rooted in the soil; and even in the middle of the semi-cultivated areas north of the Seine they brandished manorial surveys, tarnished mirrors only reflecting a tiny part of the land. There are few supporters of such a static analysis today: even in Italy Pierre Toubert has demonstrated that there were changes of site and remodelling, just as there were in Provence or Languedoc. Further north archaeology had completely overturned the theory of continuity: it is quite possible that there were continuous settlement patterns here and there – in isolated parts of the Central Massif, for example – but these were exceptions.

A floating population

To understand a phenomenon so manifestly contrary to our traditions, we must make a conscious adjustment that is by no means easy. It is difficult for us to imagine (though possibly easier than for our fathers) the constant movement within medieval peasant society, which Marc Bloch compared to that of molecules in a body. Individuals or entire groups were constantly on the move, from a valley onto a plateau or from a plain to the mountains, to say nothing of migrations, wanderings and exile – voluntary or otherwise – which tore people up by their roots and cast them from one country to another, under the tyranny of faith, the exigencies of hunger or the fear of danger. There is even proof of this incessant movement within the narrow framework of a single land-holding, where minute parcels of land changed hands virtually every generation. The causes of this permanent state of agitation escape our immediate comprehension, as indeed do other aspects of the subject: insecurity, discomfort, a sense of inner dissatisfaction and no doubt others. We, after all, react in the same way in our own troubled times. If we add the need to take refuge in the woods or gather wild berries and fungi there, or the need to sow elsewhere when the soil was exhausted, there are sufficient specific reasons to gauge the prevalence of this phenomenon.

Against this some scholars have set indisputably fixed characteristics such as the natural boundaries provided by the contours of a region, the forests which determined the extent of areas of pasturage or the antiquity of a place-name. But these arguments do not contradict my theory in the least: the formation of place-names in both Romance- and Germanic-speaking areas is much less evidence of long-standing settlement than of the concept of collectivity with a final -heim or -curtis, or the name of a Roman family ending in -iacum; in every case an expression which referred to the group, the totem they set up or the ancestor whose protection they sought. Who would have the audacity to claim that a place-name had always been rooted to one particular spot rather than half a mile away? Field-boundaries were sometimes laid out on unquestionably ancient lines, but I see these as part of a vast area of shifting culture, with huts rather than permanent dwellings, and not a static collection of adjacent buildings. For their part archaeological excavations in the Rhineland, Westphalia and the south of England have shown successive settlements on the same site before the tenth century, as many as five at Chalton (Hampshire) or Wharram Percy (Yorkshire) and others that were only occupied for a very brief period, two or three centuries before the site of the village moved. I am convinced that this is the only view that accounts satisfactorily for the anomalies found even in the Carolingian polyptychs between theory and apparent reality, between the scattered settlement of the manse and the close grouping of the réserve. Moreover, such village plans as have been established – in Germany, for example, at Hohenrode, Gladbach or Warendorf – fly so much in the face of common sense that one is forced to admit the existence of capricious, anarchic and scattered settlements. I think there is every chance that such village layouts also existed on the Mediterranean *latifundia*, if we consider the country around Aix, or Rome or Asti, for example, where the houses (*casae*) are scattered across the enormous and still undefined area of a *paroisse* or a *pieve*, as it is called in Italy. In this context we should also note that abandoned village sites, like all those excavated by W. Janssen in the Rhineland, do not imply any kind of cultural setback, but a regrouping or shift of population.

Of course this is not to deny the existence of a more substantial and fixed habitation in this kaleidoscopic picture of shifting settlement: the classical *villa* reoccupied in the sixth century, a 'barbarian' palace whose foundations reveal it also to have been a place of worship, a veritable stone church – to say nothing of cemeteries with an equally fixed site. But it is precisely these which provide me with my final argument: the graveyards were almost always some way from the eventual site of the church and were used fairly consistently over a long period; excavations in many parts of England have shown that they were often to be found at the meeting point of several neighbouring clearings, as if at the point of death they acted as a focal point for the regrouping of all those whose mortal remains were buried at an earlier period, when the cemetery was not in the middle of the fields. And who could fail to see the link here with the structure of the tribal group, indeed of the family, of which so little is known at that distant period. In the tenth century this settlement of uncertain, temporary and insubstantial character can most frequently be connected with the place where its inhabitants' remains are still to be found.

The dead, the parish and the castle

The reader should be quite clear in his own mind: by 'village' we mean a grouping of men round a fixed point dependent on the cultivation of the soil over an area whose boundaries were henceforth also fixed, but, more than that, were united by an awareness of long-term common interests. Consequently we can use the term 'village' to describe an extended settlement, but one whose various hamlets and isolated farmsteads were all dependent on an area with a perceptible unity, likewise with woodland and other similar types of countryside. Inversely, community of interest and physical proximity identified before the disruption of this fairly dense network of building in the tenth century is not sufficient to constitute a village unless it is more than the expedient use of a pre-existent pattern of settlement. What is quintessentially important for us is to discover the germ of that sense of community which was the village: 'not the walls but the attitudes of the inhabitants (*non muri sed mentes*)', as St Augustine had already expressed it. There is a multiplicity of options, but we can never be sure that a particular feature was dominant in one region, nor which stage had been reached at any one period. We must now consider this vast area which scholarship has scarcely begun to investigate.

Firstly, there is the theory that settlement has to take place round an unchanging feature. Here geographical determinism goes overboard fast: village sites were no more predestined than those of towns; first of all because we have no idea what characteristics were sought after at that period: they surely preferred light, dusty, siliceous soils, the only podzols which their indifferent tools could work. Were there not changes in the level of the water-table, which must have made one site untenable or stabilized another? Did the crossing of obstacles like rivers, mountains, forests or marshes result in a concentration of population close to the new ford, pass, forest ride or causeway; or did they avoid such places as excessively vulnerable to attack from soldiers or bandits? I could continue at length in this vein. 'Some areas are attractive, others less so', said Roger Dion and this is undoubtedly true, but with important variations at different periods – witness the *a posteriori* proof provided in other studies by the reclamation and abandonment of land that punctuates the agrarian history of rural areas like Thuringia, the Warta or Quercy, to take a few scattered examples, and which also dictated, according to the period, which lands were tilled and which left as pasture.

So let us leave nature, one element amongst many. The cemetery, on the other hand, is an indisputably fixed point. We do not yet know why a tribe chose to bury its dead in one place rather than another: perhaps because it was near an agrarian place of worship, symbol of perpetuity, indeed of resurrection, or perhaps a spring? Was it isolated, because they were afraid of the dead, out of respect for them, or from a desire to avoid grave-breaking, one of the most tenacious taboos in all human societies? These are questions for the anthropologists but they raise many more. Whatever the case, the 'field of peace' was a sacred place, protected and inviolable; it could be a refuge from the living, even an attraction in communities where the cult of the dead was a particularly powerful influence. So it was the dead who attracted the living to a particular site: excavations of very different sites – in the Central Massif, the foothills of the Alps, Lower Saxony and Hampshire – have all shown clearly that tombs antedate every other trace of human activity. Even so graveyards are not an inevitable feature – apart from the countless cemeteries that have remained isolated, what about problematical villages that have no graveyard at all, like Dracy in Burgundy or Rougiers in Provence? Here there must have been something else.

The Church was theoretically the only link between the culture of the classical world and that of the Middle Ages, but did gatherings of the faithful provide a physical framework for assemblies? Historians of the parish would certainly assent: what could be a more natural expression of communal life than adherence to the same faith, participation in the same rites at shared places of worship? Unfortunately archaeology has also undermined this interpretation: authentic villages have been found in Poland and Scandinavia dating from the pre-Christian period; and there is little support elsewhere for the establishment of a parish structure before the Gregorian Reforms in the eleventh century or, at best, the lay restitution of churches which their ancestors had either created or appropriated in the early Middle Ages. These churches under lay patronage (*église propre, Eigenkirche*) escaped the supervision of the ecclesiastical authorities and survived here and there in secular control as late as the fourteenth century, accounting for as much as six to ten per cent of the total. What of the church building itself, made of stone and defensible: did the local population gather there to discuss the matters that affected the whole community? Undoubtedly, but it is nevertheless demonstrable that there were wooden churches (similar to those of more northerly areas) in regions where stone was the dominant building material, and – like their northern counterparts – these churches were vulnerable and did not remain on the same site. I would argue that local gatherings were based on the parish structure, but only after a period of readjustment, and indeed of creation, around the eleventh century after the initial appearance of chapels of ease served by a priest and chapels on large estates and in hamlets, which were later elevated into parishes. Moreover, P. Toubert has shown in his studies of Sabina and in the Latium that right in the centre of the Christian world, a mere stone's throw from Rome, the fragmentation of the vast *plebes cum oraculis* into multiple parishes on elevated defensive sites (*paroisses castrales*) scarcely antedates 1000 or 1025. As yet there has been no general study of the chronology of the parish network, but if we analyse the evidence from villages that have undergone intensive archaeological excavation the ultimately secondary role of the church becomes apparent. Thus at Wharram Percy what remains of the ecclesiastical buildings indicates a very late development: the place of worship in the Saxon period was on the Celtic site, while until the twelfth century houses were built further north even though the stone had been used for the church since 1000. Houses did not come to be grouped near the church until around the thirteenth century, when the building was extended, then left the previous site and went back towards the site of the Iron Age settlement.

The medieval village of popular imagination was dominated by the castle, supposed symbol of 'feudalism'. In France, Germany, the Low Countries and Italy a vast survey is in progress whose aim is to establish the date of origin of these fortified sites and their occupation by garrisons. Chronological phases are just emerging – after 925, before 1080 – but there are many contradictions: castles are recorded from the very earliest times in Lorraine, Italy and the Pyrenees; about 975–1000 in Provence, Auvergne and Normandy; not until 1030–40 in Anjou, Poitou, Catalonia, Calabria, Picardy and Flanders; later still in Guyenne, England and Germany. Moreover, there were sometimes many different types of building in succession: a tower or a court-room incorporated into a motte, as at

Doué-la-Fontaine or at Douai; five different types of building between 950 and 1050 on a motte in the Caux area of Normandy. But the results that have emerged so far are very suggestive: remarkable numbers have already been identified in the relatively small areas where the inquiry has already been completed – 80 in the Caux area, 80 in the Auxois, 30 around Chartres, 50 in Quercy and so on. The great variety of structures from which these fortifications might develop has also emerged: a comital *aula* (hall) of the early Middle Ages in Anjou, the Rhineland and Devon, a *corti*, a Carolingian *mansio* or even a classical *villa* in Piedmont or the Auvergne, or from protohistoric sites such as Husterknupp in north-west Germany, on the site of cemeteries in Burgundy and the Liège area. On the other hand, the initial impression at least is that we are concerned in the majority of these cases with a naturally defensible site (the *rocce*, *colli*, *podia* and *montes* of Mediterranean and Alpine regions, for example); elsewhere the motte – a mound of earth and gravel which, it has been calculated, would only have taken 50 men on forced labour 40 days to construct to a height of 10 metres on a base of 30. So it looks as if armed forces with a defensive role gathered where there was already a settlement, which then focused on the new fortification. In places like Italy, Spain and Provence the controlling authority effected this by force – here the development of the *incastellamento* (with houses perched on the side of the fortification, secure within its walls) forced the hand of peasants scattered on the low-lying plains; elsewhere, in Languedoc and the plains of northern Europe, for example, the movement inside the walls was more spontaneous and local villagers were attracted by privileges and a ready clientele of greedy soldiers. But in all these various cases it was a lordship (*seigneurie*) that took root. Even here, however, the military aspect does not provide an entirely satisfactory explanation: apart from cases of castles without villages and vice versa, some mottes surrounded by a ditch (such as the German *Wasserburg*), had sites that defied common sense; a motte was sometimes raised above a natural peak, as if the moral implication of the first detracted from the practical advantages of the second; to say nothing of sites with twin mottes. The fortress as a symbol of justice was thus promoted at the expense of its defensive role. This has little direct bearing on the subject, however, for in both cases men were held down and gathered together in one place.

The siting of villages

Have we now found the essential link? Were villages born, spontaneously or by coercion, as a result of the building of castles? Unfortunately too many cases suggest the opposite, just as there were in our attempt to relate the development of villages to the parish structure. There are countless instances of villages built to order and then abandoned at the foot of a useless tower: in the Auvergne, the Pyrenees and Sabina there is evidence of dozens of such villages that have very quickly been reduced to the level of miserable hamlets. On the other hand it was about 1130–50 before a few huts were to be found tucked at the foot of a motte, or even within the bailey wall – a protective enclosure that had had to wait 100 years for their arrival.

These last cases are of particular interest. In fact excavations of the vast enclosures dating from the tenth century or occasionally earlier, of the royal or imperial residences of Tilleda or Werla in central Germany, and of post-Carolingian camps such as Escorailles in the Auvergne, or all the earth ringworks that are characteristic of the Anglo-Saxon or Germanic regions – all show that the oldest settlements were the workshops of domanial craftsmen active in the service of a lord; one has the impression that it was this artisan community which, at a slightly later date, attracted peasant settlements. This has been proved in the Languedoc, in the Gascon *castelnaux* and also in numerous Rhineland sites. The question of artisan settlement seems to be the key to the problem of concentrations of population with which we are concerned. While the rich villas, farms and estates (*villae, fundi* and *corti*) of classical times controlled the economy, metal-, wool- and wood-working took place within their confines for the use of the dominant social group. These were centres of activity for which St Gall provides a model plan, whose abundance and diversity is reflected in every ninth- and tenth-century inventory (such as that of St Riquier) with the granary, cellar, dairy, bakehouse, brewery, sheep-shearing pen and carpenter's workshop (*horreum, cellarium, scuria, pistoria, fenile, camba, ovile* and *scipena*). These exceptions aside, village sites have only revealed the foundations of huts whose use by craftsmen was reflected in the equipment excavated, sometimes twice or four times as numerous as the houses themselves (as at Gladbach in Germany, Kootwijk in the Low Countries or West Stow, Suffolk) sometimes found in equal numbers (Odoorn in the Low Countries, Wharram Percy, Brebières in France). Now the archaeological sites which demonstrate that they were occupied until the period of regroupment with which I am concerned, suggest that these structures were abandoned in about the year 1000: the independent craftsmen appear to have been attracted firstly to domanial workshops and, secondly, to communal workshops being set up within the village itself. I suggest that it was about 1100 that this important step took place because it was at this point, or possibly a little earlier, that the blacksmith's forge took root in what was to become the centre of the village. In Picardy, Catalonia and Normandy there are documentary references of about this date to the *fèvre* or *ferrario*, the metal-worker in the midst of country-dwellers. This was an important social and economic development, since metal-work was particularly important to all social classes, whether miiitary or religious, tillers of the soil or producers of staple commodities: the manufacture of horseshoes, pieces of armour, tools for woodman or labourer, re-enforcement of the shafts of a mill or press and many other aspects of his work made the smith the natural intermediary between the lord and his men.

It is worth establishing the chronology of the smith's arrival with greater precision, as has already been done for the Eastern Empire. The evidence of literary texts (such as Germanic epics, or lives of the saints either composed or reworked in the eleventh century) appears to show that there was a stage when a primitive artisan community (precursor of the village artisans) was in competition with domanial craftsmen. The solitary charcoal burners and hermits of the woods, who were feared for their magic and admired for their skill must surely have been busy along the river banks with wickerwork, clogmaking, charcoal burning and the tempering of steel. I would even maintain that the powerful movement of 1030 to 1100 which drew to the woods men and women fleeing from this world behind Robert d'Arbrissel, Bernard de Tiron or many others, must be viewed as one expression of the birth of a whole new range of manual skills. It undoubtedly became easier for these men to establish themselves near peasant dwellings rather than to lead an itinerant existence or live in the middle of the forest. The transport of firewood (the most important raw material) undoubtedly also became quicker and more reliable as the network of roads underpinning the entire transport system improved and expanded.

It was this last characteristic which fixed the village site most securely. With the exception of routes dating from the classical period (not necessarily the work of Roman engineers), which provided a link between towns or, more rarely, joined hamlets (*vicus*, *borgho*) to the nearest city, movement within an area of cultivated land (in particular access to wood or scrub) appears to have been difficult for a long while. On the other hand it is striking how frequently paths (*semita*, *pedanea*) joining the village to an isolated field or to the forest are mentioned as boundaries from the tenth century in Italy, slightly later in the north. This network provided the basis for the distribution of small landholdings whose plan was henceforth fixed; it was along these ways, too, that crosses and milestones were erected and we should be careful not to confuse them with the high road (*via publica*, *strata*, *calceata*) travelled by pedlars and princes. Dating a road is a risky business, unless it is in a region such as Oxfordshire, where extant hedges are some guide as to age, or in a rural area where the extent of strip cultivation is clearly evident, as in the *Ackerberg* of Alsace and Limborg, where a headland ridge, formed by the plough as it was turned, marks the edge of the field.

All the peasants had to do then was to gather together all the focal points on which their life was centred: at Wharram Percy the five centres of activity which appear to have coexisted before 1050 or 1080 regrouped as a single whole, precipitating the sudden birth of a church to replace what had previously been one of the simplest religious buildings and the re-siting of the manor in the centre of a village which had finally discovered its identity.

The many faces of the village

A large walled Sicilian town would no more have resembled a village in the Trégorrais (in Brittany) in about 1200 than it does today: the development of village structures was not chronologically determined. Nor was it dictated by geography: although the Mediterranean village perched on a hilltop seems characteristically southern to us, a village on the mountain side in the Alps or the Rouergue, or even on an enclosed site in Gascony or Bavaria, would conjure up the same sense of being shut in and of the houses being squeezed together. Nor is it a question of the materials used: the log houses of Quercy recall those of Scandinavia and the 'Roman' tiles of Provence also cover the roofs of houses in Lorraine. After so many centuries it is only the social and economic history of agrarian communities that can account for the survival of the initial structure.

The double village

First I must say something about villages on double sites, because – unless research on village sites has some surprising new developments in store for us – they are essentially an exception. They deserve an important place in any survey because they probably represent primitive, rudimentary and almost protohistoric forms of the village layout; and for that reason they are ignored by documentary historians and frequently passed over by archaeologists. Only anthropologists and geographers have paid them any attention.

My logical starting-point would be the village of the dead: when one recalls the importance of the Other World in the peasant mind at this period what more significant place than that where they waited for judgement? Unfortunately the same historians who rush eagerly into the study of the Valley of the Kings in Upper Egypt, examine Mycenean tombs or pace up and down the Appian Way, are scornful of medieval cemeteries, especially when they lie beneath our own graveyards. The archaeologist is content merely to dig up bones and gravegoods and the documentary historian does not look there for a reflection of the living world. In the *atrium*, sanctuary and field of peace, historians and archaeologists both focus on the living, despite the essential role clearly accorded to the house of the dead, the hierarchy and position of corpses which we described earlier. This is undoubtedly a line for future research that would be full of surprises.

Seasonal homes have made more impact. In the first place they have survived in the remains of stone buildings on many sites in Provence, Sardinia and the Iberian peninsula, to say nothing of the example in Africa today of the 'double life' of the shepherds who move their flocks to higher ground in the summer months. Then there are also occasional relics of the *estives* (annual movement to summer pasture) in the mountain pastures of the Alps (*alpages*) and the various regional types of chalet and hut associated with this activity, such as the Alpine chalet (*mayens*) of the Valais, the *mazeaux* of Savoy and the *estars* of Andorra; also of granaries, stables, huts and fires in the open air. A mere episode in the life of a pastoral society, but one which occupied a good four months of the year in an almost exclusively masculine group with its own rules, tasks and hierarchy. The men rarely commented on this life away from their womenfolk, always on the look-out for news from the village down below. It took an implacable inquisitor to drive the shepherds of Montaillou to say even a few words about their life in the 'summer' village high on the mountains. Silence, isolation and our own consequent ignorance also obscure the *aumuches* of reeds and rushes in areas like the Fens, the *brières* of the Atlantic coast and the Frisian *terpen* which supported an entire population of fishermen, peat-diggers and gatherers of seaweed. Dredging occasionally reveals these structures, as in the recent discovery at the mouth of the Old Rhine of over 50 huts still inhabited around 1000.

On the other hand popular curiosity about life underground has continued to the present day. Galleries with rooms opening off them marked with air vents or wells were situated along a conveniently placed limestone fissure or sometimes laboriously chipped away with a miner's bar or pick-axe. Rock falls have claimed the lives of many children eager to explore this subterranean world. Other, more durable workings are still used to cultivate mushrooms, blanch chicory or mature cheese. These activities themselves are a fair indication that we are not dealing with a random phenomenon but deliberate use by man to eke out a livelihood. More than one such underground habitat has been destroyed by general stupidity, abandoned to treasure-hunters (in the Loire Valley), or fanatical historians of prehistory (as in Quercy), or used as munition depots (as in Picardy). This succession of various uses, quickly abandoned, is probably responsible for the total lack of interest in the site itself that has been displayed by even the most serious investigators. Even after the discovery of ceramic and other remains dating from the twelfth century it has been peremptorily asserted that these were sites for the practice of 'chthonic cults of druidic origin, or, when necessary, for Cathar rites'. With their isolated locations, concealed entrances and their potential as hideouts during foreign occupation (a practice that has continued in our own time), these caves have always been thought of merely as places of refuge in time of plague or danger. However, in the valleys of Poitou and the Limousin, the two areas of France where a serious stratigraphic excavation is under way there have been surprising results. Although the chambers and passages had been opened and altered many times there was evidence of several hundred years' permanent occupation from the tenth to the fourteenth centuries, with distinct phases which compel us to reject the theory that they were used as an occasional hideout. Moreover, the plan within the complex suggests that a number of distinct groups lived there, each living in one part of the caves, with its own fire, vessels and water supply. These characteristics surely imply yet another reflection of the village above ground. But how? And in what way? It is another field for future research.

Scattered and nucleated village settlement

The contemporary geographer is more interested in the development of a settlement than in its internal structure. The medievalist, however, attaches great importance to the external appearance and position of the village.

The village with a closed plan such as still sometimes typifies long-established Mediterranean settlements is not the only product of the hilltop village that gathered men together on a peak in a manner which might, or might not, have authoritarian implications. This semi-urban development was undoubtedly an intelligent response to the limited possibilities of a steeply sloping site where the houses seem to cling to each other and whose rear elevation is as blank as a containing wall: the *borghi* of the Gulf of Lions and the Italian *castro* (naturally fortified sites) combined the use of stone (which enabled the houses to be built very closely together) and the fortified gates or nobles' towers. But although today they have almost all broken through the encircling wall of wood or stone (a process that in some cases may have started as early as the thirteenth century) this was the aspect that many more northerly villages presented: a palisade of thick posts (the *Etter* of Thuringia and the Rhineland), the *tour de ville* (town wall) of Lorraine and Picardy and the *cingle* of villages in western France all had a demarcatory role, limiting an area beyond which a different judicial system applied. For we should be under no illusion as to the efficacy of interlaced branches or pointed sticks against determined warriors with axes and torches, as the *chansons de geste* like *Raoul de Cambrai* show only too well. They were there as physical markers of a judicial threshold beyond which landholdings and grazing rights (*tenimenta et pertinentia*) were subject to a common law. This enclosure has only left a few traces on the landscape, frequently visible in the Scandinavian *byl* or the Anglo-Saxon *burgh*, but all too often eradicated by subsequent changes in the pattern of landown-ership.

Our knowledge of these enclosed villages remains frustratingly imprecise: are we dealing with a grouping that was consciously created at the end of the first stage of peasant settlement, between 950 and 1100, and endowed with a code that justified this grouping and protected its privileges? In the case of the new towns and villages of the thirteenth century, which I shall shortly consider in detail, the case is clear-cut, entailing a remodelling of the area so complete that it almost defies description. But what happened in the tenth century? The concentric pattern of roads and lines of houses was clearly determined by the limitations of the site on the edge of the Cevennes or in the Levant, but why was it adopted in Bavaria, Alsace or Westphalia?

The open-plan village, though contrasting, provides no solution, as it is not typical of an unfranchised area. Moreover, it is found evenly distributed throughout Europe at this period, as much in southern Europe as in the majority of German *Dörfer*. The houses were scattered round the church or the cemetery along the roads which patterned the land. But two fairly distinct features seem typical: within their relatively loose structure, the individual plots of land – whether they were the Burgundian *meix*, the Saxon *borée* or the Germanic *Hufe* – enclosed a garden or an orchard, or a yard (*usoir*) for poultry. This survival of one age-old feature calls to mind another feature; the Italian *casale*, the *curtis* or *mansionile* of northern France were apparently all settlements that originated within a former domain, elevated to the status of village by the arrival of church or cemetery. If a monastery had remained lord of the manor there, we should not expect a castle. What is more it was onto this main trunk that subsidiary settlements were grafted, such as the *écarts* (dependent settlements of a parish), the *Willer* and the *Ham* that are so common in the Austrasian zone between the Scheldt and the Weser – and which prevented them from being distributed entirely at random, possibly a survival of a redundant pattern of land-use, such as the Germanic *villicatio* of the Carolingian period. However, similar settlement patterns are also found in the Celtic *ran* and *mejou* of Brittany and Wales without any such models.

It would be absurd, as well as in opposition to everything I have emphasized so far, to believe in the stability of these structures for even three centuries. This fluid situation was further affected by two specific considerations. One was the progressive concentration of building in areas already settled, which in the absence of statistical data we can only judge firstly from the number of sites that were abandoned in the period of agricultural expansion (and for which there were therefore no obvious external reasons for desertion) as, for example, in Oxfordshire, Norfolk, the Eifel or the Würtemberg area in the twelfth century; or, secondly, from an analysis of datable buildings added to those of an earlier date, as on numerous English sites. Sometimes several clusters of houses coalesced round a church or manor house, as in the village of Wharram Percy which we have already considered. The second characteristic is undoubtedly related to contemporary demographic pressure and to the search for fresh cultivable ground which either followed or preceded it. This was the great wave of deliberately created new settlements which affected the whole of Europe, but especially the north and Atlantic coastline. Henceforth these areas were the most active in this respect, with Gascon *castelnaux*, the *bourgages* of Normandy and the Maine area, the *villeneuves* of northern France, *Waldhufendörfer* of the Main and Hanover regions, the *villafranca* of Piedmont and the *sauvetés* and later the *bastides* of southern France. This expansion was essentially a feature of the years 1150 to 1250 and at a stroke produced settlements based on square or circular geometrical plans, surrounded by plots of land which were often designed to be all the same size, but in some places were grouped together in *aiole* or *quaderni* in the south, elsewhere in a herringbone pattern or in strips. At this period, when there was such widespread granting of privileges to villages we should not overlook their expansion by means either of building on areas that had previously been cultivated, by encroaching on one side of an old village, or by colonizing a suburb of easy access, dykes and litoral regions. These developments were characterized by a symmetrical plan sometimes still detectable today in the relative disorder of an old village centre. Examples could be cited from Picardy, the Ile-de-France and near Durham or Cambridge.

A living structure

The city-dweller in his dark and cramped conditions distinguished different quarters in the town without difficulty but could scarcely detect them in a small village. Nevertheless the great number of surviving documents from 1260 to 1280 onwards – when the population curve began to flatten out – is increasingly enabling the historian to distinguish in the village some of the features that are clear in towns: polarities of wealth, different centres of production and communal meeting-places. We must beware of excessive zeal in this field, however: a study of the provenance of the remains of utensils (largely used for cooking) at Rougiers in Provence has demonstrated households almost everywhere without any evidence of clearly defined social distinctions. A mixture of all types of rubbish from all periods and of similar constituents was found in the ground all round

Wharram Percy in Yorkshire, in that case undoubtedly also accompanied by human waste-products. However, at the close of the thirteenth century at the latest, building evidence assessed either at the time of a disaster (as at Cagnoncles, near Cambrai) or still visible (as at Rougiers) reveals 'islands' of particular social types within the village. Similarly, throughout our period archaeological evidence pinpoints workshop sites in both a domestic and a village context: positive batteries of kilns are sometimes found grouped together as at Saint-Victor-des-Oules or La Chapelle-des-Pots; or iron- and woolworking are each distinctively localized, as at Tilleda; or it may reveal craftsmen – and only craftsmen – dwelling within the walls of a *castrum* (a village within a fortified enclosure), as in so many villages of southern France, while the peasants built their houses outside the walls along the *estars* of Gascony and the Lyonnais.

Communal meeting-places are also relatively easily established, even without reference, given our chronological limits, to the evidence from confessions at Montaillou. Virtually everywhere this was first and foremost the square (*place*), *pratellum* or green, surrounded by rows of houses called row and *coron* either side of the Channel and *linea* in Italy. This was where the herds and flocks assembled before they set off for the woods or summer pasture in the mountains; where assemblies like the assize, *concejo* or *balia* that involved the whole community were held; where the old men told tales and the children deloused themselves. The village's water supply was another focal point, but here it was the women who reigned supreme, whether at a laundry-place by the riverside or stone tanks like the two at Rougiers which held 80 cubic metres of water. Collective store-pits also imply a considerable degree of social homogeneity which may not have pertained everywhere, but excavations of deserted village sites have been sufficiently extensive (there were 14 at Rougiers, for example) to establish this as a practice in marked contrast with our own society. Although the work of most rural artisans at this period (spinning, weaving, woodwork and basketmaking, even brewing and pottery) were within the scope of the average household, the smithy demanded equipment and skill that were outside the common run. I have already stressed how the arrival – or possibly the return – of the smith to the centre of the village was a landmark in peasant history; besides, the peasants found a natural leader and communicator with their master in the man who could handle fire and repair the lord's sword. The sites of forges can be identified today by deposits of hammer scale in the ground and they are the focus of significant studies in medieval metallurgy. In a documentary context it would also be valuable to trace the slow rise of the smith in witness-lists to the edge of a different world, peopled by nobles and clerics, and which no doubt resulted in their more frequent visits to the cavernous forge where he worked, where iron, flame and tools took on an almost magic quality.

When the village reached a certain stage of development the mill was added to these meeting-places. But it always remained apart and suspect: apart because until 1200 and beyond, its machinery required running water, and the need for a mill pond and a slope dictated a site far from the houses of the village; suspect because it was the work of the lord and an expression of his power. The miller, too, was something of an outcast, seen as the master's spy and an agent of his taxation, an attitude that long persisted in the French countryside. Certainly, when they had to go and queue at the door of the mill this was a place, for women especially, to exchange news, but it was communication soured with the irritation of waiting and the fear of being swindled, with the ferment of complaint and dumb revolt. It was also a place of sin – of anger and disobedience and also of luxury, according to St Bernard who, as I have already mentioned, denounced habitual prostitution there, while St Dominic believed it should be actively opposed and sent his friars to preach at the mill.

Finally, there was the cemetery (*atrium*, field of peace), the enclosed space around the church, sometimes just large enough to contain the village tombs, sometimes – as in Brittany – raised to the level of an assembly field that covered several hectares. This sacred land was an asylum for the wanderer or the criminal, a meeting place where even the lord of the manor himself could only enter on foot and unarmed, a place for preaching and also for bargaining, common land to which all the villagers and all the faithful had a right and, of course, a place of primary importance in the grouping of the inhabitants.

The peasant home

The archaeological discoveries that in many cases began with the urban sites destroyed in the Second World War in Poland, northern France, England, the German Rhineland or the Low Countries have completely changed the study of the home and man's environment over the last three decades. Between the polarized and endlessly repeated traditional images of the magnificent castle towering above the humble cottages of the peasants that nestled in its shadow, the picture of a varied and constantly changing village community has emerged, whose history is closely related to that of the techniques and methods of its inhabitants.

From 'hut' to 'house'

The concept of a household (a close-knit group living under a single roof) as the fundamental domestic unit, is a very recent historical development. It is clearly related to the development of a family-centred structure which involved a social realignment largely brought about by the fragmentation of the larger clan or tribal unit which I have already mentioned. Striking proof of this has come from archaeology rather than from detailed studies of classical or early medieval texts, or from the rather poor visual sources of these periods. Sites that have been investigated in England, the Rhineland, the Low Countries and northern France have revealed a remarkable similarity in the structures excavated: great halls, some 25 metres long and 5 or 8 metres wide, supported by one or more lines of posts, shared between the human inhabitants and their livestock. Of course there are differences of detail between West Stow and Warendorf, Gladbach and Chalton or Odoorn and Brebières, just to take some familiar examples, but they are to be found in the means of supporting and roofing the structures rather than in their role as a place of refuge, which was the essential function of these enormous hangar-like buildings. Beside them in the open air, occasionally surrounded by earthworks or a palisade, were the huts occupying a few square metres of uneven ground and the objects found there show that their use was almost exclusively as workshops. The building group taken as a whole seems to have been put together quite haphazardly: as I have already said, these handfuls of dwellings do not qualify as villages. Finally, as more becomes known of rural society in the late classical period with its prestigious Gallo-Roman and African villas, the same picture of disorder and lack of an overall plan emerges and is also borne out by aerial photography in areas away from groups of stone buildings – in places where, when all is said and done, the rich hardly ever ventured. Historians have always been misled by the embroidered memory of classical times and for far too long have neglected the crucially important development of the peasant house. It is because I see this as such a vital development that I have made it the basis for this study.

Excavations do not reveal the foundations of peasant huts before the tenth century, with the exception of a few structures found close to princely dwellings as in the Ottonian sites of Tilleda and Werla in Germany. At the same period the great communal houses decreased in size by about half: 12 metres by 7 at Hohenrode, 4 metres by 7 at Wharram Percy, even smaller at Rougiers. Where larger buildings remained, as in Yorkshire, the Harz Mountains or along the Baltic coast, these were manors, the lord's residence, rather than the traditional, communal, fortified constructions. Individual elements from the earlier arrangement persisted, such as granaries, silos or haylofts, but they were used for storage and no longer sheltered craftsmen, women or slaves, for these workers had now returned to the home. Henceforth the main concern was not so much to protect oneself from wild beasts at night, but to lead a settled and productive life. This return of the womenfolk to their own roof is surely the fundamental reason for the great increase in female influence that is characteristic of the years 1100 to 1300. A second important fact was contemporary with this change: there were no longer fires in the open for communal cooking; even when the fire was not reinstated within the house it moved close to it (as at Rougiers in twelfth-century Provence or Chalton in the south of England), or sometimes it was housed in a separate or adjoining structure, as at Gomeldon in Wiltshire or Büderich in Hessen: in every instance it had become the property of the new smaller family group and there is no need to seek any other explanation for the use of the word 'hearth' to refer to this domestic group. It entered the living area itself in the mid-twelfth century in Brittany (as at Pen er Malo), Frisia and the Vendée, in the centre of the room at first, then placed against one wall, as at Dracy in the thirteenth century. Finally a canopy and a flue of fired bricks were built above the fire to let the smoke escape, but at a considerably later date than in noble houses; there is no evidence for this last stage, which seems so typical of the peasant house, before 1340 in Italy, England or Thuringia.

The presence of the hearth within the house created an entirely new situation as far as peasant attitudes were concerned towards the family structure and social arrangements. The women who tended the fire drew from it their power and influence; it gave the old men who warmed themselves there the opportunity to relate the history of their family and of the village and offered greater chance of survival to the little babies placed near it for warmth. Even in noble houses where they could burn whole tree trunks the wet-nurses, the elderly and the sick gathered near to the fire: they are graphically described by Canon Lambert of Ardres (fl. 1150–1200) in his account of the construction of the great keep at Ardres in 1120 or 1125. This new hearth did not impinge only on social patterns; it caused changes in the very structure of the house. The warmth of the animals which had hitherto been indispensable for heating the human inhabitants in the great communal halls of the early Middle Ages became less essential; so the entry of the hearth coincided with the departure of livestock, or at least with its isolation in an area specifically allocated when the house was built. Men and animals might still share common entrances, but they had separate eating- and sleeping-quarters and in time improvements dictated the separate disposal of animal and human waste-products. The mixed or byre-house with combined accommodation for men and animals undoubtedly persisted in the Jura, the Alps, Brittany, Frisia and the Harz Mountains, as well as areas such as Oisans, Aragon or the Hebrides, where the custom persisted into our own time; but at the beginning of our period the basic dwelling house was already in existence, with the living room where the fire burned and separate sleeping-quarters which also served as a store-room. If the ground area was available, several rooms might be joined to this initial block, radiating out from it or aligned on a nave or central corridor along which wagons laden with hay, barrels with reserve supplies of water, men and animals all passed. If there was insufficient space to do this another storey was built, for example in areas where local stone enabled the construction of solid walls, as at Rougiers, where houses six to eight metres high can only have been dwellings of several storeys which had to be subdivided because of the successive fragmentation of the family group between the beginning of the thirteenth century and 1400. But this practice was not confined to the Mediterranean: excavations at Dracy in upper Burgundy have also shown that there may have been another storey where the grain and tools were stored.

Wood or stone?

The question of which building materials were used seems absurdly simple at first sight. Wood was used for building where it was in plentiful supply and stone where wood was lacking. Unfortunately archaeological evidence does not corroborate this traditional and simplistic view, indeed further reflection undermines it: why was a village like Rougiers built of poor stone on a steep slope (which doubled the effort involved) when the top of the hill was covered with trees? Why did wood succeed stone and *vice versa* for the nine successive periods of manorial building activity at Wharram Percy between the twelfth and the fourteenth centuries? Why were log houses like those of central Europe built in the Agenais when there was a source of good quality local stone, but forests were distant?

There are more questions than answers, even within a limited local context. We shall try and sort out the jumble of facts. The value of wood as protection against the cold is well known: when the illuminator of the *Très riches heures du duc de Berry* wanted to portray – in highly improbable fashion – a dwelling in February, he painted a huge wooden hut beside a dovecot with regular courses of well-dressed stone. Where the forest was near and, most important, clearing was permitted (that is, in the thirteenth century, but seldom earlier), building in wood extended from the Baltic to the Vosges and the Dauphiné. But stone had advantages: admittedly, it had to be coarse-grained, it was slow and difficult to work, expensive to transport and, there again, it was only in the thirteenth century that well-harnessed carts carrying several tons of stone appeared; before then they needed a miracle like that of Conques, or harsh forced labour as at Ghent to transport the raw material. On the other hand the building was resistant to fire and flood, stood firmly on its foundations, facilitated the building of several storeys and offered a 'lordly' aspect: from the end of the eleventh century the church, the castle and the local manor all used it; moreover, the coldness of stone made it suitable for southern areas and also for preserving the snow that acts as a protection in mountain areas where, with a reversal that we now take for granted, the roof was made of flat roofing stones (*lauzes*) and the rest of the house from wood.

The long history of Wharram Percy shows how in reality all the varying factors of economic opportunity, local conditions and factors bearing on preparation and comfort interacted simultaneously. In practice it can be shown that intermediary types were mixed with homogeneous buildings in the same place at the same time. Examples of this kind include the typically Scandinavian or Celtic houses made of turf blocks, a type of construction still chosen in the twelfth century in the Ardennes, northern Germany and Scotland; often the earth was mixed with straw, brushwood or gravel and rammed into some kind of framework; in wattle and daub, or cob walls, supported by vertical wooden uprights or by diagonal timbers (the half-timbering of the Channel coasts and elsewhere) which were driven or cemented into either a low wall, or a beam running the length of the building or the plaster work between joists. These external surfaces were all familiar from the tenth and the eleventh centuries at Husterknupp, Hohenrode in Germany, and Wharram Percy, while in the thirteenth century they extended from Oxford to the Limagne and from the Ardennes to Catalonia. Construction might be entirely of wood, by stacking logs on top of each other as in the Vosges, the Queyras, the Tirol and Slav countries, or by the interweaving of thick branches as was customary in Ireland, or, most commonly, by joining vertical planks together (German *Stabbau*), a technique perfected equally in Denmark, Essex or Würtemberg: these methods have survived to the present day for numerous outbuildings, such as barns, storehouses, stables and cattlesheds. Stone was crushed, then set in a lime mortar (jointed bonding was reserved for fortifications after 1120–25 or for churches) and did not become widely popular until the twelfth century, later still in north-west Europe and even after the close of the Middle Ages in Germany. By contrast the dry stone walls of Provence, Apulia, Périgord and Burgundy were built at a relatively early date, but they remained crude, very thick so that they might provide a more secure foundation, or indeed support an additional storey, 70 or even 90 centimetres thick at Rougiers or Wharram Percy. The construction of window apertures posed formidable problems of equilibrium to these builders; however, a partial recess for a wall cupboard or chimney breast bestowed a greater degree of comfort upon the inhabitants. The supreme advantage of stone was that it could support any kind of roof beams, the basic timber framework that was perfected in the fourteenth and fifteenth centuries, on which a light but damp thatch of straw was placed, or laths which might, or might not, support stone plates. The Mediterranean use of curved, 'Roman' tiles which insulate the house from the heat of the sun, naturally prevailed in southern Europe, but since this practice is also found – and continues today – in Lorraine, it is a good example of the complexity of the variable factors involved. Then there are many equally widely distributed examples of plant materials used as coverings on a roof that was sharply angled to prevent rotting and in buildings of the 'cruck' type, where the roof stretches from the ridge to the ground over timbers placed at angles to each other and meeting at the upper edge, thus forming a sort of wall-less hut which we would assume to be of the most primitive and wretched kind, were there not proof of its continued use for human habitation, as well as for animals until the fifteenth century.

Self-sufficiency?

The desire 'to live off one's own' is deeply rooted: it presents man with a mythical world of self-government where he sees himself as a new Robinson Crusoe, capable of providing all his own food and meeting all the practical requirements of everyday life – although in the middle of the twentieth century the level of freedom and well-being attained by so many groups of human beings who have been left to stagnate in just such a way for thousands of years (in the equatorial forests, for example) should give food for thought. It was at precisely this level of basic subsistence that great numbers of men struggled to survive at the beginning of the Middle Ages, just as they had done in classical times. But even at a protohistoric level individuals were inevitably affected by changes in the society of groups closest to them: these inevitable patterns of interdependence, with the 'primitive' exchange of gifts (salt for iron, skins for corn) outside any commercial system or the profit motive, characterized even the poorest peasant community and continued well into later periods with evidence of broader horizons and technical developments.

These are commonplace observations, but nevertheless I believe them to lie at the bottom of the hope evidently dear to the medieval peasant, that he might live off the fruits of his labour. Historical anthropology has of course not yet progressed sufficiently for us to postulate a relationship between the intellectual attitudes of a group turned in on itself and the state of the surrounding economy. One thing at least seems clear, that the break-up of the extended family unit into small households each centred on a married couple re-enforced this desire to be independent of everyone else – unless this is to confuse cause and effect. In the area with which I am concerned this development appears to have made a considerable impression upon the peasant house. It is reflected in the internal subdivision of the basic dwelling house to which I have already referred and which was either the consequence or the cause of a more affective relationship between man and wife, and it also resulted in higher status for the woman at home. Rarely can this cliché be more applicable than in this context: it has been possible to trace the successive subdivision of groups of houses, at Rougiers for instance, and also at Dracy and Wharram Percy. It is clear from the first example that the disadvantages of this development should not be overlooked, in particular the reduction in surface area available to each couple. But when all is said and done, although it would be rash to generalize for southern Europe as a whole, the two southern examples of Rougiers and Dracy are valid models for areas of reduced space and population pressure. Elsewhere (this time with many localized examples) another phenomenon is evident, more closely linked to the peasant's desire to have everything under his own control and we must examine this case in greater detail.

This development is illustrated at a rather late date by a number of fourteenth- and fifteenth-century miniatures, and archaeology provides evidence a century earlier from the excavations at Gomeldon (Wiltshire) and Wharram Percy, as well as the region around Soissons, Flanders and the Perche (west of Paris). It is essentially concerned with the building of extensions and the appropriation of pieces of ground next to the main house, regardless of the extent to which the dwelling was divided internally. These might be the stable or the sheep-fold, the bake-house or the barn; or, in the case of manor houses, the dovecot, or a shed for barrels or tack on the side of the house itself; as well as flanking the house, they might be in the ground around it, such as the area occupied by a pond, buildings scattered across a meadow or a kitchen garden. Here perhaps lies the origin of the modern *ferme* (tenant farm) and *cense* (leasehold), often enclosed by a little wall encircling as much as a quarter of a hectare of ground. This could not be everybody's lot, of course, but it translates into the fabric of building a social, economic and moral evolution quite comparable with that of the tenth and early eleventh centuries which either followed or precipitated the building of castle mottes and the establishment of the manor as a social unit of fundamental importance. In fact what we see here is substantial evidence of a split within the unfree peasant world between *laboureurs* (those who laboured in another's service, responsible for farm implements, carts and livestock) and *manouvriers* (more substantial peasant farmers rooted in the extended family house); and also proof of the desire of this second group to have everything at their disposal that they required for their household's subsistence since, unlike the lord of a manor, they did not have the option of requisitioning what they needed by means of seigneurial or public powers. The development of a rural artisan class and the specialization in certain types of essentially speculative activity, such as stock-breeding and growing dye-plants were very closely bound up with these complex structures, but again it is impossible to be certain about their place within the scheme of things: did functions dictate structure or *vice versa*?

From then on, but with an evolution so slow as to be barely perceptible, the communal character of rural life gradually declined, although still reflected in open fires, enclosures for cattle and communal silos, while the 'hearth' became the natural basis for taxation. I think we should reverse the usual path of the financial historian and study the regrouping of houses and the birth of the 'house' and 'household' (as we looked at the village earlier) before the first indications of fiscal activity are examined. We still have to ascertain what a royal agent might hope to find in these houses.

Rich and poor

In 1298, after an attack by soldiers had ruined their village of Cagnoncles near Cambrai and their barn there, the monks of the abbey of Saint-Sépulchre held an inquiry and then drew up a list of the damage done, house by house, with estimated costs. The buildings were valued at just over 300 *livres* with a dozen of them called *manoirs* assessed at 60 to 90 *livres* and which I would readily identify with the large, composite house structures previously discussed. But what is most instructive is the list of chattels burnt or taken away: grain, of course, clothes, kitchen utensils, harness, bales of wool, cloth and pieces of armour. These were sometimes found in the very humblest of dwellings. For once this sheds more light on a family's *catel* (their moveable goods) than the results of excavation which are always reduced to the remains of imperishable objects that are usually broken.

Hidden thresholds of comfort

Through their size, the quality of construction, the presence of a threshold and the discovery of several hearths, the keys for numerous pieces of furniture, of hinge pins and locks, houses provide the most concrete evidence for an assessment of the level of wealth of their occupants: more so than written documents like the *questes* or *fouages* of the fourteenth and fifteenth centuries, which are in any case at the end of our period and the product of fraud, error and forgetfulness. There are various means, some more reliable than others, of establishing the context of peasant life. They include inventories drawn up in southern Europe after an individual's death, iconography (admittedly often showing the noble who commissioned the work in an unduly favourable light), traces or remains of utensils when, as at Dracy, a terrible fire forced the inhabitants to flee without their possessions. Before we investigate certain aspects of this picture in greater detail it must be emphasized that there is virtually no basis for an exhaustive description: too much escapes us – the importance of a secret hoard, for example; the existence of supplies and utensils in the open air, the value of land which is almost impossible to assess accurately in relation to household goods. Moreover, there is no possibility of a serious chronological survey since the majority of the surviving evidence dates from the end of the thirteenth century or later. The earlier period is shrouded in ignorance.

Apart from the building itself, movable goods seem to constitute the touchstone of wealth. More precisely, the possession of certain objects increased a man's status. A bed was one such object, for the straw mattress on a wooden framework (where five or six slept naked beneath covers of coarse wool (*burel*, *tiretaine* or *keute*), children and adults together with surprising promiscuity) was supplanted here and there by the footed bed and sometimes by one with closed curtains or sliding panels, designed to conserve heat rather than out of any sense of modesty, although such sentiments may have originated here; these were beds for two with sheepskins and perhaps bedcovers too. Very small children would sleep with their parents despite the risk of accidental or (according to malicious gossip) deliberate suffocation. The chest also played an important role, since it proclaimed that the owner had valuables to lock away: fine clothes for feast-days, metal dishes or possibly jewels. It also served as a store for reserves, a bench for guests or for story-tellers in the evening. Some fifteenth-century examples of neither seigneurial nor urban provenance have survived. The rest was of no value: there was a trestle table, seats from blocks of wood or bales of straw, while cupboards built into the wall or fitted into a corner were integral parts of the building. There is iconographical evidence for wooden pegs, metal fire-dogs or a hook for a pot in the chimney, ornate oil lamps, sometimes a candlestick, a glass vase, shutters for the windows made of oiled cloth – these were some of the more humble constituents of rustic decoration. The economist or anthropologist will expect a statement about the peasants' implements, but here the potential for error is enormous. Apart from the great uncertainty that surrounds the dating of eroded metal objects, and the very poor state of preservation of domestic ceramic and pottery material, it is highly likely that virtually nothing has survived from outside the domestic context proper – none of the tools used by agricultural workers or craftsmen, which would be fundamental to any assessment. Can we draw any conclusions? It is important to remember that we cannot date blades of knives, sickles and bill-hooks, the shoes of donkeys or horses, augers, planes, hoes, buckles from belts, hooks, nails, keys or iron bands from barrels. No fewer than 1,000 of these iron objects were found at Rougiers – two thirds of iron, the rest of bronze. Spindle-whorles and whetstones are legion and everywhere pins, combs, necklaces and pieces of mirror underline the preponderance of feminine activity in the home. Cooking pots and storage jars offer a whole range of types whose classification is still being studied by the experts – pots, basins, stew pots, porringers, jars or bowls, whose polychrome glazes of varying constituents sometimes offer more conclusive evidence of date than physical tests. Sometimes broken implements from refuse pits, as at Rougiers, or their inclusion in the rubbish dumps sited at intervals in the fields, as at Wharram Percy, are a more fruitful source than the floor of a house. This all has a certain interest, but in my present field of reference domestic tools do not appear to classify their users: only the possession of a yoke for oxen introduced a fundamental distinction, and this is a point to which I shall return.

Anyone living in the nineteenth or the four previous centuries would have been able to distinguish the rich from the poor by their clothes. The egalitarian approach to dress in our own period should make it easier for us to appreciate the same situation in the central Middle Ages (1000–1300). The little evidence we have for peasant clothing comes from literary evidence, painting and sculptures, lists of beautiful items reserved for a bride's trousseau and here or there fragments of leather, buckles and hooks or the bodies of a handful of fourteenth-century Danes mummified in the ice or peat bogs of the extreme north. Two dominant strands of thought, both essentially 'modern', emerge from this varied body of material: dress was functional, unvarying and the same for everybody. Admittedly men wore leggings caught in below the knee and women a long *cote* or tunic, but apart from this detail, jacket or jerkin on top, bodice or shirt, hooded coat, *botillons* (short leather boots) or clogs and next to the skin underclothes which were doubtless also similarly cut for men and women. In winter they piled on every piece of clothing they possessed, topped if possible with an animal skin worn with the fur, fleece or hair inside. On feast-days a bonnet (*chaperon*) or coiffe replaced caps and women's hoods, perhaps with a finer dress for the woman and a belt for the man. But only a few rich peasants would sport a jacket like the lord of the manor's decorated with braid, or own a fox or beaver fur, or ermine. It is noticeable that if a peasant was in debt he was more likely to pledge implements than clothes, a reflection of the money-lender's lack of enthusiasm for the latter and a reminder that at the beginning of the fourteenth century the estimated value of a rich trousseau for a peasant marriage seldom exceeded 20 *livres*, the cost of three horses.

Eating habits

The question of medieval food is one of the most vexing, given its importance in any serious appraisal of the man and the worker, but it must also be one of the most poorly documented aspects of the Middle Ages. For the little we know concerns noble, clerical or urban life, while both financial and didactic literary sources are content with generalizations. When we add that we are quite ignorant of the dietary role played by food gathered in the woods or fished from a nearby pool, and know even less of the role of the henhouse and the kitchen garden, let alone the quantities that these sources provided, it might seem wiser to ignore the subject.

But archaeologists especially have tried to remedy this situation in the last 10 years and since this book aims to stress new developments, the little that is known had better be reported.

In the first place, we have another problem in the very compartmentalized nature of the medieval economy and findings from one place are clearly invalid for another. This absence of real contact at the peasant level is an important characteristic in the history of food: it explains the persistence of localized famine even when there was extensive trading in the same area; wheat, wine and animals were all in circulation, but they went to markets in towns and hunger continued to prevail in the surrounding countryside. Lists have been drawn up of these sudden periods of dearth in which the weather was a primary factor; but these are only mentioned in monastic chronicles and it is only in the mid-thirteenth century that sudden price rises are occasionally blamed. Despite our probable areas of ignorance, the impression is that the character of these shortages actually changed between the eleventh and the fourteenth centuries. From the late tenth to the middle of the eleventh century these were profound and widespread disasters; they affected huge areas, sometimes (around 1030) the entire continent; they were invariably accompanied by 'plagues' (apparently forms of cholera and dysentery, but in any case deficiency diseases to which the cemeteries bear plentiful witness); their initial causes may perhaps have been climatic but their length and seriousness seem to stem from a system of production that was still incapable of responding to increasing demand. For this is also the beginning of the period of population growth that we discussed in the previous chapter. The narrative of Raoul Glaber for the great famines of 1030 or 1035 has a nightmarish realism in the context of the undernourishment of so much of the world's population today: he describes emaciated limbs and distended stomachs, voices barely audible and the final decline into a coma. It may not be true that they cooked and sold human flesh at Tournus, or dug up corpses or killed children, but all these stories were conceivable and prompted by desperate hunger. These total and recurring famines can be contrasted with those of the twelfth and early thirteenth centuries which were generally localized, short in duration and were not extended by medical complications. A list would include the years 1106, 1125, 1144, 1160, 1172, 1196, 1209, 1224–26, but although this is not the whole picture, only part of Europe was affected each time. Moreover, these isolated setbacks to otherwise increasing prosperity were partially alleviated either by the intervention of the Church or rulers, such as Charles the Good of Flanders, who organized the distribution of supplies, or alternatively by measures forbidding stockpiling of grain in the towns – designed as much to forestall any revolt that might jeopardize the established social order, as to punish speculators. It was undoubtedly the relatively mild character of these episodes, followed by a long period of stability which explains the horror-struck reaction of north-west Europe to the failed harvests in the years between 1315 and 1317. It appears that this time the towns were more seriously affected since they paid a heavy price in the form of large numbers of undernourished immigrants. When crop levels returned to normal the peasantry of regions such as Flanders, that had been hardest hit, revealed a vigorous demand for social change, a sure indication that famine had departed. The shortages that accompanied the brutal onslaught of the Black Death are outside my brief and were of quite a different kind that was to be characteristic of the later Middle Ages.

My second observation is at the most basic factual level: the daily requirement of a man or woman engaged in hard agricultural labour in regions as climatically varied as Scotland and Sicily would have been between 2,700 and 3,200 calories, depending on age and sex. The state of malnutrition, however, only pertains when the calorie intake is below 1,700. Establishing the adequate calorific level is one problem, but there is another familiar today, namely that of establishing a balance of fat, protein and carbohydrate in the diet, otherwise deficiency diseases will unleash not only intestinal and liver complaints, but also diabetes, impaired muscle activity and mental disorders. Our knowledge of the nutritive principles of the medieval economy as a whole and also its ecological system is insufficient to solve these problems: the demand for cereals at all costs placed a disproportionate emphasis on the role of flour, porridge and bread, to which were also added flours obtained from lentils or vetches grown in the fields. This was their principal foodstuff, rich in carbohydrates: 'This century was stuffed with peas', said Lynn White of the tenth century, when the first population increase took place. The evidence of ninth-century texts, giving details of diet in monasteries, or food allowances for labourers in the thirteenth century is surprising: between 1.2 and 1.7 kilograms of cereal products was consumed per person daily, a calorific intake of at least 2,000 or 2,500. Other sources confirm these figures, such as the 1 kg loaves distributed in Flanders when there were shortages, or even the 900 g average consumption of bread of the French peasant in 1900. This 'staple' was accompanied by the consumption of a startling volume of wine by the whole population, women and monks as well, which might be as much as one and a half or two litres a day and, although these beverages were undoubtedly only mildly alcoholic, they added another 1,000 or so calories a day. If we add vegetables and dairy products a total of over 6,000 calories was reached in ninth-century Corbie and 4,400 at Beaumont-le-Roger in 1268. This would be enough to feed two or three of our own contemporaries and more than enough to jeopardize the medieval peasants' health, too, because of the deficiency in animal protein. Although animals were kept in the woods, the sheep and cattle were scraggy and the pigs more fat than lean. Evidence from village sites and refuse pits that provide informa-tion about the food consumed in twelfth-century Jutland and northern Germany indicates that between 80 and 95 per cent of the animal bones used for meat came from domestic animals, principally pigs and cattle; with the probable exception of eggs, insignificant quantities were provided by hunting, fishing or the poultry yard. These circumstances resulted in a very low protein intake and an inevitably unbalanced diet. This is probably why so much importance was attached to vegetables rich in peptides, such as onions, leeks and garlic, that are relatively neglected today.

At least one distinctive feature emerges from this survey: the medieval peasant's diet was essentially that of the classical period, bread and something to go with it (*companaticum*), wine and *potage* (a mixture of leaf- and root-vegetables grown in the open – not unlike a modern pottage); Germanic culture had introduced beer, Celtic culture fat and onions, but the general framework had not changed and did not alter until the beginning of the twentieth century: indeed it still survives in Sicily and some parts of Ireland. Their diet was unbalanced, excessive (some three to four kilograms per day) and nutritionally poor, which explains *a posteriori* the disastrous ravages effected by a sudden shortage or epidemic on a malnourished community.

Life and death

This depressing picture is brightened only by the availability of wild foodstuffs in woods and marshes, which explains the eagerness with which the peasant sought these out. The noble could supplement his diet with venison and buy expensive fish. This distinction in dietary habits merits more consideration than it usually receives. Here, after all, are two men living in the country, both engaged in physically demanding work, one at war and the other in the fields. Did the difference in diet have any connection with the power and authority that the one exercised over the other? Did the noble rule because he ate more meat? The question is not superfluous, even though it may never be solved: descriptions or visual representations of the lord are quite common, those of the peasant much rarer, but there are the same distinct characteristics beneath the gloss of scorn or caricature which was the peasant's inevitable lot in these socially biased works. The noble had a fine frame and strong arms and legs; he is credited with feats of physical prowess that verge on the incredible, but skeletal remains and surviving pieces of armour suggest men generally smaller than today and this is re-enforced by evidence from monastic graves. More detailed pictures show a pale face and fat belly. The peasant was represented as little better than an animal, no doubt because his beard and hair were unkempt and he washed himself so little. He, too, was not tall, but had a thick trunk, broad hips and spindly arms and legs. Was there really a visible difference between them? It seems unlikely, but this is certainly an area that merits anthropological enquiry.

The study of illness may furnish some part of the answer. This area of history has barely been outlined, but there is no lack of concrete evidence, even for early periods: the evidence of graveyards comes immediately to mind, where examination of detailed evidence and an investigation of calcium and fluoride levels in bones can reveal the pathological cause of death according to the skeleton's age. It is hoped that a technique along these lines will shortly be developed to discover the blood group of the deceased. Accounts of miracle cures or of pilgrimages to places renowned for their curative properties abound in saints' lives or *exempla*: the fact that they are entirely fictitious is quite irrelevant because they offer a valuable insight into contemporary attitudes. Finally, chroniclers often wrote eye-witness accounts of the deaths of secular or ecclesiastical princes and contemporary analysis shows that they provide sound diagnosis: Louis VI's dysentery, Philip Augustus' cirrhosis, Barbarossa's stroke or the combination of angina and tuberculosis suffered by Charles V are just a few of the most famous cases. At the same time there were scrofulous diseases and cases of infantile paralysis, general debility and hydropsy, which were commended to the care of the Virgin and the saints. It is clear that the lower classes fell prey to congenital diseases stemming from malnutrition or constitutional disorders, while the nobles were victims of various kinds of intemperance or excess.

Death came in other guises, but they were ultimately less prevalent than has often been believed. Plague had disappeared and its return bisected the history of the medieval West. Cholera, as already mentioned, made some inroads, but without widespread effect. St Anthony's Fire (where hallucinations accompanied by fatal convulsions are provoked by ergot, the fungus in spurred rye) caused panic from Avignon to Lorraine between 1093 and 1109, but it could not be called an epidemic, if only because it was rare for more than one man from a village to be affected. Leprosy was endemic and contact with the East caused it to become more widespread. It has been calculated that some three per cent of the population was affected. Its dreadful reputation is well known, but the situation is less dire, however, if we remember that at this period (when leprosy was incurable) many lepers left their leper house and returned to normal society, suggesting either benign forms of the disease or mistaken diagnosis. Tuberculosis has always been rare in the country and did not appear until leprosy was dying out, in about 1320–40, and the two baccilus would appear to be mutually exclusive.

There is little evidence of smallpox, cancer or alcoholism, the other great scourges of our own and our parents' generation, either because we have failed to recognize references to them, or because death was caused by so many other means that these were superfluous.

Our contemporaries have the impertinence to call the Middle Ages a period of violence, but in fact there are far fewer broken limbs, fractured skulls and smashed ribs in the graveyards of this period than in the previous centuries. The explanation is simple: after the year 1000 war became a minority activity and this small armigerous group were now well protected by body armour and more frequently taken prisoner than killed. It is possible that the incredible exploits of Roland or Gawain were no more than the poet's expression of regret for the days when killing was the rule. When killings occurred – and occur they did – emotions ran high and the fact was registered. Murder and everyday violence remained: the court rolls for some English counties, recording accusation, trial and sentence, have recently been studied in this context – and such an enquiry could consider virtually any criminal offence in the area. The crime rate was shown to be lower than that of the nineteenth century, but higher than our own. The most interesting conclusion of this study was that the hope of personal advantage was the dominant motive for rural crime, far exceeding passion or jealousy. Moreover, these were very often collective crimes and the victim older than his assassins. It is a plot worthy of a nineteenth-century peasant novel and what, indeed, is surprising about that?

Two areas remain obscure: that of suicide, of which we still know virtually nothing, even in the fifteenth-century village (and this silence is still characteristic of contemporary society) and infanticide. The Church attempted to classify both deliberate abortion and the suffocation of the new-born under the heading of infanticide and a thick mantle of canonical condemnation conceals reality from us now. Were more female than male children eliminated in this way? Was it the result of the promiscuity between master and servant that was habitual until the nineteenth century? Should we see this as a brutal method of population control? These are difficult questions and can be no more than sketched out with the present state of knowledge.

They were family affairs and the burial rites described earlier are sufficient to underline the taboo nature of this subject.

The terms that we have gradually assembled in this chapter – village and house, rooms and hearth – were to define the framework of peasant life for a long while. Although they changed with the passage of time and varied from area to area this structure was henceforth to represent the basic social unit of rural life, whose work I shall now attempt to assess. But before we finish this section we must remember that some men were excluded from this social regrouping. By definition these rootless individuals *sans feu ni lieu* (of no fixed abode) escape the historian today as they did the tax official and the recruiting commissioner. They were not so much shepherds or innkeepers who lived on the edge of the village but were an integral part of it, as men of the road, pedlars, minstrels and itinerant herdsmen who slept rough at the foot of the crosses set up at the entrance to the village and who passed through in the hope of finding lodging, work or some kind of good fortune. There were also men who lived in the woods – hermits in caves or huts made of branches, consulted by lovers and the sick, or dangerous bands of thieves and outlaws lying in wait for passing merchants or stray sheep and cattle. They were held in check by the wolves and wintry weather rather than by the gallows or the lord's serjeants. But the village was their enemy and pillage was soon to become a common problem.

3

Work

The history of the medieval countryside is punctuated by the rhythm of the 'labours of the months', a theme so unvarying that it was a constant iconographical feature from late Antiquity to the *Très riches heures de Jean de Berry* (*c.* 1416): with monotonous regularity wheat, vines, woods, the hearth and hunting were tirelessly copied and recopied from Amiens to Modena with no concern for reality. This was to ignore the relatively small regional variations, but – far more importantly – it took no account whatever of developments that took place within this period. Just as we have seen changes in the peasant house and village, so the peasant at work did not repeat the same actions with exactly the same tools in precisely the same setting as a thousand years previously – a thousand years, moreover, in which he had constantly struggled to overcome nature and in which success was often followed by setbacks. This picture of a continual struggle can easily be divided into distinct chronological periods.

The face of the landscape

Initially the untamed wilderness stretched in all directions. We have only to read Duby:

There were great empty spaces that gradually opened out into vast expanses to the west, the north, and the east and finally became all-enveloping. There were tracts of fallow land, fens, meandering rivers and heaths, woods and pasture and all the degraded forms of woodland which followed brushwood fires and the itinerant cultivation of charcoal burners.

Great spaces devoid of human life, little clearings where those who tried to extract a miserable living from the soil came and went; and all around lay the maquis, the *garrigue*, the forest or the steppe. Why persist in denying a fact clearly borne out by the low level of the population, the poor quality of their tools and even a vocabulary which distinguished the land under permanent cultivation (*ager*) from that which had been abandoned (*saltus*) – the 'infield' and 'outfield' of contemporary geographers? The landscape of Roman or Carolingian times and of the Celtic and Germanic periods also presented these contrasting aspects.

The significance of uncultivated ground

The historian is not always in a position to reconstruct the characteristics of the primitive world at the dawn of European history, but there are grounds for hope that this may one day be possible. Charles Higounet has already sketched an outline with his very detailed textual study. Palaeobotany also provides fresh approaches: in the Low Countries and in Oxfordshire hedges encircling land under cultivation have been dated; at Middelburg and in Alsace the headland ridges (*Ackerberg*) gradually built up by the action of the plough as it was turned at the edge of the field have been precisely dated and the age of the terraces that cover so many slopes in cretaceous areas has also been established. Above all there has been systematic analysis of pollen in fossil deposits. It originated in the study of some exceptional peat bogs in Belgium and north Germany and has now covered the entire north-west of Europe and the alpine regions. Unfortunately there have been few such studies of southern Europe and we consequently know little of this aspect there.

A picture of typical characteristics gradually emerges. But before describing them we must call to mind some of the common features of Europe in about the year 1000. The language itself is full of silences and ambiguities; we are not even sure of the origin of the word *foresta*: is it the Latin *foris*, implying that the area was outside man's control? Or the Germanic *Föhre*, a plantation of firs? Should we ascribe different, specific meanings to the terms *silva*, *boscum* and *lucus* in the vocabulary of a pedantic scribe? Moreover, these wooded areas were in reality zones of mixed vegetation, and we can take the *mescla* (the Mediterranean maquis) as a typical example: beech and oak predominate to the north of the Loire and the Danube, beeches to the east, chestnuts to the south, both kermes and holm oaks on the edge of the Mediterranean, and a few conifers in most regions but certainly in far smaller numbers than today. The maritime pine, the Italian cypress, the spruces of the Vosges or the firs of the Harz are all sixteenth-century introductions. Besides, these tall species of tree were smothered by an undergrowth of thorny woods and ferns; since no-one thinned the woodland or tended the soil, fallen tree-trunks, swamps and hollows made some parts of the forest impenetrable and dangerous. Moreover, this was the home of wild boars and wolves: the fear these animals aroused only echoes now in the pages of children's story books. Elsewhere the forest was predominantly swampy with wormwood, plantain, bramble and hawthorn, occasionally an isolated clump of trees, hornbeam, willow, elm or lime, or a patch of broom, gorse or lavender. The appearance of the forest was affected more than it would be today by the character of the soil – the degree of acidity, whether it was clay or sandy, the amount of rainfall and the rate of drainage; it explains why in England the word 'forest' (theoretically royal forest) was used for all fallow land. For here is one last and fundamental distinction between the Middle Ages and our own time: it is true that the forests, maquis, rabbit warrens and heathland were not cultivated, but they were an indispensable source of food, grazing ground for animals and also a refuge for a whole crowd of misfits and exiles: in short, an area seething with wildlife, a reservoir of primary foodstuffs and one of the pillars of the medieval ecological system.

But medieval man did not see these vast spaces that encircled him as a frame that threatened his existence. The German and

Scandinavian forests covered a vast expanse, stretching from the Oder to the Carpathians, from Bavaria to the Arctic Circle. They accounted for two-thirds of the surface area in Germany and it was possible to walk for several days without meeting so much as a clearing. It was not only the mountainous regions of central Germany that were covered by forest, but also limestone areas and even glacial morain, the mossy uplands of the Ardennes and spongy swamps, where oak, birch and conifers all flourished. But, perhaps partly because of its very size, the forest was an integral part of the Belgic and Germanic world: the forester's axe was also the traditional weapon of the Saxons; the fine iron spears of the Germans were tempered in the forest where Weyland the Smith reigned with supernatural powers; Wotan held court there and it was a place of safety where the legions of Varus or, later, Charlemagne himself might be surprised. Further west, along the entire Atlantic coast, the woodland was thickly interspersed with moors and sandy heathland from Scotland to the Basque region, on granite rocks, sand or glacial gravels. Sea-mists hung there and confused the traveller, putting him at the mercy of goblins and wicked spirits, in the power of Merlin or Melusine: in these parts the forest and moor were symbols of danger and evil, places such as the Forest of Brocéliande (with dragons braved by Lancelot and Gawain), or the questing knights lost in the Forest of Braconne, the haunt of hermits who had prophesied and threatened from Perceval to Charles VI of France (whose first attack of madness occurred whilst hunting in a forest in 1392). Further south these phantoms disappeared, but that did not make the *garrigue* or the maquis cultivable ground; the rocky outcrops and impenetrable woods were only good for sheep and goats; after the year 1000 it does not matter whether the deterioration of the Mediterranean region was the result of bad land-management in the classical period or whether there had been a continual and growing trend towards the desert state since the beginning of our own era. At the moral, social or economic level these areas did not exist and this was no small matter since they removed from potential cultivation two-thirds of the available ground. When we add to that the marshes beside the rivers that meandered along with their pools, ox-bow lakes and springs, halting soldiers and merchants alike, the stagnant waters near the coasts where malaria-bearing anopheles swarmed, or the precipitous slopes of Mediterranean hills where there was no longer arable land, it is easy to understand the peasants' fear of the wild and their longing to free themselves from the natural world that dominated their existence.

'Scratching the surface'

There was, as Georges Duby has said, the merest 'scratching of the surface' before the beginning of the period with which this book is concerned. Neolithic man may have made great strides when, during that long period, he mastered the principles of systematic sowing, introduced the ard and the sickle, as well as making the first clearings for the express purpose of cultivation, later used by the Iberians, the Celts, the Italiots (Greek settlers in ancient Italy) and the Germans. Marc Bloch certainly thought so and it is a justifiable assumption, but unproven. Historians are not in agreement about what happened at the dawn of our own period after the achievements of these first 10 centuries and I have already alluded to these conflicting opinions in our discussion of settlement. A researcher who thinks in terms of Cicero, public roads and the vigour of Roman urbanization cannot imagine that the countryside was not organized on a similar basis; he looks everywhere for evidence of systematic planning and persuades himself he has found it far from towns – even in Brittany – whenever a piece of land appears to have been laid out on a grid pattern, however crudely. It is useless to draw his attention to the total lack of evidence of settlement away from the *villae*, which are essentially exceptions, although he maintains they are the rule. Adherents of this school of thought do not attempt to deny the great leap into the twelfth century that it demands, but argue that this was a return to an earlier situation after dramatic setbacks. They are blind to the essential contradiction between this view of the early Middle Ages as a period of cataclysmic disaster and their belief that Roman influence on language, law and attitudes continued unabated. Adopting a slightly different position are the devotees of Charlemagne, principally German historians, who tend to confuse the honour of their country with the endeavours of one particular family from Liège. For them the ninth century is the high point in the history of the countryside: from a few clearly nonsensical prescriptions and from scraps of inventories left by a handful of religious houses and possibly lacking any practical basis, they extrapolate a whole range of achievements in methods, yields and cultural progress that Europe would otherwise only attain in 1900. Other scholars (largely Belgian or English, but with an increasing number of French amongst them) have stressed the poor quality of the soils, especially sands and podzols which exposed the weakness of their tools, or the disjointed and sometimes inconsistent patterns of seigneurial exploitation; they have pointed above all to the fact that documentary evidence leaves us totally ignorant of 99.5 per cent of the land of the Carolingian Empire.

Yet it would be wrong wilfully to contradict the golden vision of the Carolingian enthusiasts on every point. We have evidence for the conquest (possibly the reconquest?) of uncultivated areas; more importantly, of the moving spectacle of the obstinacy and almost desperate determination of a small group of men, monks whom education had raised to positions of influence. They succeeded in overcoming the perspectives of a family of Frankish warriors and establishing a state, with its own currency, commercial structure and policies, even though there were neither men, tools nor money sufficient for the undertaking. All the developments that take place after 950 or 1000 prove *a posteriori* that earlier there could only have been a theoretical impetus and a few localized attempts: in other words, worthy endeavours with little practical result.

On the other hand, it must be emphasized that the social structure of the early Middle Ages ultimately provided the foundations necessary for further development. Stimulated by the Viking and Saracen raids of the ninth century, and by those of the Hungarians and the Moors in the tenth, the desire for plunder grew to such proportions in this warrior society that the Church was seriously concerned and it always coloured summary judgements on the anarchy of the period. This chaos was in reality highly productive, for the corollary of pillage was the ritual gift-giving of the lord to his followers and the subsequent expenditure of large sums on projects dear to them; the raids and reprisals were followed by alms and munificence, the beginning of a procession of changes and the awakening of a dynamic new spirit. The importance to the countryside of the Carolingians lay in this rather than in any pseudo-Renaissance of interest in classical Latin; they and their own people, no less than the last 'barbarian invaders' who crushed their hopes, undoubtedly disturbed the surface of a world that had gone to sleep.

This interdependent process cannot perhaps entirely explain the increasing rate of change that followed, which was sustained for 250 years. We must take other factors into account and I can do no more than sketch the outline of a question whose solution continues to escape us: what was the reason for the awakening of rural Europe, the rise in population and production and ultimately European expansion across the globe; what prompted this series of interconnections so crucial for the history of the human race? External influences, such as Islam, would only affect trade and intellectual attitudes and would not explain why the expansion continued for so long. The almost inevitable development of 'feudalism' from an obsolete and virtually slave-based economy neither could nor should have stimulated a military and mercantile development that was sustained long after the seigneurial system itself had disintegrated. This is why contemporary historians are examining ecological evidence very closely: pollen analyses which enable us to trace marine and glacial movements suggest that we should look for the causes of a considerable change in man's biological environment. Over four centuries even small variations in temperature or rainfall levels can produce considerable changes in plant cover and also in animal and human behaviour.

Whether it should be viewed as cause or effect of European expansion, the population increase sharpened the problem of the relationship between the human and the natural world, between untamed land and the tiny plots in cultivation. Decalcified skeletons from cemeteries of the eighth and ninth centuries show that hunger was affecting an increasing number of the population, but fear still held them back from the edges of the woods. After 950 it disappeared in the face of necessity with the burst of energy that led firstly to an assault on bushes and then copses and long-established woodland. This impulse was combined with a growing consciousness of *homo faber* and of the Cluniac and Gregorian attitudes to manual work as an offering to God – although it would be impossible to unravel the intricacies of this inter-relationship. It was also combined with the interest of a growing number of peasants to whom newly reclaimed ground was promised at a fair price, and finally the influence exerted by a lord interested in estate management upon the men who worked for him. But it is clear that at the same time there were curbs which sometimes brought this progress to a halt and setbacks here and there: people were afraid to reduce the area available for grazing, to make a break in the natural line of protection (Caesar's *murus nativus* which surrounded village and castle); they were also reluctant to restrict the opportunities for hunting, picking fruits and gathering fungi which were all an important part of the role played by woodland in contemporary society. At the end of the tenth century peasant society embarked on a prolonged inner struggle against the old prejudices that had circumscribed their ancestors.

The daily round

The reader will expect me to discuss the process of clearing the land, which Marc Bloch saw as the principal legacy of the medieval period to our own. This will be discussed in due course. But it is important not to take the easy option and accept the conventional view unquestioningly. For some, like the peasant farmers of the German forests, settlers on a recently established clearing or the peasant fishing communities along the coasts, this was a daily task. But not for everyone: the majority stayed on land that had long been in cultivation and it is what they were doing that interests me, for man has to be in control of his immediate environment before he can master new lands and make them productive. To my mind this persistent toil, of which very little is known, is more important than the pioneering work which, although always spotlighted in texts, trial records and new place-names, undoubtedly affected no more than a fifth of the land surface of Europe.

Equipment

Anthropology has made advances beyond the wildest dreams of Bloch or Lefebvre-Desnouettes and there have also been some particularly fruitful excavations. Traditional texts on this subject teem with intractable problems: the pedantic scribe anachronistically uses *aratrum* (ard) in an area we know to have been cultivated with a mouldboard plough, a careless scribe refers laconically to 'land', 'harness' and 'work' without further explanation, while an over-zealous scribe uses the Latin *bladum* (corn, especially wheat) to denote any kind of grain simply because his source used *blé*. Moreover, statistical evidence is very poor before 1250, to say nothing of our complete ignorance of the local value of a *sétier* (a measure of grain), a *journal* (a day's work) or an *hommée* (amount of land, meadow or vine a man could work in a day).

An understanding of the soil itself is of cardinal importance: apart from a selective study of plants, everything hangs upon pedology (the study of soil structure and origins). It is some years since Roger Dion sketched a map of favourable and unfavourable soils encountered by a worker on the land in classical times – what his modern descendant would call warm or cold, light or heavy soils, terms that in fact reflect his ability to use these types rather than their intrinsic qualities. So the dusty, grey and acid podzols that are poorly regarded today and considered best suited to re-afforestation, were the soils most generally worked until the eleventh century because the ineffectual ards then in use could scratch the surface sufficiently to prepare the ground for sowing. They were ill-suited to cereal crops, however, and even less to grazing. Brown earths on the other hand – the rendzina often formed through wind erosion, reddish alluvial soils and pale yellow loess – all provided excellent meadows and land which was easy to work, even though they had a calcareous substratum. The woodland and scrub growing there still had to be grubbed out and the ground itself turned over. As for black chernozem with its high carbon content, this was forbidden ground in the early Middle Ages, too thick and sticky to be worked successfully and soon trampled to a morass by cattle, while to our mind this is a soil that cannot be bettered. It is not difficult to understand why it was so necessary to feed poor soils and work good ones.

'Feed poor soils'? It is more easily said than done. Man has probably learnt from experience since protohistoric times that the quality of these soils could be improved by marling or liming. Indeed, we see landholders obliged to do so after 1225 or 1250, when competition from his neighbours' harvests forced a more active pursuit of profit on the lord of the manor. The use of the marl-pit still had to be organized, possibly by means of compulsory carting services. Other processes appear to have been simpler: denshireing (that is, burning cleared weeds and turf and spreading the resultant ashes upon the land) or burn-beating a second crop (burning the stubble and spreading the ashes upon the land), digging in lime or even brushwood on land that had lain fallow for several years – all these techniques are still employed in many parts of the world, and were regularly used in the eleventh and twelfth centuries when a new piece of ground was brought into cultivation and had to be enriched. But these practices had to be backed by crop rotation and long periods when the land was left fallow, and this had in effect been the practice in the classical period when there was a favourable ratio of men to cultivable land. The use of animal or plant manures is also by far the best means of feeding the soil. The Roman writer Columella (*fl.* 1st century A.D., author of *De re rustica* and *De arboribus*) praises many farmers for using this method and once more it is a familiar practice throughout Asia and even in parts of Europe today. Evidence from many English sites shows that human waste products and food remains were spread all over the area round the peasant's plot. Further areas might be covered with soiled animal litter or dung mixed with leaf mould, but in this case the animals had to be kept under cover and not allowed to graze in the woods. Pigeon-dung (*columbine*) was highly valued and so scarce and sought-after that from the twelfth century the lord of the manor made it his exclusive prerogative to keep a dovecot and collect the dung from it to manure his orchard. These practices alone would not have sufficed, so they also resorted to grazing on the fields, notably by sheep whose dung has a very high nitrogenous content. Since they were generally banned from the woods because of their devastating effect upon bark and young shoots, they were put on the bare ground within a moveable enclosure such as is still used today. It would surely have been more profitable to make use of cattle dung, not only available in larger quantities, but also more easily incorporated into the soil by the trampling of the animals' feet. And if the small area of woodland available to them was limited by felling or by the more acute concern to preserve large forest trees or hunting grounds, it would surely have been more sensible to have released an area of fallow land for pasture where they could have fed on weeds and the second hay crop. It is possible that the methods of crop rotation I shall shortly discuss had their origin in the need to provide grazing land.

Now we must tackle the problem of agricultural equipment. For even if it is improved, soil will not feed a continually growing community unless it is deeply worked, more especially if part of the area in cultivation had to lie fallow each year. There has been great emphasis on this first step in agricultural progress in the Middle Ages, although in fact it was too often disregarded. While Carolingian treatises tell us nothing on this subject there is documentary evidence of an increasing number of technical terms to denote the successive stages in preparing the soil after the year 1000. These references antedate the thirteenth-century English treatises on agriculture (Walter of Henley's *Husbandry* and *Fleta*) which are always cited because there are no French or Italian sources of this kind until the fourteenth century. (This should not, however, be taken as an indication that these areas were in any way technically backward.) In mid-August the land was dug with a spade, hoed twice in September and October and finally ploughed with a pair of oxen. After 1150 this third and final stage was repeated. This was called *tercier*, since hoeing was seen as the first stage in the process. Harrowing after sowing is first documented after 1080. The process of working the land is well documented, especially in areas where it was heavy and in recent cultivation, but the question of drainage – essential if the crop was not to rot – remains largely unsolved. We do not know when the development of agricultural methods which permitted this were introduced: it is generally accepted that from the classical period onwards the land was worked cross-wise, that is the furrows ran in two directions, cutting each other at right angles, to ensure that the entire area was thoroughly worked. More significantly, this practice meant that autumn rains could not run off heavy soil, not to mention the difficulties that rutted and waterlogged ground presented to cattle and peasants alike. Ploughing in long, gently curving strips admittedly prevented criss-cross working of the soil, but it enabled the soil to dry naturally. Rather than the use of a particular tool, as Marc Bloch believed, it was the nature of the soil and its cultivation in rectangular plots that determined the division of land into thin strips.

Plough and mill

At seminal points in this discussion I have referred to the tool used for ploughing. This deserves closer attention, for it was an essential element if not in agrarian progress at large, at least in the improvement of the sedimentary areas of north-west Europe at the expense of the light, dry soils of the south. The ard cannot get a grip on heavy, rich and fertile soils: even with a metal ploughshare, a wooden cone – whether it was pushed or pulled – could only scratch the surface of a friable soil. The effort required to exert sufficient pressure to make a fairly deep furrow was exhausting and the ploughman had to go slowly, in time with the walking pace of his oxen. The soil rose behind him in two ridges of equal height and tended to fall back into the furrow – whence the need for criss-cross ploughing, which in turn dictated sowing broadcast and the pitiful triple yields of the classical and Carolingian periods, if we ignore the patently absurd claims for returns made in ninth-century documents. This was the picture that enchanted Virgil; it was the despair of Palladius and Columella who vainly counselled other methods. They encouraged the ploughman to tilt his plough so that it entered the ground at an angle and the soil was better aerated. Did they know of the other plough which was being developed and which they could have seen north of the Alps in Rhetia, present-day Bavaria? This had an asymmetrical ploughshare, possibly with sloping handles (this point is uncertain), a very thin wooden coulter and a mouldboard that turned the soil over on one side only, tearing the earth out of the ground. The word *ploum* used by the Lombards to describe this tool in the sixth century was undoubtedly the German *Pflug* and the Saxon *plough*. However, the oldest asymmetric ploughshares have been found in Bohemia and Poland, dating from the eighth century, then in the Rhineland and Savoy from the ninth and tenth centuries. Perhaps because here and there it was provided with a wheel-carriage in front, like a small cart, it appears as *carruca* (French *charrue* = plough) in tenth- and eleventh-century texts. It was only adopted very slowly and did not immediately displace the ard, to judge from fossilized furrows in the Low Countries, which show that both types were employed at the same time. When did the mouldboard plough displace the ard? From 1050 or 1100 the term *charrue* is used for stretches of land north of the Seine and in England, suggesting that it was firmly established in these areas. It was never used in the Mediterranean region: it did not appear to offer any advantages on the dry soils of the coastal plains of southern Europe. This was above all a tool for new, deep and heavy soils and one sufficiently precious to be accorded the same protection as houses in laws promulgated to keep the peace in the German Empire in the mid-twelfth century.

Do we need to spell out the direct and indirect results of using the mouldboard plough? There was a progressive decline in southern European agriculture in comparison with areas where the new tool was used, producing yields of five for one at Cluny in about 1150, eight for one in Picardy a century later and as much as 12 for one on the Flemish borders another century later – four times as much as in the time of Charlemagne or of Virgil. Then there was also the consequent importance of the smith, alone capable of repairing a tool largely composed of metal: from 1040 the smith levied a tax on such repairs from the valley of Aosta in Savoy to Saxony and Forez. In Metz the job of *sochier* (maker of ploughshares) was one of the most popular forms of employment. Then there was the role of the horse, with muscles for jumping that also made him good at pulling a heavy machine out of muddy ground, but also skittish and expensive, which is probably why the English peasantry always remained suspicious of the animal and continued to use four pairs of cheaper oxen as they had always done. Finally, we must not overlook the rift that the new plough opened up in the peasantry between those who had the wherewithal to harvest twice as much in half the time and the poorest, still tied to his ard (the *éreau* of Poitou or *Ehrling* of some areas of rural Germany). On the other hand, we can certainly reject Marc Bloch's hypothesis which attributed strip-cultivation to the mouldboard plough because of the supposed difficulties encountered turning the machine round: it can scarcely have been a simple task to turn an ard drawn by eight oxen!

When Marx, in the nineteenth century, saw the mill as the crucial point in a particular mode of production he stressed that its economic role ante-dated all social effects. We must pause here. In itself the grinding of corn by machine did not constitute a technical revolution: milling by hand at home was exhausting but equally efficient. To digress slightly from our theme therefore, we should emphasize the multi-faceted impact of harnessing a natural force rather than its immediate effect upon agriculture and, of course, the alienation experienced by a large part of the population because of the profits that accrued to the owner of the machine. We are very well informed about the history of the mill: the principle of one millstone turning on another that was stationary or *dormante* and crushing grain, olives, bark and other materials dates from the earliest classical times. The apparatus could be operated by slaves, camels, donkeys or horses: it was used in the days of the Pharaohs and still employed in twelfth-century Carcassonne. On the other hand, harnessing the power of the wind, of river-water or indeed the sea (for the Middle Ages attempted even this) involves the transformation of a vertical or oblique movement into a horizontal one, with vanes or sails receiving their impulsion on a different plane from that of the millstones. This difficult process had undoubtedly been mastered in the classical period: Varro, Vitruvius and Palladius all describe the relevant geared mechanisms, as well as the construction of vanes that would produce a head of water or make a sluggish stream run more quickly, and the moving axle on which the windmill shaft turned so that it might come as close as possible to the lightest breath of wind.

However, they did not take the next step of generalizing the process, possibly because of the irregular patterns of wind and water in the Mediterranean region or the great numbers of slaves. Moreover, the cost and the technical expertise required were increased by the need to find lead for the gears, iron for the tie rods, tree trunks for wooden wheels and huge stones of identical size for the millstones. This situation prevailed for a long time and even in the Carolingian period references to mills are rare and generally confined to raptures when one had been sighted.

They began to be built in considerable numbers in the eleventh century. There are several examples from tenth-century Catalonia, Italy and central and eastern Gaul, which suggests continuity from classical times, but it is impossible to generalize from this evidence. In England, 5,624 mills are recorded in Domesday Book (1086), about one for every four villages. The numbers grew after 1025–30. In Picardy a century later, for example, 300 references are to be found in a far from comprehensive series of documents and they were gradually introduced everywhere. The middle of the twelfth century witnessed two important developments: firstly the Cistercian Order apparently made the provision of mills on its land a standard feature, encouraging many other lords to follow suit; secondly, by placing either hammers on a camshaft or a metal saw on a system of rods the mill could be used to beat iron (from 1115–30), saw tree trunks, split stones or full cloth after 1170. From then on it became one of the most vital pieces of equipment in the medieval countryside, not just because it saved time or moved predictably, but because it enabled the various stages in a process that had previously been carried out in different places to be centralized at one point. We will discuss later the fact that the mill must clearly also be seen as a means by which the rich and powerful controlled and later constrained the other members of society. The cost of a mill inevitably confined ownership to an elite which it then further enriched as they charged others for using it, or even forced them to do so.

Production

Repeated working of the soil and better implements resulted in greatly increased yields from the old lands and meant that there was a rapid transition from scrub to crop on newly reclaimed areas. It would be logical here to enlarge upon minor contributory improvements, but I think they are secondary in this context. They include shoeing horses, the use of harness and horse-collar to yoke animals in pairs across the shoulders and (after 1175) in a string one behind the other and the development of pivoted cart-wheels. These are all 'inventions' with which the Middle Ages had somewhat rashly been credited, since (as in the case of the mill) these things were all known to Antiquity but had not been exploited, probably because of the vast resources of slave labour. Having made such strides in working the soil (only bettered by the advent of the tractor) it is all the more surprising that the western peasant did not make similar improvements to the process of harvesting. Here, too, there was a classical precedent and there is a very famous fourth-century bas-relief from the Rhineland showing a kind of reaping machine pushed by men and animals cutting the standing corn in front of it. There seems to have been nothing comparable in the medieval period: reaping was done with sickles, cutting the stalks at thigh-level, possibly to enable the tendrils of vetches and other leguminous plants to remain twined round them and possibly to provide a second crop which the very poorest could gather, or so that the soil might later be enriched by the rotting straw. The subject has been much discussed but it is impossible to draw any definite conclusions. The same applies to threshing with a flail: there seems to have been little use of other techniques (though even these seem somewhat primitive to us), such as the rolling of a cylinder pulled by horses on the threshing floor, or treading the grain – a crude method, but one which was considerably more efficient than the flail.

Once the grain was threshed it had to be stored, according to type, for consumption by men or animals, for each crop had its own particular uses; barley, for example, was unsuitable for horses, who much preferred oats. These, however, were only eaten by men in porridge or fermented to produce an every-day beer called *cervoise*. The diversification of species may have been accidental: there is nothing to suggest that, for example, the decline and subsequent disappearance of the ancient spelt of classical times and its replacement by wheat in thirteenth-century Belgium was the result of a deliberate policy. It is much more likely that the choice was determined by such factors as the ability of a particular plant to grow in the soil or the possibility of higher returns, or by the demands of the rich for white bread, supposedly better – something our own times have shown to be a case of taste and fashion. There are no grounds for going beyond these tentative assertions; even less for statistical claims. In this field we must also treat with scepticism some documents that have long been considered decisive. If we read the accounts of the Burgundian *bailliages* of *c.* 1340, wheat and oats emerge as the staple crops; unfortunately, an accidental fire at about this time in a peasant house on a slope behind the Burgundian village of Dracy shows that the grain store (destroyed in the fire) consisted essentially of rye, with some millet. We will therefore say no more than that wheat – of which a dozen species are known today – gradually advanced, despite the strain it placed on the land and a merely average yield, because it provided flour of the highest quality which, the peasant was confident, would achieve a high price once the lord's needs had been met. Barley on the other hand was grown less, increasingly confined to southern Europe, where Italian *polenta* preserves the memory of good thick soups prepared for men and cattle alike; there is no indication that this robust cereal crop had replaced oats in the manufacture of beer before the fourteenth century. Rye was still thought of as the cereal of the poor: hardy and giving good yields regardless of the type of soil or method of cultivation, it was only the acrid taste of its grey flour that was responsible for its gradual retreat to the cold, Hercynian soils where it is still to be found. The horrors associated with the ravages of ergot at the end of the eleventh century, which we have already mentioned, do not seem to have had any impact on its cultivation. The growing demand for beer and the increasing use of horses resulted in more oats being grown. It was also useful as a human foodstuff – porridge in the British Isles and Picard *grumel* – but it was its inclusion in the cycle of crop rotation after 1130–70 that resulted in a sudden increase in the area devoted to the cultivation of oats.

Each of these species had its individual requirements and had to be sown and harvested at different times. Oats would tolerate very late sowings: a *blé de mars*, *mars*, or *trémois*, they would say, referring to its rapid germination in March. There were different species of barley that could be sown at every season, but winter sowing was essential for wheat and rye. In cold or wet areas it was useful, if not essential, to exploit a number of these possibilities in order to mitigate the effects of a very severe winter when the grain rotted. In this case a second cereal sowing of oats or barley was made in April. This was a sound approach as long as only part of a large area was cultivated and the remainder allowed to rest, at least for anyone who held a large piece of land. This is how I would interpret allusions in Carolingian documents to winter and spring cereals, rather than make rash assumptions about triennial crop rotation in the ninth century. What is quite certain is that repeated sowings of wheat quickly exhausted the soil and a period of rest was imperative. The land was therefore allowed to lie fallow and the plants that grew on it later dug into the soil to replace the nitrogenous and carboniferous elements that the wheat crop had removed. Crop rotation was consequently essential and there is substantial evidence for this practice on poor soils in the twelfth century, on the 'wastes' (*gastes*) of England, Forez and Hurepoix. This was the principle of the Italian *debbio*, a rotation system that extended over a 10-year period. The introduction of unrestricted grazing on uncultivated ground was probably an important step, since it implied a half-pastoral and half-agrarian organization of the village economy. In Italy or Flanders grazing on the fallow land might last two, three or four years.

When an itinerant existence was replaced by fixed settlements and cultivation of the surrounding land, the population also increased and the development of a more systematic form of land-use became essential. The most commonly adopted practice was to let the land lie fallow every other year, a prudent measure and one long-established in Italy, Castile, Languedoc and Poitou. Where the soil could be deeply worked there were higher yields, and in areas where the risk of a hard winter was greatest a cycle of winter sowings followed by spring sowings and then a fallow period evolved. It was no longer a haphazard progression dictated by failed winter sowings but was determined by assigning a specific crop to a particular piece of land. The certainty of one, and probably two, harvests was advantageous for men and animals. Broadcast sowing of leguminous vegetables (peas, beans etc.) amongst the cereal crops, barley in particular, could also be planned. Work was also more evenly distributed throughout the year. On the other hand, the disadvantages were obvious: ploughed land was reduced by a third, by two-thirds if one of the two sowings was lost. The effects of prolonged arable cultivation could only be offset by repeatedly working the soil and by manuring it with grazing-stock on the fallow land. This last feature demonstrates a clear relationship with the reclamation of the forests (which reduced the size of the usual grazing grounds) and the use for pasture of land not currently sown with cereal crops.

We should be careful not to assume that there was anything regular or generalized about this method of growing cereal crops. It is true that there are some ninth-century references to *saisons* (seasons) and later to *soles, royes, delles* and furlongs according to region. There are many indications of this from 1116 in the Ile-de-France and Picardy, 1150 in the Cluny region and the Beauce (south of Paris) and from the late twelfth century in England and Burgundy. But the essential steps were only taken much later: on the one hand, biennial or triennial crop rotation had to be established – something that clearly only the rich could do before 1250 or 1260; on the other, the entire area had to be divided in this way, either grouped together in compact blocks or singly amongst the individual strips, which could only happen when the entire village community decided to entrust their grazing animals to a communal herdsman, in 1280–1320 at the earliest. Even then it is not clear what happened to the tenants or freeholders who owned only one piece of land: did they stop eating one year in three?

The struggle against nature

For 200 years the European peasant tried to break the stranglehold of the wilderness that encircled and oppressed him. It was a constant and heroic struggle, but one with clear results. It is impossible to gauge the work involved, for the extant texts preserve only contracts (admittedly full and detailed) between two rich parties, one of whom was the Church (hence the preservation of the document), but we know nothing of all the rest, the unwritten labours of the individual which were undoubtedly the major part of the undertaking.

How and why?

Whenever two parties set out in a written contract the conditions under which newly reclaimed ground should be cultivated, economic interest can always be adduced as their motive, even if there were conventional references to the salvation of souls as well: for the one it was to clear the trees (*eradicare, exstirpare*) and free the ground for cultivation (*ad arandum, ad colendum*); for the other the prospect of a good yield of tithes from the new land (*novales*) justified sharing a valuable right. Silence unfortunately covers all details of the future operation; we know only the drift of their intentions and nothing of the real motives behind this search for new land: a surplus of man-power that had to be put to good use? Increased demand for plots of land from a growing population? The need to control an area where wood, the most important raw material, would be within easy reach? Or, as is increasingly accepted for all these initial stages, concern with improved use of both the land left for animals and that devoted to the production of foodstuffs for human consumption? Nor should we underestimate the desire to return to one's roots which re-occupation of land once cultivated and then allowed to revert to its wild state represented: traces of Gallo-Roman or Celtic occupation have been discovered here and there in the *artigues* (as the newly cleared ground was known in Gascony), as well as in the *plans* of northern France and some of the Belgian *kouter*.

We are better placed to describe the methods employed, not because descriptions have survived, but because they are those still used in many parts of the world on land new to cultivation. First the land was denshired: the undergrowth and smaller tree trunks were cleared with a hoe and then burnt, enriching the soil which was subsequently turned over to grazing, at least for a while. Then the ground around large tree trunks and roots was thoroughly dug; only then was the tree pulled up by pairs of oxen, after the woodcutters had been at work for a long while. In woodland between four and six years had to elapse before the land, duly worked and enriched, was ready to cultivate and corresponding delays were allowed to the leaseholder before any economic return was expected of him in Kent, the Ile-de-France and Bohemia. That was in good, rich soil. Other conditions might present more problems: by the water's edge or in the marshes of the English Fens and the Brière, the low-lying lands of Flanders or in the pools of Languedoc, the Crau (southern France) and the Marenne of Poitou. In these regions the land had to be drained, extra soil transported, the necessary dykes built, then carefully maintained and sometimes broken at a specific point if the pressure from the sea (the Flemish *zegang*) became too great. All these waterlogged areas (*moere, étiers, meersen, schoeren,* as they were called in the different regions) could only be used for sheep and occasionally rye and, even on a collective basis, the undertaking was so costly that it was only the very rich, such as counts or monks, who could control the vast herds of sheep and cattle whose numbers ran into hundreds. The morain gravel of the Valley of Aosta, the Dombes (south-east France) and the Allier (central France, formerly the Bourbonnais) and heavy alluvial flood plains, such as the *bonifachi* of the Po, the *teppe* of the Saône valley, the *carrèges* beside the Garonne never lost their tendency to flood, despite the earth and gravel banks that protected them, like the *turcies* of the Loire valley built between 1080 and 1160.

I hesitate to place the Mediterranean slopes ravaged by water-erosion in the same category, but the building of small walls to contain terraces of soil (called *ciglioni* and *gradoni* in Italy) must have been exhausting for the men who had to hoist stones in baskets up the steep slopes, strengthening the irrigated and cultivated plains (*huertas, orts*) with the roots of living plants or olive trees. From the Spanish Levant to Calabria they had to be perennially alert, to decide when it was necessary to canalize a torrential stream, or to dismantle parts of the stone walls in its path.

Until very recently it was only written sources, short in detail, that provided information about the way in which work on the land was organized, and then only if there were fairly exact stipulations in the contract: uncultivated land was leased with tithes reserved, perhaps to a group of peasants or to a lord who made filling his granaries a higher priority than preserving traditional hunting grounds. These leaseholders (*locatores*) in their turn often leased plots of land for clearance to workers who had come from elsewhere, either individually or as a group; they might be woodcutters, woodmen or labourers. Paid assistants are also documented. This was a reflection of the fact that land reclamation was one of the few medieval enterprises that reached a level requiring division of labour and specialization. It is often said that the leaseholders paid rent from the produce of the land under various share-cropping agreements (*champart*, *agrière*, *mezzadria*) of about 10 per cent of the total produced. But there are many widely distributed examples of fixed contracts, both of money payments and payments in kind. It is clear in any case that payment of a proportion of yields provided a safety-net if there was a very poor harvest and also shows how the lord of such an area would participate in the venture in order to attract others.

I would like to provide dates and measurements of surface-area, but this is virtually impossible for the historian. The villages that developed in these clearings (reflected in the many place-names ending in *-rod*, *-ried* and *-schlag* in the Germanic area, *-rupt* and *-sart* in northern and eastern France, *-ronchi* further south, besides the many *neuville* or *villafranca*) provide the basis for a detailed map, but the microtoponymy has still to be examined in detail, the evidence of aerial photography assessed and plant and pollen remains analysed. In our present state of knowledge this seems to me the most plausible interpretation: an initial phase when all the different sorts of undergrowth – heathlands, brushwood, alder thickets, beech-woods, wastes and other uncultivated areas – were colonized through small-scale and possibly illicit individual effort. This can confidently be traced back to 975 in Catalonia, 1020 or 1050 in the Mâconnais, Flanders, Auvergne and Poitou, towards the end of the century in Picardy, the Harz or Piedmont. These smaller enterprises are lost from sight in the period of contracts which can be pinpointed with some certainty to 1150–80, as a good third of the surviving documents from this period in Maine, England and Picardy refer to forest clearance. Reclamation of land from the sea and standing water also occurred at this time and the concentration of newly founded village settlements is greatest. After about 1180 or 1200 (but progressively later the further east one goes) there was some slackening of seigneurial effort and a litigious period began, with lawsuits over contested tithes, boundary disputes or the abuse of justice, when lords wrangled amongst themselves or the men of one village all supported one of their number accused of 'furrow-filching', in other words pushing his plough a little bit over the edge of his piece of land in order to acquire an extra furrow. Reclamation by individuals resumed (if it had not continued all along), witness the large number of plots of land bearing the names of the men who had first worked them and who can, in some cases, be identified.

The trend ceased when, in the mid-thirteenth century, an equilibrium – however fragile – was established between the community's need for cultivable land and its forest and grazing requirements. In 1315 or 1330 land was still being reclaimed in central Germany, Friuli and the Alps, but these archaic and backward areas were exceptions.

The effects

I should like to quantify the area reclaimed, but this is an extremely difficult task. Here and there the surface area of a pool that was drained or a low-lying field, or polder, won back from the sea enables us to make exact calculations: some 150,000 hectares along the French Atlantic seaboard, slightly more in the area between Boulogne and Frisia, a little less on the English coast. But apart from these exceptional cases we have no information about the extent of land reclamation in mountainous areas, on flood plains or even in areas where access was no problem. The total seems very low if we add up all the sparse documentary references or deductions from a map for a specific area: for Picardy this came to scarcely 40,000 hectares. There should be further examination of *cadastres*, old boundary lines and the evidence of aerial photography. In many regions this has been scarcely outlined. We have to rely instead on estimates based on the meagre evidence of boundaries, field divisions or the species of plant remains. Should we say 10 to 15 per cent reclaimed land for areas of established occupation – the sedimentary basins of north-west Europe or the interior plains of the south? Or more, perhaps 25 or 30 per cent, in England, Germany and mountainous areas? The de-afforestation of wooded plateaux was undoubtedly the most important single characteristic. Even where large tracts of forest survived, inroads were always being made and each part given its own individual name – in the Paris area alone Laye, Yvelines, Cuise, Loge, Cruye and Biere fall into this category.

Another important characteristic, however, is more easily detectable on a map and that is the intensive settlement that followed the woodcutters into the open clearings, on earth banks or along slopes that had been cleared. This effect was so widespread that it would be possible to maintain that many lords were prompted to support these enterprises by a desire to create new centres or exert their rights. Whatever the case, these new settlements, populated by settlers from a distance and the younger sons from nearby villages, seem relatively emancipated to us, free from a number of the restrictions that continued to limit their neighbours, until they in turn invoked the new village and demanded identical treatment, threatening to leave the old settlement if this was denied them. The village might be populated mainly by labourers, where the houses were built in a row along the path that ran through the forest, with each man clearing the wood at the back of his own plot, the typical pattern of the German *Waldhufendorf* and the 'herringbone' settlement of geographers; or it might be nucleated, surrounded by a palisade, as in so many *sauvetés* in Aquitaine or Lombardy; or again the settlement might develop gradually in the expectation of future demand for plots of land, an expectation that was sometimes unjustified and is reflected in the odd plans of some villages today. But the fringe activities carried out by individuals or families could only produce large isolated houses (such as the *borderie* of Poitou or the Provençal *cabaneria*), if we ignore for the moment the areas where individual enterprise tended to compartmentalize the countryside. I shall return shortly to this possible origin of bocage, with small fields amongst patches of woodland enclosed by trees and hedges on raised banks.

We are on surer ground when examining the social effects of the new settlements. Their inhabitants almost certainly enjoyed greater freedom. For some who had previously been anchored within the rigid structure of an old village it undoubtedly also meant increased social status: the possession of peasant freeholds by those who a short while before had been chafing at strict seigneurial control was a marked characteristic of the late twelfth century. In 1100–1120 60, 50 and 40 per cent of the documentary references to the status of land for Catalonia, Picardy and Franconia respectively, speak of *allodia*, *hereditaria* or *patrimonia*.

This increase in the influence of the peasant may have been responsible for the fairly generous contracts made with the newcomers, and later with their former neighbours in the old villages. When a lord wanted to attract labour, whether he held lands in eastern Germany, Burgundy, Champagne or Maine, as the *locator* (leaser of land available for cultivation) he had to make it an attractive proposition. These terms were sometimes written down and occasionally survived: besides individual freedom there were various privileges and a fixed rate was established for taxes whose level had hitherto varied. The form of these contracts is clearer in the south: the practice of *complant* extended to the new areas, envisaging ownership when all or part of the land had produced two complementary crops for several years (vines and olives, vines and cereals or cereals and fruit, for example). The same method had been employed in the ninth century in the Catalan *aprisio* or the *escalio* of Languedoc to ensure that the Spanish peasants fleeing from the Moors settled in one place. The exceptionally favourable conditions presented by *complant* and *champart* share-cropping agreements and the offer of various freedoms and privileges explains why some of these developments took place on a huge scale: 180 households settled simultaneously near Verona in 1186 and more than 100 at Jouy in Champagne at the same time.

One obvious question has to be answered. If these newly reclaimed lands were expected to do no more than provide subsistence was there not a danger that insufficiently fertile soil would be cultivated or that there would be a serious shortage of land required for other purposes, such as grazing? As there has been such small progress in pedology, only archaeological evidence can enlighten us on the first point: even before the desertions of the fifteenth century (which obviously occurred first in isolated areas where the land was least fertile) setbacks can be documented in regions as diverse as Italy and the Rhineland when agricultural expansion was at its height. Here and there groups of peasant settlers were forced to return to the lands that had long been cultivated, because of the exceptionally meagre yields from cereal crops on soil that was too poor for anything other than grazing. The area available for grazing was inevitably reduced by the reclamation of woods and wasteland and, as I have explained, was offset only by allowing some ploughed land to lie fallow, so that sufficient food for the community had to be produced by more intensive and scientific cultivation of the remaining fields. This balance was not achieved everywhere, and where it did not exist the 'vicious circle' that operated in the medieval economy began to impel these dislocated rural areas towards a critical shortage of either arable or grazing lands.

It must be emphasized, however, that these potential dangers did not prompt the first protests over the abuses of land reclamation which were voiced between 1255 and 1290 in north-west Europe; they stemmed rather from lords whose hunting grounds were threatened, or communities deprived of their common pasture land and sources of collectable wild food (fruits, nuts, fungi and so on). In the first case the lord could only resort to enclosure and the protection of pieces of woodland, parks, warrens or spinneys, which thus further depleted the area of grazing ground as well as that available for clearing. As very large expanses were required for any self-contained hunting ground this option was only available to those of high rank, such as the king of England, who increased the area covered by his 'forest' considerably after 1270, or dukes and earls after 1280 or 1290. One of the aims of demarcation in the forest (so that for a while at least all men and animals were excluded from one part of it) may have been the regeneration of especially vulnerable species: this was often the result of ecclesiastical and notably

Cistercian initiative. The controlled and rational exploitation of woodland with the practice of staggered felling was therefore the primary result of the abuses of forest clearing. Even before the French royal *ordonnances* of the fourteenth century this was one of the most positive results of the struggle between man and the forest. On the other hand, it is not entirely clear whether enclosure within the forest was such a wise move as far as hunting was concerned. By setting traps, lures and nets on the small area left to them the peasants ensured that a minimum of complementary nourishment reached the poor man's table, while the 'great beasts' whom it was dangerous to approach remained the prerogative of the 'noble' hunt and stayed in copses and spinneys. This disruption may have led to some degree of zoological imbalance, but unfortunately there is no means of establishing this. It is possible that refinements in the art of hunting after 1250–70, notably those associated with the use of falcons, even before the appearance of hunting manuals in the fourteenth century, are a reflection of the hunters' concern for improved methods of tracking disappearing species. As for the peasant's concern about the abuse of forest clearing, stemming from the reduction of the area of land available for gathering wild berries and fruit which were part of his diet, there is no precise evidence since we have no idea how important this food reserve was. Once again it is the *a posteriori* evidence of the appearance of fruit trees and vegetable plots round individual dwelling houses (the *pourpris* of northern France, the *ferragina* of Languedoc and the *orts* of Provence) which may be indications of a return to traditional lands for foodstuffs that had previously been found in the wild. They are found from the twelfth century onwards in the Mediterranean area, considerably later (the early fourteenth century) further north.

I have dwelt at length on the sometimes negative effects of clearing in order to emphasize some of the underestimated results of this great movement of agricultural expansion. The positive consequences have always been stressed; it is sometimes forgotten that there was also an undeniable dislocation of the natural equilibrium and if we fail to recognize this fact, we run the risk of ignoring an important cause of the rural economic crisis of the later Middle Ages.

The conquered land

Let us consider the situation in the mid-thirteenth century, when the unfortunate consequences of assarting were scarcely apparent and there was a balance between man-power and grain yields. At this point we can assess this important aspect of medieval agrarian history, namely man's control of the soil – the corollary of the settlement which had both preceded and given rise to it.

Systematic mixed farming

Doing a little bit of everything was one of the unchanging characteristics of European agriculture up to the last century, but this practice is gradually disappearing. For many centuries, and above all in the Middle Ages, the absence of any buffer stocks, the uncertainty of long-distance transport and the impossibility of controls on a wider scale forced individual communities to be self-reliant. The peasant had to make the most of all that nature offered and if she failed him, nothing was to be expected from his neighbour. This requirement (as well as the notoriously parrot-like characteristics of the Carolingian scribes) undoubtedly explains the uniformity of ninth-century agricultural writings (like the capitulary *De villis*) offering the same advice and listing the same plants from Frisia to the Campania, despite the intrinsic improbability of this situation. It also dictated the precept (which only died out at the beginning of the fifteenth century, as the taste for *vins forts* – strong wines – decreased in towns and noble households) that vines should be planted as far north as Scotland or Norway. This was not, as has been unthinkingly repeated, so that the priest should have a supply of wine to celebrate mass (two or three vines would have sufficed for that) but because once the eucharistic needs had been met the remaining grape juice provided the populace with the healthiest drink available. We know nothing of the quality and taste of wine grown in such conditions, of course, though much can be supplied by the imagination!

However, I have already pointed out that most of the cleared land was given over to arable crops, which formed the basis of contemporary diet; the rest of the *companaticum* (apart from the role of wild plants and what was provided by animals and poultry) consisted of leguminous crops, peas, vetches and lentils sown amongst cereals. It was only in the semi-arid Mediterranean areas, or in northern Europe during the later thirteenth century, that part of the cultivated land was systematically set aside for a particular crop. Indeed, in the south the poor quality of the Italian maquis and of the *larris* and the *garrigues* of Languedoc and the Iberian peninsula eliminated entire sections of the land, as surely as if they were sterile: irrigation was essential for the *orts*, *viridaria*, *rivages* and *ferraginalia* which developed along the edge of the great rivers of the Mediterranean, where vegetables, dye- and textile-plants were grown; or vines might be planted with olives or chestnut trees in areas too steep for any other complementary planting. In the north the dykes and slopes were used only for the cultivation of flax or hemp, or of woad for dyeing; on the other hand after 1220 or 1230 market gardens began to be cultivated amongst the boggy waters of the slow rivers, vegetable gardens which from the thirteenth century were called *hardines* or *hortillons* in Flanders, Picardy and England.

The progressive but irregular practice of crop rotation which we have already discussed undoubtedly provided an incentive to develop improved agricultural methods so that there was no reduction in crop yields when only two-thirds or half the area was cultivated. Now we come to a critical issue: what was the grain yield at this period? For although it is quite impossible to attempt to give any kind of global production figure, we must try and establish the *ratio*, that is the relationship of seed corn to harvest, bearing in mind that comparisons with modern figures are highly misleading since we know very little of the exact botanical nature of the species sown. In the classical period Varro and Columella, with scant concern for practicalities, drew up a table of yields which was copied by Carolingian writers and then reproduced, clause by clause, by *Fleta* in the thirteenth century: barley gave an eight-fold yield, rye seven-fold, wheat five-fold and oats four-fold. These are distinctly optimistic figures, especially in the context of the barely developed techniques of Carolingian agriculture. For although there are some glimmers of future improvements in the polyptychs, for example, or the famous inventory of the taxable lands of Annappes, reality was much harsher, with a three-fold yield at best. From *a posteriori* evidence of the first half of the twelfth century (in other words after a period of significant developments) the data from the accounts of Cluny or Winchester show that they were still far from achieving the classical ideal, with yields of 2.5 for oats, 3.8 to 4 for wheat, 5 for rye and 6 for barley. The figures are low, even if the sequence of species is the same. The thirteenth century was therefore the crucial point: after the middle of the century there were five-fold yields of wheat in Lorraine and Languedoc, eight-fold in Picardy and the Ile-de-France; around 1315–20 even 10- or 12-fold yields were achieved in good years. This was dazzling progress but we should bear two major reservations in mind: on the one hand the whole of southern Europe seems to have been unaffected by these agrarian improvements, with only three-fold yields in the Alps of Provence and five-fold in Tuscany. Even allowing for the fact that the population levelled off very quickly here, this shortfall provided a potent explanation for the seizure of the neighbouring countryside by towns affected by severe food shortages. On the other hand, even the high figures for northern France represent mediocre yields in real terms: at best they represent only some 10 or 12 hundredweight per hectare, a figure admittedly comparable with that of the late nineteenth century, but without the dietary contribution made in the later period by meat and dairy products, foodstuffs that were in very short supply in the Middle Ages.

We should give greater consideration to the non-existence or at least great rarity of naturally occurring flat meadowland which evidently led to a great concern that every bit of potential arable ground should be cultivated. But this increased the problem of the provision of adequate pasturage, which was a vital ingredient of peasant society, indeed of all medieval society, for warriors and travellers as well as the tillers of the soil. The numbers of grazing beasts were swollen by the clearing of woodland that had previously provided pasture for them. Admittedly, the practice of grazing on fallow land provided a palliative, as I have already mentioned, but the disadvantages of this practice quickly became apparent, to say nothing of the constraints on the community as a whole that it involved and in some places it was difficult to sustain. Once the animals had consumed the scanty vegetation growing on the fallow land there was no other food for them; land had also to be set aside for hay to provide fodder in the winter, as well as for leguminous crops. But where was this land to come from if not the area already set aside for arable crops? Setting aside unbroken or common land at the centre or on the edge of the village for pasture seems to have been the most satisfactory solution. Animals grazed freely amongst the houses and between the *communia* shared by the richest owners of livestock on these open spaces, variously called green, *pratellum* or *Allmende*. This practice must have started at an early date, since an English royal statute issued at Merton in 1236 theoretically forbade the practice; but it was adopted on a large scale on the Continent at the end of the thirteenth and the beginning of the fourteenth centuries in Picardy, Hainault and Normandy. If we add that these were precisely the regions which utilized fallow ground for leguminous crops, there is an additional reason for keeping cattle, horses and pigs in a stable or yard round the family house when they could not be led onto what wood or common land remained.

Unfortunately there were numerous areas where it was impossible to develop such practices because commons had never been established or because the soil was too poor for pasture. Once again southern Europe was worst affected and there was a marked reduction in animal husbandry in this area from 1250 onwards; in mountainous areas herds could be taken to seasonal pastures in the summer; elsewhere there was a perennial threat of famine and shortages which, as we have observed, did nothing to mitigate the effects of poor agricultural practice. In this way grazing played a pre-eminent role in medieval life.

The supremacy of grazing animals

Herds of grazing animals are often neglected in the study of the medieval economy and yet they were crucially important. I have already frequently referred to the importance of animals in the ecological structures of the period and to the important links between the flocks and cultivated land, between grazing animals and the countryside at large.

It is therefore particularly disappointing that there are only the most fleeting allusions to herds of animals before 1300: the size of a flock of sheep (numbering some 2,000) belonging to a Cistercian house, for example, or that of a manor of the bishop of Ely, where there were 40 cattle, 60 pigs and 120 sheep. Scraps of information of this kind make it impossible to attempt any overall estimate or generalizations as to the species involved. The only figures that can be deduced with any confidence (and they are not insignificant) concern the relative numbers of different types of animals kept, bearing in mind of course that there will be local variations. At the end of the eleventh century, for example, Domesday Book (though by no means a comprehensive survey) records 1 horse for every 3 cattle, 10 pigs and 30 sheep; in Poitou in the early twelfth century 15 sheep are recorded per head of cattle and there are similar figures for Champagne around 1150. The scarcity of horses revealed by this early evidence is borne out by the tariffs of tonnage until well into the thirteenth century and the prevalence of sheep is explained by the intensive use of wool and hides. On the other hand, archaeological evidence provides information about their use as foodstuffs: the bones found in northern Germany and in Burgundy dating from the twelfth and then the fourteenth century show that more beef was consumed than has generally been believed, accounting for 38 to 60 per cent of the whole, while pork was more stable at between 27 and 32 per cent; however, virtually the whole of a pig might be eaten which was not the case with beef, since they were generally slaughtered after a working life, rather than especially fattened. On these sites there are also horse bones, showing that here at least there was no taboo on horsemeat; wild animals accounted for some 11 per cent of the total, reflecting the active role of the hunt. And of course we are completely ignorant of all kinds of dairy produce.

This is a very sketchy outline, reflecting the lack of information in the sources before the mid-thirteenth century, even in English manorial accounts. The evident changes in animal husbandry and their effects are more informative. One might expect a progressive reduction in the number of animals as settlements became fixed and tillage more extensive, but this is not the case. The growing importance of the horse in cartage, ploughing and in knightly training appears to be directly linked to the increased number of sowings of oats: this crop positively invaded the fields after 1125–60, supporting crop rotation as well as providing the fodder needed by the horse for his exertions. Moreover, there was a sharp rise in the price of horses, or rather the prices, since a clear hierarchy of types was established between the *destrier* or war-horse and the *roncin* or rouncy used for cartage and as a pack animal. This reflected an urgent need and, in a second phase, a satisfactory supply. Prices rose from one to three *livres* between 1140 and 1180 (a 300 per cent increase), from three to six *livres* around 1220 (a rise of 100 per cent) and then from six to eight *livres* (a 50 per cent rise). The growth of herds of cattle was probably less spectacular: using the same scale of estimates the price of a bullock in northern Europe or a buffalo in the south was only a few *sous* around 1100 and did not reach a *livre* until the mid-thirteenth century. One has the impression that providing sufficient plough beasts (as was the practice in England or at Cluny) was a higher priority than the provision of meat or dairy products. But the most important point is that the primacy of grazing stock was linked to two other kinds of traditional European animal husbandry.

This development was less closely related to the pigs who would continue masters of the remaining woodland until the fourteenth century and whose slaughter in December was the prelude to Christmas and the celebration of winter. More like wild boars than our fat, farm-bred pigs, the medieval hog was a dietary mainstay of the poor; there were few households without one and the sow's remarkable fertility is renowned. Consumption of mutton was very limited, on the other hand, even in Mediterranean areas where the shortage of meadowland often made it impossible to keep cattle. Sheep were kept for their wool; they were therefore one of the most important elements of an intensive pastoral system which was a major influence on farming and daily life. Just as earlier we saw that vines were planted everywhere because they were indispensable, so it was with sheep. Considerable numbers are documented in the fourteenth century, for example, with flocks of 30,000 belonging to the same owner in England; in Castile there were one and a half million sheep when the *hermandad* or fraternity of shepherds was created in 1273, three million before the introduction of the merinos prior to 1350, five million a century later. Although historians have always placed the increased economic importance of sheep after 1350 this was in fact a much older trend. On the one hand, because of their voracious appetite, sheep were banned from woodland and a section of arable land had therefore to be set aside for them; on the other, their survival on the most meagre vegetation resulted in some areas which could have been irrigated being given over to sheep; finally, because of their prolificity and robust constitution it was possible to keep enormous wandering flocks. These features combined resulted in two important characteristics of the medieval economy. There were no longer the vast estates of the Roman period, roamed by grazing animals and watched over by slaves on horseback; but on areas where, either as a result of the natural paucity of the soil, or because of grazing by wild animals in the classical period, only short grass and scrubby bushes would grow (the *herms*, *frosts*, *causses* and *mescla* of Italy, Corsica, Castile, Languedoc and the Central Massif or the mountainous, wooded soils of the Atlantic coasts): here the sheep reigned supreme and the herdsman or shepherd was a figure apart, isolated from the village and vaguely suspected of witchcraft. On the other hand, in regions where soils were largely of a different type, there was large-scale movement of grazing stock. When transhumance was merely a question of leading the herd up the mountain to a grassy summer pasture there was no adverse effect on arable cultivation. But very often long distances had to be travelled: there were seasonal movements of flocks from Quercy to Béarn, for example, and from Andalucia to Old Castile. Movement on this scale needed explicit control and regulations governing their route and resting places appeared from 1200 onwards; of these the Castilian Mesta is the most famous, regrouping animals from all over the province into huge flocks in which the big graziers, military orders, Cistercians and Spanish grandees predominated. The animals moved slowly along tracks used every year for this purpose (*drailles*, *cañades* or *tratturi*, as they were called in Aquitaine, Castile or Lombardy). These paths were wandering and indirect, with many branches: the animals trampled the fields, broke fences, devastated the young crops and tore bark from the trees. Their passage infuriated the peasantry every year and provoked an avalanche of interminable lawsuits from 1180 onwards that only stopped in the nineteenth century. However, although sheep were destructive, they were also a source of wealth; the shepherd might be disapproved of, but he was protected by powerful individuals; wool, even short and harsh, had no serious rival before the cotton fabrics of the fifteenth century. As a result the pastoral economy (particularly those elements relating to sheep) which had already effected many changes in the organization of farming was an important influence on the shape of rural areas.

Paths and plots

The rural landscape is one of the most enduring aspects of the legacy of the Middle Ages. The imprint left there by medieval man is only gradually being effaced by the vast changes in land-use effected in our own period and still provides the basic structure for rural life today.

I have always stressed the importance in the history of settlement of the period when a maze of cart tracks was established in the countryside, which still form the basis of our road transport system. For this to occur there had to be a dominant centre to provide the hub from which various paths radiated, giving access to arable land or uncultivated areas. Afterwards (or perhaps before this stage) the inhabitants had to achieve full control of the land and eradicate all trace of the old routes across the wilderness and wastes. During the period of itinerant cultivation these were the means by which men reached their isolated plots surrounded by wasteland. It was also essential for the importance of the Roman road system (with an essentially urban-oriented plan) to diminish; this often coincided with an increased use of even older routes which were more useful to the medieval peasant. Certainly it has been observed with satisfaction that the evidence of aerial photography in particular shows how the layout of plots of land continued to follow the Roman pattern, especially in Mediterranean areas where Roman influence had naturally been strongest. However, I am far from convinced that this was the case north of the Loire, and it was surely not universal, as supporters of this theory would have us believe: at any rate it left no mark on Germania or Brittany. It is extremely difficult to establish even the broad outline of the network of medieval tracks. This area of agrarian archaeology remains extremely hazy; what is required is a study on several levels, not only systematizing documentary references to roads (which are more common than is generally supposed), but also taking into account parish and communal boundaries (which often ran alongside a path that still exists), examining the oldest *cadastres* and dating hedgerow vegetation. The few studies of this kind that have been attempted have done no more than prepare the way for a comprehensive survey that would permit a history of landholdings.

Documentary references to the nature or shape of areas of cultivated land are very rare indeed before light is shed on the subject by the Swiss and Italian *cadastres* of the late thirteenth century and then by the more comprehensive evidence of the early fifteenth century. Field archaeology has only supplied a few isolated examples in Alsace, Limburg and Yorkshire. This absence of hard fact has produced a superabundance of theories. I have already referred to that of Marc Bloch, which linked the division of land to the tools used to work it and is today rejected on technical grounds. Bloch's initial observation on the clear distinction between areas where the land was divided into thin strips and others where the units were large squares, is nonetheless valid and there is as yet no obvious explanation. Leaving aside areas where land division was clearly dictated by geographical constraints (such as narrow fields with terraces or edged by woodland), or by convenience (such as isolated fields in the middle of uncultivated ground, heathland or mountain pasture, which were roughly oval in shape so that they might be enclosed more easily), the two types of land division appear to have co-existed. The question of size is irrelevant: some strips in northern France were only 10 furrows wide, but over 100 metres long; others were 6 times as broad; they might vary in overall size from a few hundred square metres to 20 hectares for one tenant. These observations are as true for plots grouped together as those scattered over the open fields. Once criss-cross tillage had been abandoned there was no technical advantage in either pattern. The solution must lie elsewhere: at present socio-judicial explanations are favoured – judicial in that field division into strips (a product of the systematic division of inheritances) was a fairly accurate reflection of the peasant's concern that his plot should be no steeper, nor the soil poorer than that of his neighbour; social because the breakdown of the large family unit lay at the root of the success of such division and linked strip-fields with areas where there was a marked fragmentation of family groups. This observation is strengthened by the documentary evidence of such fragmentation into several plots on Carolingian estates (*manses*) in northern Europe, where there was an increasing trend towards smaller units – quarter-virgate, *huitée*, *vergée*, *Vierteil*, as they were variously known in England, France and Germany. Since these were also areas where there was marked, large-scale technical progress, strip cultivation soon became the norm – incidentally supporting Bloch's theory. All these characteristics were particularly telling in areas where strip cultivation predominated (and still does in some cases), in the sedimentary basins, coastal areas and flood-plains of northern Europe.

Conversely, in Mediterranean regions estates remained intact; the planting of vines, olives and trees encouraged large plots of land, the family unit remained much stronger and technical progress was halted mid-stream. Communal identity was also less highly developed and there was consequently little impetus to pool neighbouring strips of land for rotation-cropping or common grazing. Here the square plot reigned supreme in the *quaderni* and *aiole* of Italy and Provence, where rectangular plots are documented with a shorter side three-quarters the length of the longer side.

Obviously there are exceptions to this generalized picture in the terraces of southern France, for example, and the vineyards of the north; but, most importantly, it ignores a problem that was to become crucially important in the fourteenth and fifteenth centuries, that of enclosure. At some point (when wheat was growing, for example) peasants would erect wattle fences round their fields to protect them from the adverse effects of indiscriminate grazing, either of their own accord or because their master instructed them to do so. In steppes or mountainous regions a little wall would be built to separate the field from the surrounding moor or mountain pasture. This practice has been recorded since classical times and continues in many parts of the world where the land is only under partial control.

On the other hand, growing hedges permanently between two plots of land or along a road was a new practice of uncertain origin. It is not clear when it appeared: 'Celtic' precedents have often been cited to explain the presence of hedges in cold coastal areas like Brittany or Kent, and Danish origins have been postulated for some English counties and the Caux (Normandy); but it is possibly more helpful to see it as the enclosure of arable areas in the middle of grazing ground, rather as peasants took measures to protect their crops from straying animals in areas like Aragon and Gascony where the effects of transhumance might be devastating. Enclosures to protect Mediterranean *complants* are a separate issue, as indeed are vineyards, which were universally enclosed. All these long established factors explain the enclosure of plots here and there, but they do not account for the creation of bocage (mixed woodland and pasture land) with a continuous landscape of compact plots individually hedged. (No doubt the practical difficulties of enclosing a narrow strip of land had some influence on the shape.) There has been endless debate amongst historians as to the causes of this movement and its extent. There are indications of the enclosure of previously 'open' countryside after 1230 or 1260 in England or northern France and in the Perche (northern France), slightly later in Hainault and the Rhineland, while we know that it became a powerful and irreversible movement in England after 1400. This outline ignores areas where bocage, with its small fields enclosed by hedged or wooded banks, reigned supreme – parts of Wales, Brittany, the Vendée (Poitou) and parts of the Central Massif – since the pattern appears to have been established at an earlier date. All the other explanations put forward for enclosure are of very limited use: it has been ascribed to individualism – but can we really assume a valid comparative framework for peasants in regions as diverse as Brittany and the Thiérache? Systematic sheep-rearing may provide an explanation for England but certainly not for the Vosges or the Vendée. It evidently provided pasture for cattle in fifteenth-century Hainault and Normandy, but not in Brittany and, indeed, cereal crops were grown on many of these plots. Despite many studies we are unable to generalize from soil type, economic structure, local attitudes or climate. The only point that seems to emerge is that men positively wished to enclose their lands in this way, either because it made animal husbandry more profitable, because they wanted to be their own master and refused to rotate their crops with other peasants', because they rejected participation in the wider community or simply because they needed the protection afforded by enclosure. It seems likely that the bocage was established in successive stages, even in areas such as fifteenth-century Hainault, where it made a sudden appearance and was rapidly accepted: at first there were isolated enclosures, and then the open land in between was gradually filled in and used either for grazing, where the soil was cold, or tilled straightaway, as in England.

In surveying the peasant's daily exertions in the context of his seasonal labours (a vital component of my argument), I realize that I may have glossed over contemporary developments in the rural economy. It is certainly possible to plot the progress of new techniques or the slow extension of land cultivation, but geographical variations have a greater impact here than elsewhere and they must be emphasized if any useful conclusions are to be drawn. Agricultural progress in southern Europe may have reached its peak sooner and was also checked at an earlier date; or, to put it differently, the conflicting interests and resulting stalemate that stemmed from this very expansion were felt most quickly and acutely in these areas – the problems of largely unprofitable livestock, poor returns on cereal crops and the limited development of mechanisms within the community to help and support the struggling peasantry. If my brief had extended beyond 1350 nothing would have illustrated this inequality better than the peasant revolts of this period: risings in the north were structured and coherent; their participants had enough to eat; in the south desperate and secretly plotted outbursts were made by the starving peasants: northern Europe saw battles and oppression; the south the slow decay of rural communities. For the social evolution of these two areas was also distinct and so we shall leave the peasants to their daily round and turn to their masters.

4

The Lord

In old-fashioned textbooks the 'lords of the manor' epitomized the Middle Ages and the centuries with which we are concerned in particular. Many of the pictures evoked are no longer accepted, of course: we no longer see the serf 'tied to the soil'; nor his lord riding roughshod through the peasant's crops or amusing himself with the seduction of shepherdesses. But for all that he remains crucially important in any picture of day-to-day rural life. If the term 'feudalism' is inappropriate for this period (because of its ambiguity, if nothing else), that of 'seigneuralism' or, more euphonically, 'seigneurial regime' is an entirely valid expression. Directly or indirectly every peasant was affected by the crushing tutelage of the lord in his castle.

Imprisoned in the village

I stressed earlier that one of the cardinal points in European history was the establishment of peasant settlements round church, cemetery or castle. I could have added that from that point onwards the peasants led their lives within the very narrow framework of these tiny communities, under strict control and locked within their own small unit of the 'seigneurial' system, the natural corollary of the regrouping that had occurred. Nevertheless, it remains one of the most obscure areas of medieval social history.

The emergence of the lord

Theoretically there should be little hesitation about the date at which this occurred, although local variations account for certain discrepancies – in the early tenth century in Catalonia or the Auvergne, the late tenth century in Provence or Sabina, the first decades of the eleventh century in central France from Poitou to Burgundy, a little later further north and as late as the twelfth century in Picardy, England and Germany. It is possible that these dates may be a reflection of the surviving sources which are much richer for southern than for northern Europe at this period. But this reservation does not affect the principal conclusion, that there is a clear correlation between the appearance of the lords of the manor and fixed village settlements.

The stages of this process are less clear: castle-building was undoubtedly a dominant feature but, setting aside ecclesiastical lordships that had no castle, numerous fortified towers were evidently built where there was no settlement, either at that time or later: Canossa, Quéribus and Château-Gaillard (Normandy) all fall into this category. Conversely, there were some lordships without keeps until a very late date. I have already observed that the military significance of castle-building has been obscured by its symbolic value, but we can safely say that, where they were built, this was clear evidence of the appearance of a seigneurial power on the scene. The inquiry into medieval fortified sites currently under way in France facilitates chronological analysis: 50 castles have been listed from before 1100 in Poitou, 60 in Lorraine, 90 in Provence, but only 10 in the Mâconnais and 12 in Picardy; outside France, on the *rocce*, *podia* and *colli* of Italy, Spain and Languedoc there were dozens before 1050. But a fundamental step in their development eludes us: nowadays much emphasis is placed on the great importance of the peace-keeping institutions that gradually emerged between 990 and 1110, appearing first in central France and moving north and south, finally spreading to other countries. It seems highly likely that it was the building of mottes (castle mounds) and the dangers which they presented to the Church and to weaker, unarmed members of the community (the *inermes*, as opposed to the *milites*), that stimulated the leagues of self-defence which became widespread in the West as a result of sworn peace treaties, supported by councils held in the locality. In any case, since rulers (reluctantly supported by the Church) took the initiative in building more castles from the late eleventh century onwards, it is equally possible that the relatively small number of castles which prompted the peace treaties were far outnumbered by those which they provoked.

In these circumstances even the salient characteristics of the emergent dominant group remain obscure and historians have been unable to establish any consensus. The traditional explanation of 'the breakdown of the Carolingian state' followed by 'feudal anarchy' has generally been abandoned. Apart from the fact that anything other than the theoretical existence of this state has yet to be proved, the supposed breakdown, often accompanied by the unquestionable devolution of public rights to individuals, demands an explanation and it is certainly not to be found in the traditional grounds of Norman raids and the supposed pusillanimity of Charles the Fat. The solution must be sought elsewhere and there are numerous possibilities. The first sounds the keynote: the inability of a centralized system (given the shortcomings in both technical and human terms of this period) to tackle urgent, local problems and, equally certainly, the absence of all economic ties between neighbouring regions other than those that were purely fortuitous, such as a ruler's visit or requisitions for an army. These characteristics all kept, indeed in some cases redirected, the horizons of justice, defence and subsistence within a local framework, that of the region (*pagus*, *pays*) or even of a group of villages. The prince and Christendom were not forgotten, nor did respect for them diminish, but economic pressure and the shortage of knowledgeable administrators forced dependence on their local representative, such as the count or the bishop, or their agents. Some have even believed that Carolingian rulers encouraged this devolution, seeing it as the only means of control available to them. If we add that the free rein Carolingian monarchs gave their localities coincided with the first stirrings of economic expansion – a little more man-power, money and local vigour – we undoubtedly have the basis for a theory of tenth-century fragmentation grounded in dynamism, rather than deficiency.

For all that, the problem remains. These men were called *dominus* (master) much more frequently than *senior* (*seigneur*, lord, meaning literally 'older man'): who were they? The differences between various theories is clearer now. For some this authority is rooted in the quasi-mystic aura of royal origin shared by all such individuals: they were the ruler's dependents, relations whom he often placed at the head of an honour, an office provided with a landed endowment, where after 875–900 they established their family seat and in the most legitimate and 'familiar' way gained control of the royal castle and the administration of justice there. When, in the Carolingian period, their ascendancy was established, they were referred to as *nobiles*, exceptional individuals accredited with every possible virtue. Other historians do not believe that this delegation of royal authority and subsequent ascendancy were essential. In their view the crucial factor was the lord's ability to protect and control a *sauvement*, or place of refuge: a man who received part of the king's revenue as a gift for services rendered could recruit men-at-arms whom he paid for garrison duty; he either built on his own initiative or (and this was apparently more usual) obtained authority for the construction of a tower (*castellum*) in which he could lodge these knights. Soon he himself became part of the very enclosed clique of specialists in warfare (an activity now so complex that it required an elite), responsible for feeding and exercising all his men and making arrangements for their free time, warding off aggressors and controlling excessively powerful elements. Yet another group of historians emphasize the increasingly close bonds formed by oaths exchanged between the free men who surrounded the group of especially favoured retainers, dependents in the service of a more powerful lord. It is true that vassalage and its accompanying ritual have their origins in the seventh century, but these practices only came to be generally accepted in the tenth century. Not because, as has so often been asserted, they extended from one end of the aristocratic ladder to the other; nor because written references to such acts of homage add something genuinely new to our knowledge of bonds between the king and his counts, and between them and lesser lords; but because the character of these rites, at once worldly and formal, resulted in the formation of familial controlling groups, of 'artificial relationships' between little groups of men who were ready to assist each other and who controlled the rest. One final characteristic stems from the rest, namely that the individual who imposed his authority upon those around him was rich, with plenty of lands and dependents. The manorial form of homage, *commendise*, gathered men round him in the expectation of food, protection and assistance; his stronghold (*firmitas*) was a rural centre before it became a castle. Like the patrons of late Antiquity he was the essential link between the ruling power and ordinary men: to fulfil this function he needed no royal blood, nor did he have to be knight, vassal or *vicomte*, he had only to combine the demands which he as master could make upon his tenants – demands of service or payments in kind – with those to which he was entitled if political power (the *ban*) was genuinely devolved upon him.

If all these cases were clearly distinguished there would be no need to rehearse them in this way. In reality – and especially before 1150 or 1160 – all these factors grew in importance, mingling here and there: one individual whom we know to have been a knight chose not to use this title because that of count or even *dominus* (lord) seemed more dignified; another administered in his own lands rights of justice to which he had no title, but complied as a vassal with the demands of his lord; in Germany it was possible to be serf and knight simultaneously; finally, in yet another case, a man might hold some lands as an allod and be tenant, vassal or lord in others. By the end of the twelfth century these distinctions had admittedly weakened. Knights, office-holders, vassals and their lord, great landholders, allodial or otherwise, all converged in one 'noble class' whose juridical privileges were not always clear, but who, by virtue of their descent, preserved their aristocratic status, which revealed merely a scale of wealth and obscured all origins.

Faces of the master

Perhaps we are drawing over-hasty conclusions, for the peasant (whom we must not lose from sight) saw his masters in a different light. He was the man above all others, who had their support.

This was the case at both ends of the aristocratic scale, from the holder of a tiny allod to great lords. The former was always hard-up and the desire to keep up appearances in dress, hospitality and his house inevitably soon outstripped his meagre income; he met his ruin in the supposedly 'good old days' of St Louis (Louis IX), because he had no effective means of exerting pressure on the men who simply leased land from him and over whom he had no judicial or military rights. He continued to live in a very small fortified manor house (*maison forte*) with privileges that brought no real advantages; often no more than a raw squire, he was a hard task-master, but knowledgeable about the land and his animals, very close to his peasants and almost always at hand. At the other extreme counts, dukes and castellans were never there, always on journeys, or at war in the service of the king or coming to the assistance of one of their own vassals; as their lands were vast and scattered, their appearances in each were rare. When a great lord did appear his presence was undoubtedly felt: he demanded lodging for his voracious household, emptied granaries, addressed his men and delivered judgements. But as soon as he left his power once more became indistinct. Admittedly, after about 1230 or 1250 in parts of north-west Europe, such as England, it became more common to farm out distant parts of the demesne (*domain*); five out of six Oxfordshire lords had adopted this practice at the beginning of the fourteenth century. The farmer of these lands was generally a local man rather than one of the lord's officials. He took very seriously all the rents, tallages and essentially regalian taxes on markets, measures, transport in time of war and duties of watch and ward to which his lord was entitled, but for all that he was a peasant, however successful, to whom even the humblest had access.

Feudal or not, the lord of a handful of villages (sometimes only one or two) occupied the centre of the stage. He will be my model as I now attempt to assess the demands he made upon the community. He had a castle on a motte, delivered sentence publicly, visited his lands, summoned men to fight or do guard-duty, exercised rights over the coinage and when necessary levied taxes on the mills and forges that he built. In his castle he received impecunious relatives, vassals serving their *estage* or guard-duty, and men-at-arms who ate huge amounts and squandered his resources. Those of lowest rank were worst – the servants and minor officials whom the lord sent out to collect money due to him or to summon the peasants, an office they performed with arrogance and brutality. As a result resentment was less commonly directed against the lord himself than his household (*familia*) and these servants in particular. Moreover, it sometimes happened that multiple lordship was shared amongst several brothers (*frerèche, parçonnerie* or *pariage*, as it was occasionally called) if an inheritance was particularly difficult to administer, a practice that tended to encourage opposition and undermine authority. The burden imposed on the peasants only became heavy when exceptional demands were made on their master by his immediate overlord or by the king, such as payment of feudal dues or high military expenditure. In other areas, such as the Catalan *dominicatura* or some German castellanies, there was automatic payment to the count of a significant proportion (say five per cent) of what was paid by the peasants. For the lord clearly recouped his expenses from them. Nevertheless, without suggesting there was even any kind of tacit agreement between the lord and his men, the situation remained fairly stable for nearly 200 years, say between 1090 and 1260 (from the end of the troubled phase that accompanied the establishment of lordships to the beginning of the period of economic and social breakdown), which is itself a highly significant fact.

Even this relative consensus did not pertain in our two last examples of medieval lordship. Only the Church believed the myth of her gentle governance, set out at length in writings which had long had a purely ecclesiastical audience. In fact the lordship of a monastery, cathedral chapter or collegiate church was extraordinarily exacting: theoretically, of course, there was no military service here and ecclesiastical courts demanded money rather than blood; but just as many tallages were levied to maintain their barns, still-rooms and mills, and if a felony was involved the 'secular arm' was always more than ready to go to the assistance of Christian justice. Even worse, the master was faceless, no more than a holy name, difficult to insult, above the world, making his demands through men who were themselves anonymous and sacrosanct. Moreover, these requirements were very harsh indeed because the Church's estate-management was efficient, meticulous and conservative: every little item was known, weighed, recorded and claimed; there was no opportunity for peculation, no hope of understanding between these men of God who could read and write and the impressionable peasants. There were compensations: accounts show that at the beginning of the fourteenth century the monks still disbursed six to ten per cent of their revenue in alms at the door of their monastery, to say nothing of the inestimable gift of their prayers. On the other hand, between 1050 and 1200 there was an increasing number of restitutions of tithes by the secular lords who had appropriated them at an earlier date, a trend which made the requirements of ecclesiastical masters still more exacting. After about 1160 the Cistercians were the harshest masters once the first brief halcyon period after their foundation had passed: not because they oppressed their peasants, for the few they had were waged, but because they regrouped holdings, ejected tenants and enclosed their land as part of the policy of independent administration and optimal direct exploitation over which historians have long enthused, forgetting the deserted hamlets, fragmented landholdings and peasant debt.

The *avoués* (advocates), secular lords and theoretical defenders of an unarmed Church, were even worse. As guardians (*custodes*) of the most famous monasteries such as Farfa, Cluny, San Cugat or Saint-Victor, kings and counts had played an admirable role, but after about 1000 the practice began to be abused, with an increasing tendency to delegate the office to generally mediocre *sous-avoués*, *vidames* and *Vögte*. This had a disastrous impact on the peasants: the *avoué* claimed ecclesiastical immunity in the exercise of his rights over all the inhabitants of his lands, whatever their form of tenure – allod-, copyholder or vassal; he levied military taxes, built castles, extended the range of fines of justice already imposed by the monks and modelled his additional demands on those of ecclesiastical landlords. As a result these vultures were opposed by the Church itself as much as by the peasantry in the area between Champagne and

Thuringia where this practice was most common: it slowly decreased after 1095 in Lorraine, 1120 in Champagne and 1140 in Bavaria and the Church's representatives gradually abandoned their financial claims and rights to high or low justice. But it did not die out entirely for another hundred years.

An analysis of this kind traditionally demands consideration of the position of the townsman (*bourgeois*) in the country, but this phenomenon did not really appear before the middle of the fourteenth century. Men from the neighbouring cities were to be found in the nearby villages: they were very often relations of a peasant living there permanently and their activities in this rural context were very limited, with a small plot, a few animals that he might hire or farm out – nothing that would impinge significantly on village life or the rural economy. The rise of the *bourgeoisie* since the Mycenean period, regarded as axiomatic by all historians, had not yet attained possession of barns and grain-stocks in 1350.

The lord's powers

Seigneurial demands have traditionally been presented in terms of the juridical spheres in which they were exerted. The *ban* (an ancient Germanic word of uncertain meaning which we might loosely translate as the power to enforce one's will) is consequently seen as operating in the fields of defence and military requirements, justice and the maintenance of public order and, finally, the economy, including control of production. I shall attempt to explain the varying degrees of control exerted by the lord on the peasant community in other terms, if only so that we arrive at a better understanding of the origins of these powers and their uneven distribution.

Vigorous peasant resistance in fact developed during the period when these powers were devolved or usurped and there are echoes of this movement for more than 50 years, muffled under the cloak of 'heresy' gladly provided by the Church. The resultant picture of these complaints suggests there was already a hierarchy of protest. It seems that in the first place country-dwellers resented the abuses brought about by newly introduced military requirements: the evil practices (*malae consuetudines*, *malos usos*) of which they complained were the exactions, requisitions and obligatory carting services (*carrea*, *corrogata*) which had only previously been demanded of them as lessees. From then on such innovations were, it has been claimed, imposed within the context of administrative units that in practice probably meant very little to them: the English hundred and the *centaine* of much of France, or the *vicaria*, *viguerie* or what was known as the *ager* from the Limousin to the Dauphiné. These were subdivisions of counties (*comtés*) which, it is believed, were related to levies of men and military requisitions. In a different context, the restrictions on communities which accompanied new settlement in the south of Europe seemed to the peasant population to lack any real justification and expressions such as *exactio*, *tonsio* or *tallia*, besides more placatory terms like *bede* and *questa* gave a bad name to this enforced protection. Since for all that the notion of military service by free men had not been abolished this was clearly a justified grievance. So this first phase was accompanied by the building of castles on mottes (often by forced labour) and assemblies of knights and *bellatores* (warriors) gathered round one powerful man.

A second phase focused on restricted access to uncultivated land. As I have already explained at length this affected the whole community, but the smallest landholders above all. Restricting such access was a policy adopted by some landowners, others insisted on the payment of fines (*droits de usage*), foreign to both Germanic and Romano-Barbarian codes. At the same time, because woodland was an essential resource for the aristocracy who were in the process of grouping plots of land together, the very richest were resuming control of the land and determined to make it financially viable. Judicial fines were raised and their use extended, an arbitrary policy that had serious implications for the semi-pastoral economy of the high Middle Ages because it could have such a severe effect on the initial stages of assarting.

On the other hand there seems to have been no concern initially over personal status or judicial framework. In the latter case it is well known that lawcourts were gradually abandoned, first by small plaintiffs, then by the parties to minor lawsuits.

The tendency is marked in the case of the comital assize or *mal*, but also affected more or less bastardized forms of earlier general courts of free men, such as the *colloquia* of the Iberian peninsula, or the Lombard *arengo*. However, the substitution of castle-based, indeed seigneurial lawcourts for those of count or *vicomte* apparently aroused much greater resentment as an over-simplification of justice. As for individual status, justice has long been done to Marc Bloch's theory that this reduced the peasantry to a general state of serfdom; many allod-holders were undoubtedly forced to accept an overlord, by paying rent for their lands or holding it as a fief and there are also examples of very widespread decline into serfdom, as at the time of the Norman Conquest in England; elsewhere the practice was rare. Since, moreover, such claims to economic control could only be made at times such as completion of a mill, accumulation of lands in the hands of a single owner or as a one-off measure, it is obvious that any study that aims to document chronological phases and periods of intense constraint cannot confine itself to a purely judicial field.

Let us first consider the force of the lord's moral authority: his 'noble' life-style, his conspicuous consumption with expenditure on tournaments and the hunt, horses, the overflowing table he kept and the noisy escort that accompanied him, with his sword and banner – these were all superficial signs that symbolized his place far above even the richest of the peasants. It would be wrong to see these things merely as manifestations of misplaced pride, for it was by his appearance that the lord demonstrated that he was of a particular order and that he was indisputably entrusted with the mission of a Christian knight. Although there are examples of lords murdered by exasperated peasants these are rare and were universally condemned.

The lord was able to impose his will in many areas by his control over men on his lands; he authorized and levied fines on peasant marriages and not only – as has long been maintained – the marriage of unfree men. From Flanders to Saxony and in Spain a *maritagium, merchet, laudemium* or *bumede*, as it was variously called, was paid when a man married. The men had military obligations, whether in the Saxon *fyrd* or the Spanish *caballeria*, with duties that involved provision of personal armour and service; elsewhere they might also have to present arms, however basic, carry out patrols or, at the very least, clear the castle moat and provide forage, with heavy fines of 60 *sous* for any attempted evasion. In France or Spain he had to attend sittings of the lord's court (the *plaid* or *concejo*) for it was only in England and the Empire that allod-holders (English sokemen and German *Schöffenbarfreien*) continued to take their cases directly to the court of the count or earl. In his court the lord sat on the bench, attended either by men of solid worth (*probi homines, prudentes viri*) or legal specialists (*jurisperiti, sculteti, causidici*) and passed judgement of all kinds. The scale of fines went from seven *sous* for disrespect or refusal to pay the fine imposed to the most serious crimes, which might be punished by death but more probably by mutilation – the punishment for crimes that threatened law and order rather than morals, such as arson, abduction, rape or murder. Since their judicial rights were an important source of revenue for many less fortunate lords, control was strongest in this sphere and at a later date in the history of lordship it was here, too, that the break was to be most apparent.

From the individual we pass easily to the family group, for the taxes that theoretically paid for the *custodia* or *tuitio* (protection) by the lord were levied on the 'hearth', or household. However, whether it was imposed only on freemen (as in northern France) or on everyone (as in southern Europe) it could be a total for the entire village and the amount levied varied according to circumstance, sometimes 100 *sous*, sometimes 20 *livres*, depending on such variable factors as seigneurial building and wage payments. This explains why setting a regular fixed payment became one of the major concerns of peasant communities in the twelfth century: from 1150-70 in northern France and Lotharingia, later elsewhere. 'Aids', on the other hand, could never be fixed since they were defined by feudal obligation and irregular by their very nature. They were levied when their master was ransomed, departed on crusade or on the occasion of his daughter's marriage and the knighting of his son: all these expenses were passed on by the vassal to his men. In reality, the feudal aid was a relatively late development, dating from well into the thirteenth century, that is the period of problems in seigneurial administration.

But it was on production that the lord's eagle eye lingered longest, and every decade saw an increase in the revenues derived from it and changes in the way they were levied. There were the tithes which were still enjoyed by 8 to 15 per cent of the laity in most dioceses in northern France and the Low Countries at the end of the thirteenth century; and, like any other landlord, the lord of the manor collected ample rents from the holdings of his men. Some dues were crucially important: rights to a tax on the sale and transfer of land (*lods et ventes*) and on entry fines (payment on purchase or inheritance of land). Income from such transactions increased steadily throughout the thirteenth century, accounting for as much as a third of annual income from property, the equivalent of the 'relief' paid by anyone inheriting a fief. Rights of the lord to part of an inheritance (the English heriot, French *mainmorte*, German *Todfall* or Italian *mortario*) were more contentious, since they impinged on an individual's conception of his status as a free man, which is why this death-duty tends to be seen in the context of serfs, although many examples affecting free men could be cited from Germany and the Low Countries. Then there were taxes on buying and selling (whose various types, rates and practices defy description) and on access to woods, marshes and fish ponds, which were generally calculated as a proportion of the whole in the twelfth century and later levied as a specific cash sum. Their precise value was only established after bitter claims and counter-claims, for this was an area where agreement was crucial but exceptionally difficult to achieve. Finally there were the obligations (*banalités*) of a specifically seigneurial character, whereby the lord required that as much as a tenth or a twelfth of the produce should be sent to his mill, wine-press or even his bakehouse, giving him real control of production, especially since he also dictated the terms by which it could be measured. Restrictions of this kind could not be imposed overnight and this was one of the least well known. Although, as I said earlier, these expensive machines appeared during the eleventh and early twelfth centuries it seems that it was not until 1200 that the lord felt he could make it compulsory to use them. Enforcement resulted in vigorous opposition and interminable lawsuits, like that between the abbots of St Alban's and their peasants, which lasted more than a century. It could be said – and this is a point to which I will return – that the lord won the day because time was more valuable than money for a small proportion of villagers (the richest), who preferred to pay the miller than use the mill themselves at specific times. In fact it would not be an overstatement to say that it was essentially by selling them time that the lord gained control over his men.

The division of land

The importance of seigneurial exactions and the brutality that could sometimes accompany them, does not show 'feudalism' in a good light. But we cannot possibly understand the concept if we see it merely in terms of the more or less willing acceptance of requirements of this kind. A more detailed examination of the patterns of landownership on which the 'feudal system' was based is obviously essential.

Did the lords control the land?

The agrarian historian cherishes the almost invariably vain hope of reconstructing a full picture of landownership. This is virtually impossible before the fifteenth century (when the first *cadastres* provide more systematic information) because of the disorganized nature of landholding and the vagueness with which boundaries were defined. For earlier periods one has to accept a crude analysis of social groups in an attempt to establish average areas of holdings. On the other hand, we are relatively well informed about the ownership of land and stages of expansion, especially in the case of church lands whose history can be followed after the tenth century in the bulls of confirmation in episcopal registers.

The richest members of society saw a marked increase in their income from landed sources in the eleventh century; for even when a monastery sold off a wood or a marsh all that was conceded was the right to make use of it (the lawyers' *jus utendi in re aliena*); newly reclaimed lands, on the other hand, brought them a new tithe (called the *novale*), rents or judicial revenues. In addition to this and quite apart from income connected with newly assarted lands, the eleventh and early twelfth centuries were clearly characterized by a deliberate attempt to increase the revenues from land and this was one of the newest concepts to emerge from the muddled 'domanial system' which (putting aside the question of its putative Carolingian origin) consumed endless quantities of time and resources. The level of land-transactions is a sound guide to adjustments in landed wealth and at this period it rose steeply, exceeding alms and purchases. Regular and secular canons increased in number at this period, but Benedictines of all observances were as zealous in their exaction of every due related to mill, vineyard and fish pond, or the pursuit of a lapsed tithe, assiduous in levying tolls and taxes. The Cistercians went further than this since it was the policy of their order to assemble large plots of land into 'granges' which they managed themselves. Since virtually nothing is known of secular practice in this period except when land was ceded in favour of the Church, it is impossible to make any comparisons; in the twelfth century, however, there seems to be a similar upward trend in secular income from these sources, while that of the Church appears to have remained at the same level: for example, it has been calculated that to have the resources to arm and equip himself without undue hardship a Burgundian knight in c. 1180 would have had to own about 30 manses (or some 300 hectares) and at the same time an English lord or a Silesian colonizer would also have to possess this amount of land to cut a respectable figure in the service of an earl or count. However, many English manors covered an area well over 1,000 or 2,000 hectares. What is more, here too wealth and power resided in rights to bridges, tithes or judicial fines. It seems a reasonable assumption that for a moderately sized landholding of, say, 3,000 to 4,000 hectares, seigneurial rights, those derived both from patrimony and from allods seized, the 'reserves' exploited through labour services or wage-labour came to about 20 to 50 per cent of the value of the land itself. These figures can be obtained without great risk of distortion for England, southern France and Italy.

The thirteenth century – at least before 1275 – however, saw these vast estates whittled down. The causes are easily established: the weakening of patrimonies was both the result of the increase in the number of alienations to the Church during the periods when there were so many ruinous crusading expeditions to the east, and in every case, the poor return from land in terms of ready profit which led the 'noble' to parcel out most of his landed capital to obtain the liquid assets which were increasingly necessary. This took place on such a scale that it would be tempting, though inaccurate, to speak of the mortgaging of all their reserves. Thus, for example, a knight's equipment in about 1260 could only be sustained by those with the income of 150 manses (in contrast with the 30 of 80 years before). This was virtually the sole cause of the bitterness displayed by the lords of the manor when they sold their privileges to the highest bidder. They even ceased to exact labour dues that brought in little or no return, preferring to sell their rights, for everyday tasks at least ('weekwork' in England), although others such as harvesting ('boonwork' in England) continued to be seen as reflections of the master's wealth and were consequently insisted upon.

These were the circumstances that produced an intense seigneurial reaction at the end of the thirteenth and beginning of the fourteenth centuries. The urgent need for ready money, exacerbated by the first currency manipulations, did not only affect knights or improvident landlords; they also affected the Church. Income from public taxation (such as the tenths frequently exacted by the rulers of England, France, Naples and Castile from the Church after 1260–80) doubled with the constant extensions of state justice: *baillis*, *sénéchaux*, sheriffs and *gobernadores* took cases to their own courts, instead of using seigneurial lawcourts. The lords responded to these encroachments in two ways: either they made a conscious effort to increase the profitability of their estates with better management at the risk of creating a powerfully and potentially destabilizing group of salaried peasants within the village community; or, alternatively, if they had neither the will nor the means to pursue this line of action, they resigned themselves to tenant farming and tried to protect themselves against looming debt or sales of their land by raising quit-rents or judicial fines. The ruin of a whole section of the landed aristocracy had begun: they eschewed the expense of knighthood; accepted the imposition of rents in perpetuity, sold property at a distance or – and this was the worst solution – decided to restrict the rights of marriage and inheritance to the oldest son. Here I can do no more than outline the effects of policies such as these, which were to be moral and psychological as much as economic. Only one is of direct relevance to our subject: the peasants judged the 'seigneurial contract' to have been broken.

Or did the peasants?

We know relatively little about noble ownership of land and information about peasant wealth is no more abundant. Nevertheless, there is a great deal of evidence from the mid-fourteenth century and later that clearly shows that the peasant sphere of production was quite as well developed as the noble, if not more so, and that it was on the peasant's activity that progress and production essentially depended. This statement must be qualified, however, for we do not have the means to assess peasant exploitation of the land before the twelfth century: by then a strong movement for peasant emancipation was intensifying, but it only affected part of peasant society and the inevitable corollary of growing prosperity for some was a decline in the fortune of others. The situation requires close scrutiny.

We know virtually nothing of the early Middle Ages. The evidence of the polyptychs of the ninth century and the Lotharingian or Italian *censiers* of the tenth and eleventh shows rural society in the middle of an evolutionary process. Old Carolingian terms are no longer used in their original sense: 'manse', 'hide' and 'hufe' no longer refer to a household's landholdings tied to certain compulsory services – if indeed this had ever been their meaning in southern Europe; the terms *quartiers*, *huitée* and *Viertel* disappeared and where a scribe wrote *meix* or *mas* he meant no more than an established landholding. This fragmentation was undoubtedly an easier process when the manse was composed of scattered pieces of ground. It had many causes: dislocation of the family group, improvements in agricultural method so that the same yields could be obtained from a reduced surface area, demographic pressure resulting in over-population. Whether they occurred simultaneously or in sequence, it is striking that these phenomena coincided with the grouping of men in lordships as well as with the period of western economic expansion. Our picture of peasant farming is made up of small units, even landholdings comprising no more than a few hectares. Calculations have been made to establish how much land was needed to support a household with children at the beginning of the thirteenth century: ignoring variations in equipment and the quality of the soil four to six hectares is thought to have been the smallest viable surface area for subsistence, a quarter of the Carolingian manse.

The provenance and composition of peasant wealth are still more difficult to determine, for besides the continuing mobility to which we have already referred, research is also bedevilled by the imprecision of contemporary vocabulary: did *courtil* only mean 'garden'? Was a *mansura* or *masura* a piece of land set aside for cultivation? Was an Italian *casale*, like a Burgundian *meix* or *cap-mas* of the Cevennes, a piece of land with farm and buildings? An English or Norman manor was a lordship, but a Picard *manerium* was no more than a landholding, to say nothing of the essentially juridical confusion that led to pieces of land in rural Aquitaine being called 'fief'. We will end this depressing list. The only area on which some light is shed by land-registers (*terriers*) or straightforward documents of sale seems to be that of the terms of lease, and here differences are established which merit discussion.

The *censive* (rented holding), whether it was a former peasant allod now rented from a lord, or part of an earlier manse, was by far the most advantageous form of land tenure. As the demand for labour services declined in the twelfth century and the lord's need for liquid capital grew, so these peasants were no longer required to perform these duties or pay dues in kind, but to make money payments in return for the land they held. We do not know how or when these aggregate sums were established: the variations between them defy straightforward explanation, but were doubtless affected by variables such as the quality of the soil, equipment available, the terms of the rent and the date on which possession was taken. On the other hand, the fixed rent was a once and for all payment and any increase or supplement was regarded as a complete injustice and resisted as such. Henceforth a rented holding was transmitted normally, once the duties on the transfer of property had been paid: the land could be sold, granted to someone else or shared between several individuals on payment of a small indemnity to the lord. If the latter attempted to take it back into his own possession – and, as I have said, he was ready to exercise any such supposed rights in the thirteenth century – he ran up against the principle of a genuine hereditary reversion of the land to an heir, however distant. It is only a short step from this situation, and one that had perhaps already been taken, to thinking that there was little to choose between a rented holding and peasant ownership. Only the occasional survival of labour dues, such as the *laborancia* or *manualia* of southern Europe or sometimes of heavier obligations, such as English 'weekworks', remind us that this was a tenancy.

The Italian *livello* and the Pyrenean *escalio* differed only in that, on the one hand, the tenant's obligations were set down in a document (*convenientia, libellus*) and, on the other, because there was a 30-year lease on the cultivation of land – a time-limit that was purely theoretical, as it could be renewed. As for leases for mixed arboriculture (*baux de complant*), which were very common in southern France and along the Italian coast, they brought the peasant advantages that were very different but ultimately of equal value: a strict obligation to mixed farming (*coltora promiscua*) with substantial payments in kind, which might be up to 50 per cent of the crop, but on the expiry of the lease (which might last thirty years) the land was divided, with the lord granting ownership of at least half to his tenant. I have already stressed the advantages that leases of this kind conferred on both parties when new land was being reclaimed.

The tenant was less favourably placed as far as crop returns were concerned: payments in kind (the *terrage* and *herbergage* of northern and western France) could be a fixed sum that corresponded to an old piece of land from which the owner still expected to feed himself; but more frequently it was calculated as a percentage (the *champart* of the Ile-de-France and the Namurois), a tenth or a twelfth (the *agrière* in Aquitaine, the Spanish *tasca* or the Italian *quarta*, which might range from a sixth to a quarter or even a third of the grape harvest).

Originating in Italy before the fourteenth century, the final development was the *métayage* (*mezzadria*, *ad medietatem*) system whereby the owner provided seed or stock and was entitled to half the yield. This benefitted the tenant if the harvest was poor – and there might be virtually no return from land still covered with tree stumps; on the other hand, the owner profited from good harvests. What disadvantaged the tenant in the long term – and especially where *métayage* pertained – was the obligation to provide seed, tools and draught animals which were originally supplied by the owner but were later sold or hired out by him. This is why the spread of *métayage* can be seen as a reflection of acute peasant demand, either because of a shortage of land, a growing number of landowners, or population pressure.

In other forms of tenure a renewable lease operated (sometimes short term – three, six or nine years in areas where triennial crop rotation was practised) and the rate was renegotiated at each change of tenants. The lease might of course be for the tenant's lifetime or, as in the case of English leaseholds, for the lifetime of several individuals. But the formula which the landlords sought to impose was the holding of land at farm with or without a written contract (English copyholders are an example of the latter), on a short lease. This appeared in England after 1086 and took the form of fixed rents to be paid over a specified number of years (*mesaticum*, *feorm*, farm); after about 1140 many English monasteries, including Ramsey, Glastonbury and St Alban's applied this *firmarium* to about half their manors. At the same period Abbot Peter the Venerable of Cluny farmed out some 20 *domaines* and Abbot Suger pursued the same policy at Saint-Denis. After 1180 the practice was common in the Rhineland and Saxony and, as I have already said, it was adopted by many lords at the time of seigneurial reaction in the thirteenth century. It offered the obvious advantage of freeing the lord from practical involvement while securing him a regular, guaranteed income and even offered the opportunity of securing higher payments if circumstances were favourable when the lease was renewed.

Despite these obligations the tenant farmer, for his part, could run things his own way, without supervision and accountable to no-one for the land he held. If he was resourceful and clever there were opportunities for speculation. It was generally the most comfortably-off peasants whose livelihood was secure who were tempted by this possibility: if they succeeded they became the most important men in the village. Tenant farming thus helped to accentuate a social split to which I shall return.

There was therefore some relationship between social standing and type of tenure. But we should not overlook the fact that wealth and equipment were vitally important. In this context the last decades of the thirteenth and the beginning of the fourteenth century give us a rough idea of the progressive differences in the level of peasant wealth. Demographic pressure undoubtedly varied, but there was always insufficient cultivable land and this, combined with the practice of partible inheritance, resulted in the continual fragmentation of land that reached impossible proportions: in Picardy, the Ile-de-France and Languedoc there were increasing numbers of plots of 500 square metres or barely more, which hardly sufficed for the needs of any kind of a household; at the same time access to the lord's woods was increasingly disputed and even more heavily taxed. Without being dogmatic we can suggest that between 10 and 15 per cent of the peasant population were driven to extreme poverty and some 40 to 50 per cent possessed less than the four hectare minimum required to support a household. At the other end of the scale the top 5 to 10 per cent of rich allod-holders and enterprising tenant farmers ran the village and took the lead. It was also they who were in a position to wring from the lord the legal and financial concessions which determined their levels of wealth and freedom.

Wealth and freedom

The conditions of a lease, the quality of the soil and the extent of seigneurial exactions brought divisions within the rural population that became more marked in the course of the thirteenth century. Whether they were the concomitant of developing peasant enterprise in the marketplace or resulted from it, or whether they were by-products of increased freedom, they were also a direct consequence of the lord's deliberate policy.

'Rent' and surplus

When a lord had full manorial rights his responsibilities were, theoretically, equally heavy. If we portray him as a shark or a parasite or even (as some have done) a 'terrorist', we are viewing the situation in terms of modern rationalism or nineteenth-century positivism. It is only too easy to forget that, at least until that crucial turning-point, the late twelfth century, the warrior (*bellator*) and lord whose divinely directed activities exposed him more than most men to the formidable temptations of money, bloodshed and sexual indulgence, was also entrusted with the grave responsibility of providing protection for the local community, sitting in judgement and keeping the peace; he enjoyed none of the aura that surrounded the priest; in the execution of his difficult task at least he was in no sense 'privileged'. It was a task, moreover, that was expensive as well as very difficult: in the first place because the large-scale distribution of largesse was an inevitable requirement of his rank and status, and because he had been taught that the sin of avarice (*avaritia*) was worse than that of pride (*superbia*); finally because the expenses of his equipment and of building, repairing and maintaining the fortress that protected the community, besides the mill (which was an important source of revenue) and the cost of seigneurial justice could reach huge sums, like the 3,000 silver marks of Berzée castle (in the Namurois) in 1155. This was the reason for all the levies and exactions that we have just discussed, his 'feudal rent' which could only be obtained by demanding more work from his men.

At the time this basic tenet of the seigneurial regime would certainly not have been viewed as corrupt or tyrannical: the lord's men wanted their livelihoods to be protected and accepted that this price had to be paid. It is difficult to calculate the sums involved, which undoubtedly varied according to time and place. One plausible estimate suggests 20 per cent of the harvest was reserved for seed corn for the following year, 10 per cent went in tithes and as much in rent for the land; tallage (*taille*) might account for as much as 20 per cent and another 10 to 15 were needed for judicial fines, taxes on commutations and casual dues, in all three-quarters of the yield from his land might bypass the peasant completely; the rest had to provide enough for his household to eat and, ideally, something to save for new equipment, draught animals or poultry. Figures such as these provided the basis for the estimated minimum four to six hectares required for a household's subsistence. But the situation was naturally also affected not only by the resources offered by nearby woodland, but also by the quality of the harvest: a peasant in the Italian province of Sabina had a far lighter burden of dues and other payments than a Picard contemporary (amounting to some 40 per cent of his revenue), but his thin soil produced yields that were not even half that of his northern counterpart, taxed at 70 per cent: the latter's surplus was thus in fact larger.

Unless they could somehow produce more, neither of these peasants would have surpluses to sell at the local market, which was the only way to obtain tools and other necessary articles. Initially – and this was also a time when there was little contact between different parts of the countryside – only the lord in his castle was in a position to buy things from a passing pedlar or borrow from a Jewish moneylender; he alone could send a cleric or steward to the town to procure things that could only be found there – a set of fine harness, jewels, fur or valuable horses. There was little commerce within the local community – the lord sold his old wine and then the new vintage before everyone else, he might re-sell a few blocks of salt or animals he could no longer use. Those who were in a position to buy from him doubtless discharged their debts in hides, woollen stuffs or clogs. But the smith had to be paid and soon the butcher as well; if a taste for finance led him to countenance the purchase of service dues or the commutation of labour services the lord bought supplies, animals and fabric woven in the cottages; and the money that he paid then, or when he employed a mason, a roofer, a maker of furniture or a labourer found its way back into peasant homes, where some of it was spent on new purchases, as well as the inevitable taxes. Thus began the long history of the market economy.

The appearance of village markets was definitely a major advance in agrarian history. It is certainly paradoxical that its development should be linked so closely to the organization of 'seigneurial' production since the concepts of profit and competition that it introduced into human relations were to destroy the very fabric of that system. It is not easy to date its earliest appearance precisely, nor to distinguish between trade which really had no impact on the rural community and that which impinged significantly upon it. Various ninth-century cartularies anticipated a weekly market, such as were found elsewhere (amongst the Saxons, for example), but the merchants (*mercatores*) who did business there seem to have dealt largely in urban, even luxury goods. The impression remains that in the eleventh century, when the peasants performed carting services for the lord, they carried to the town surplus foodstuffs, especially wine, besides metalwork produced in the village. In the towns of the Iberian peninsula in the twelfth century the *foro* (fair) and the *mercadel* (market) were found side-by-side but quite distinct from one another, with goods that were not produced in the countryside sold in the *foro* and eggs, grain, wool and wood bought and sold in the *mercadel*. Overall, the mid-twelfth century seems to have been the period of greatest prosperity for the village market, when commutation of labour services and compounding of tallage were also widespread: even so we know virtually nothing of its organisation.

The lord was the instigator of these markets as well as their patron and most important customer. It was his measures they used; covered markets had to be built (of which many from this period survive) and sometimes the lord had his tithe barn or his cellars nearby; his officers supervised all transactions and there is much evidence of the conflict between the peasants and the lord's agents over the capacity of barrels, level or heaped measures and the quality of grain. Practical, if typically urban measures, such as the construction of stalls or sales in a shop, were only adopted very slowly: there are some scattered examples from the Gâtinais (Poitou) in about 1180 and from Leicestershire and Bavaria in the mid-thirteenth century. These rural markets flourished everywhere with the exception of Italy (where the town reigned supreme), the Italians preferring instead to trade at places of transhipment such as the banks of the Tiber, where the villagers gathered to protect the jetties designed for the loading of grain. If times were troubled or the countryside dangerous, commerce was centred on the parish, churchyard or cemetery. Finally, we should not overlook – even though it is, strictly speaking, outside my brief – the fact that in an area of specialized production such as wool, cattle, wine or salt, a village market might reach the proportions of a small fair. Examples are to be found in southern Provence, Languedoc, England and Franche-Comté, and commerce on this scale often preceded the granting of a town charter. The market revealed the gulf between rich and poor in the village that was just beginning to emerge and it continued to emphasize this contrast, with the lord and prosperous peasants on one side and peasants who were much poorer – whatever their juridical status – on the other. Urban expansion was accompanied by a sharp increase in demand for foodstuffs and raw materials. At this stage the burgeoning town did not drain the surrounding countryside, which still had sufficient resources to supply food for itself as well as the town. It has been estimated that a very small town with a population of, say, 3,000 (of which there were many throughout Europe) needed to draw on an area of 10,000 hectares for its supplies of wine, grain, meat and wood. When infertile ground and the requirements of the peasant population are taken into account, urban demands affected an area with a radius of some 15 kilometres from the town itself. This did not present a serious problem if such towns were only found every 30 kilometres, but if they were closer than that, or their population higher, the soil in the surrounding area poor, or if it was difficult to import goods from further afield, then the difference was made up by speculation and shortages in the towns (a subject beyond the field of this study). In the countryside it also led to undue pressure from urban purchasers, stewards, serjeants, townspeople and professional speculators, to say nothing of the effect of ravaging armies upon peasant supplies, such as despoiled the Sienese *contado* from 1250 onwards. The long-term effect was a steady rise in prices, in the village markets especially: the price of a measure of wheat trebled almost everywhere between 1180 and 1220, then doubled again by 1270 and that was with a normal harvest. Prices increased dramatically when there were shortages, as there often were around 1225, possibly as a result of excessive demand; only the lord and the richest villagers could face this with equanimity, for it was only they who had surpluses at their disposal which they could then sell at an inflated price, increasing the gulf between themselves and the less well-off, and able subsequently to replace their equipment and invest the profit.

So in the thirteenth century money was of vital importance, even in a system initially based on reciprocity of service. Absence or scarcity of money was of more importance than the extent of a man's holdings or his status as a freeman. In order to sustain an acceptable economic level many peasants had to resort to additional paid work, little jobs in the winter when there was little to do on the land, domestic work at the castle, soon followed by periods of temporary employment in the town. Others were forced to sell up or excluded from a shared inheritance and lived off their daily wages alone, earned at periods when labour was in high demand – especially when the grapes were pressed, the land ploughed, harrowed and then hoed, as well as at harvests, hay-making and grape-picking – but the sums involved seemed paltry in relation to the period over which they had often to be spread. The introduction of wages (hallmark of the market economy) inevitably led to the disintegration of the seigneurial economy because it introduced the idea that work was a saleable commodity. Significantly, the Cistercians played an important role here since they refused to have tenants (nor, after 1195 or 1205, lay brothers (*conversi*) because they lacked both the means and the will for the task) and so were forced to resort to hired labourers, sometimes on a regular basis. There were agricultural wage-labourers from the very beginning of the twelfth century, witness the description of artisans at work by the chronicler Lambert of Ardres, but it did not become a widespread practice until about 100 years later. Even then it remained, in contrast with the town, a poorly paid and unpopular practice: a reaper's daily wage was only a few pence, compared with a shilling for work in the town. The low wage-levels stemmed essentially from the lack of specialization or division of labour which, as I explained earlier, was the foundation of the rural domestic economy.

But a man with low wages or an inadequate income from land-rents was liable to fall into debt. We know much more about the king's mounting debts or the sums owed by clothworkers than those of peasants. To fund a crusade or pay a ransom a lord would borrow a sum of several hundred pounds in the town, which his officials were slow to repay; but borrowing on this scale was unheard of in rural society. On the contrary there is only scanty documentary evidence of peasant loans: some are disguised because the contingency was covered by one of the clauses in a normal leasehold agreement. The so-called contracts of *gasaille* or *mégerie* in southern France, which resulted in the owner of a flock of animals giving up his ownership and half of the increase in stock, were hidden loans; agreements made with a *nourkier* in northern France (whereby he bought the animal and sold it back after fattening) were not unlike the deals done by English 'woolmen', who bought the wool still on the sheep and resold the fleece at a higher price. Sometimes the loan was more obvious: even after it had been officially banned in 1163 the practice of 'mortgage' was adopted by more humble members of society as well as widely used by the seigneurial class. Under this arrangement an individual pledged his property for a sum to be repaid at the end of a specified period, generally several years, during which time the revenues from the land were the property of the creditor. However, it is probable that a loan secured on chattels was the most common form of borrowing and of this unfortunately no written evidence survives: the money borrowed from a wandering Jew and repayable in a few weeks, from a more affluent neighbour who would accept labour in exchange, or from the parish priest. Some lists of loans survive from the second half of the thirteenth century from Italy, Catalonia, Provence and Lorraine: the borrowers were mainly town-dwellers, but some peasants also feature, taking out a loan around February and repaying it in August, after the harvest.

There were some who were unable to meet the rising level of taxation, while others were not in a position to sell any surplus at a market; in short there were many who found themselves unable to repay their debts. As a result money had a more insidious effect on the structure of society, for because these men seemed different from others, because they were weak and unable to benefit from their status as free men, they were consequently treated as unfree and, without any legal justification, that is what they in effect became.

The paths of servitude and freedom

A famous Carolingian text supplied public officials with a rule of luminous simplicity: 'There are only two categories of men: freemen and the rest'. This view made up in clarity for what it lacked in precision and was no longer appropriate in the eleventh century. Firstly, because the concept of freedom was a complicated one: the idea that it was conferred by carrying arms, taking a seat at a lawcourt, paying taxes to the state and being in a position to order one's own life and belongings was no more than an ideal of lawyers well-versed in Roman law or Germanic and other law codes. In practice this long-established scheme of things was disrupted by facts such as degrees of wealth that inevitably discriminated between individuals, concepts of hierarchy and, at the least, moral dependence. This was true to such an extent that it could be argued no-one was free, not even kings or emperors, since their hands were partially tied by the precise contract entered into with their subjects, made by the king in his coronation oath and by the emperor in the *professio* or declaration that formed part of the imperial coronation. There were therefore only degrees and kinds of freedom and the number that a man possessed determined whether he was more or less free than his neighbour.

These components were still highly dependent on ancient custom: men who presented themselves at a muster in a leather cap and padded jacket, armed with a pike, felt themselves to be free men, although this equipment was totally inadequate for contemporary warfare. What is more, as in nineteenth-century America or some parts of the world today, the peasant was a soldier: in Spain he might be a foot-soldier or fight on horseback and certainly neither *peones* nor *caballeria villana* were mere figureheads. Outside the Iberian peninsula, indeed, the constant threats to many communities in the fourteenth and fifteenth centuries reinvigorated local defence, itself a symbol of freedom. Then again, although a man could not always attend a lawcourt himself, he could make his views known through his representatives there: in Italy the Lombard *arengo* offered a forum for the whole community; in England the 'frankpledge' was a sort of collective examination of conscience; in northern France the courts of *aloiers* or freemen passed sentence, and in the Empire the *Schöffenbarfreien* covered miles in order to attend the count's assizes. Whatever the system, a free man could go to law, demand a judicial duel, or pay a champion to fight for him and appeal to established custom. From the eleventh century onwards an entire legal system, restrictive yet flexible, was constructed upon this framework and this provided the surest defence of individual liberty: in England 'common law' was invoked from 1100 onwards; at the same time that Pope Urban II ruled that the count of Flanders had wrongly applied local custom (*usus patriae*) rather than natural justice in one of his judgements. These customs (*consuetudines*) were inevitably the result of a series of arbitrations and compromises, influenced to a greater or lesser extent by the texts of the early Middle Ages, whether in Saxony, Alemannia or northern France. Further south, agreements (*convenientiae*) and declarations of pleas played the same role in Italy and Catalonia.

But it was at this juncture that other elements were introduced: a man had to live somewhere permanently, be an inhabitant (*manant*), since a permanent dwelling was the rule; indeed he had to possess a livelihood, or at any rate to be considered solvent and also capable of being called as a witness or to stand surety. The concept of bodily freedom, however, was greatly weakened: even if taxes on marriage and inheritance are considered exceptional, compulsory labour services can only be seen as a shackle on individual freedom – and how should we view the homage of one man to another, or peasant commendation (the practice whereby one man placed himself in the service and protection of another)? The Church complicated the matter further, forbidding consanguineous marriages by canon law, although these remained common in such isolated communities.

It is essentially artificial to present society, as Robert Boutrouche has said, as a series of labelled pigeon-holes: any outline of the social hierarchy is inevitably simplistic, but nevertheless valuable for the overall view that it presents. At the apex of this pyramid of freemen came the allod-holder, who might be known by any number of names – *aloier*, freeman, sokeman, *Freibauer*, *libero del re*, *estagier*, *arimann*, *homo exercitalis*; he comes at the top because, even though he was subject to lordship (to which he owed military service, tallage and various other taxes) he was not limited by the terms of a lease, less vulnerable to arbitrary requisitions than other men, with greater individual freedom. The exact size of this social group has been much debated and it undoubtedly fluctuated: reduced by personal commendation, or conversion of freely held property into leaseholds when times were hard, its numbers grew when new land was brought under cultivation. This phenomenon is apparent everywhere to some extent – in Germany, where the emperor relied considerably on their military support, in Aquitaine and in Burgundy. In Picardy and the Mâconnais in the mid-twelfth century knighthood brought a large number into the lowest ranks of the nobility. It was probably also at the same time (about 1120–60) that tenants could discharge their obligation to pay rent by a lump-sum payment (the *tasca* of Languedoc, or *donum* in England); and peasants approaching the end of a *complant* lease were in the same position. It has been estimated that 60 per cent of the peasantry were in this situation in the Cluny area in about 1120, 40 per cent in the Bordelais or Picardy slightly later and almost all those in areas bordering onto Islamic lands in the Iberian peninsula. In the thirteenth century, however, their numbers fell sharply: but it is possible that their apparent disappearance in fact reflects the small number of deeds surviving after 1240–60, or that they adopted a very low profile because their position was so precarious.

The tenants, to whom this description essentially applied, were a far from homogeneous group. The variations which we have already discussed in the terms of leasehold, in wealth and in taxation, fragmented this group and there were further variables as a result of marriage and inheritance taxes, or the lack of them, compounding for tallage, commutation of labour services and so on. An individual's origin resulted in further distinctions if, for example, they were former allod-holders, unfree men who had been enfranchised and placed on a plot of land or descendants of former small-holders. Some cases deserve specific mention: many tenants of the Church (who, as I have said, were often poorly treated) were forced to pay special dues – in wax (*cerocensuales*), for example, or a poll-tax of several pence paid to the patron saint of the church to which they were subject. There are examples of this practice from Catalonia, as early as 1040, as well as Bavaria, Thuringia, Flanders and Lorraine; in the case of some rich and powerful monastic landlords it has been estimated that 70 to 85 per cent of the peasantry were in this position. English villeins (almost 65 per cent of the population) were happy to remain unfree, because although they paid the *merchet* and *heriot* (marriage and inheritance taxes) and were strictly controlled by the edicts of their manorial court, they enjoyed many of the privileges of the enfranchized, with the right to attend the sheriff's court and to serve in the Anglo-Saxon *fyrd* (army), but they paid a heavy price in economic terms, notably in the extent of labour services. The position of 'foreigners' (*hôtes*), peasants from elsewhere (even a bare mile or two away) who settled on new land, varied greatly. In the twelfth century they were indispensable and granted all kinds of exemptions, payments and liberties; they were accepted in the religious life of the village and indeed on common land; and there is some evidence from northern France of their presence at lawcourts. On the other hand they were not allowed to build 'beyond the crosses', that is, within the village itself, but confined to the area outside and the woods. This limitation, together with their eviction on the least pretext from common land in the thirteenth century, meant that this category was often considered unfree, or at least treated in the same way as travelling strangers, the *aubains*, *forains*, or *horsins*, who were not considered part of the community for at least three years and whose goods might, under the terms of the notorious *droit d'aubaine*, be seized by the community if they died or broke the law.

The problems of the unfree and of serfdom are quite as complex as those affecting the nobility. Contemporary terminology itself is unclear; unless qualified by *corporalis* (which is unusual) *homo* alone is of no significance, *servus* is rare and ambiguous, *capitales* is sometimes used to describe ecclesiastical tenants. The appellations *quotidiani* or *Leibeigen* are a surer indication of serfdom but are seldom found before the thirteenth century. Moreover very little is known of the origins of this social group: apart from the *donati* (individuals, usually women, who were given to the Church with all that they possessed) or the rare instances of those saved from capital punishment, we know nothing at all about the origins of the majority – indeed Marc Bloch, 40 years ago, maintained that this applied to the peasantry as a whole. Were they classical slaves who had been given limited freedom, as the unchanging four pence poll-tax (*capitatio, chevage, capage, cabezagio, gavelich*) seems to imply? Or had they been free men who had gradually slid into a state of increasing dependence, justifying marriage and inheritance taxes which might also be levied on free men? Had their rights been transferred, either by persuasion or by force, as the Normans did in England? The debate also centres on the precise nature of the obligations of serfdom. There is an increasing consensus, however, that the payment of *chevage*, or poll-tax, was one of these, and also that the conditions of serfdom resulted less in the loss of economic or judicial rights than in humiliation and discrimination at the personal level – publicly flogged, set upon by dogs, excluded from courts of justice, with their offers of marriage rejected and deemed unworthy of carrying arms – maybe these things were the epitomy of *pensum servitutis*, a burden more often transmitted through the female than the male line. On the other hand, historians now generally agree that after the eleventh century the numbers involved were fairly small: between 10 and 20 per cent in Domesday Book and Bavaria, slightly more along the Loire Valley and in central and southern France, less in northern and central Italy; the figure was a high as 30 or 35 per cent in the Meuse, Rhine and Weser valleys, while it was unknown in Brittany, Normandy and Picardy and the Spanish *criados* were almost non-existent. On the other hand, it is often asserted that in the thirteenth century economic pressures caused the descent of many formerly free men into servitude, reviving a situation that had become rare because of the extent of individual and collective enfranchisement in the twelfth century. The term *deuxième servage* (second serfdom) is often used for such cases (although in fact the condition was more economic than judicial), but the expression is unhelpful since the chronology and geographical distribution of the so-called 'first serfdom' are barely discernible.

Scholars have shown particular enthusiasm for small and poorly defined social groups: the English bordars and cottars are a case in point. They comprised some four to five per cent of the village population in about 1180, were terribly burdened with labour services and excluded from the *fyrd*: were they serfs? What about the *colliberti* documented in consistently small numbers the length of the Atlantic coast from Wessex to the Landes: were they semi-servile or on the verge of enfranchisement? Since they are only documented between 1025 and 1163 it is perhaps not a very crucial issue. On the other hand, it is important to remember that slavery pure and simple, where a man had no more rights than an animal, continued to exist on a scale long undreamt of by historians and which the Church pretended to know nothing about. As in classical times, prisoners of war were very common in the Mediterranean, supplied by forays against Islamic territory, despite the risk of retaliatory raids: they were taken as domestic servants throughout the Iberian peninsula, confounding all notions of social hierarchy since, for example, the bishop of Lisbon had more than a hundred in 1170. Then there were the Nordic forms that survived in Wales, Ireland, north-east England and Scandinavia: variously termed theows, kotseths or thraells and frequently women, they were bought and sold in Dublin, Bergen and Uppsala either to Slavonic Europe or to the Islamic East. This nefarious practice was deeply rooted: numerous canonical prohibitions between 1102 and 1400 had no apparent effect and the trade continued. Furthermore, the probable descendants of Mediterranean prisoners, or possibly classical slaves (the *massips* or *mancipia* of Provence and *homines de criatione* of Spain) lived in a Christian environment, working as shepherds, domestic servants or kitchen hands.

Finally, there is the important question of the Jewish community. We know that they were well established in Spain, Italy and Languedoc, but there were also sizeable communities in England and along the Rhine. It must be emphasized that – contrary to general belief – these were not exclusively urban groups. About 1170, especially in southern Europe, Jews appeared in the countryside, the owners of flocks, salt-marshes, orchards and vineyards and consequently playing an important part in village markets. They are even to be found holding land and cited as witnesses far away from the cities. But the late twelfth and the thirteenth centuries saw the start of persecutions and banishments, followed by the segregation that resulted in the concentration of Jewish communities in specially reserved districts in the towns.

It is quite clear that all the social categories discussed in these last paragraphs checked the collective progress of the village towards self-management and the development of its own rights. They acted as a brake, more or less forceful, on the dynamism of the community as a whole, sometimes halting its further development entirely. But when there was a substantial accumulation of wealth and liberties and when, too, their lords felt impelled to slacken their control – either as a result of changes in their own social attitudes, or because of economic necessity – it became possible to negotiate a balance between lord and peasants. It is this balance between the two powers that dominated the medieval countryside that we must now assess.

5

The Fully Developed Village

The steady fragmentation of communal possessions in Europe (which had already begun in the north in the nineteenth century and today has affected most southern regions as well) makes it hard for us to appreciate the strength of a man's ties to his village and the way in which he experienced an almost bodily involvement in the defence of its interests, or the power of a common stock of knowledge and a shared folklore. Communal solidarity, conviviality and family ties still play a part in our society, but they no longer provide the basis of a peasant culture characteristic of a specific region, or of a single village. Progressive equality inevitably entails the severing of roots, beginning with nation states, continuing through education and now culminating in identical and universally accessible modes of communication. We have therefore to make a considerable adjustment if we are to recreate the vigorous fabric of village life at this period.

Awakening

Urban historians, perennially on the look-out for the first signs of the development of an 'urban mentality' – for as early as the fourth century St Augustine had made his famous comment, '*non muri sed mentes*' (minds not walls) – have frequently found them in the terms generally used to signify a group of town-dwellers: there are countless examples of *burgenses*, *cives*, and *urbani*.

Unfortunately, this line of enquiry cannot be followed by the rural historian: it is not that terms such as *homines, manentes* or *pagenses* were devoid of sense; on the contrary, they were overloaded with significance. The resulting elasticity of such expressions is probably responsible for the historiographical tradition from Augustin Thierry (1795–1856) to Pirenne (1862–1935) and a number of contemporary historians that sees the fully developed village as no more than a pale reflection of the mature town. This is, almost literally, to put the cart before the horse for, without the countryside, even the Roman town was no more than an empty shell, because both the chronological pattern and the character of grants of liberties place the countryside in the forefront of social developments and, in my view, make it the driving force behind moves towards emancipation at this period.

The bond of belief?

This verbal confusion inevitably makes the search for the origins of the village tentative in the extreme. I have already said that the basis of the village group lay in the dawn of communal identity that occurred when several smaller family units settled permanently in one place. This development should probably be placed at the end of the ninth or, more probably, in the tenth century. But what else can we say? What bound men together in this newly founded village unit? I am inclined to stress the importance of the Church, even if its primary aim was not to strengthen the rural community.

Two particular forms of settlement were undoubtedly prominent in the earliest and most influential villages. Their sites centred on the dead, or on a parish church which might or might not be near an area of asylum, the *atrium* which I have frequently mentioned.

However, even these basic assertions are problematical and controversial. It is generally admitted that the isolated cemeteries of the early Middle Ages were abandoned in favour of new burial grounds which are still in use today, and there is abundant archaeological evidence for this development. There is far less certainty, however, surrounding the construction of sacred buildings in both wood and stone: there are numerous examples, especially in areas where Christianity was long established, of a foundation in the early medieval period, sometimes on a sacred pagan site; and there is evidence of 100 or so foundations from this period even in areas like the Rhineland, where Christianity did not really become established until the eighth century. But I do not see this as incompatible with the adoption of a fixed settlement: the sacred building existed, the houses did not and this is still the case in sparsely populated regions today. It was rather the parish structure, I believe, which did not exist – its complete reorganization is documented in central Italy, at the heart of an old Christian area. With the *incastellamento*, the *plebes cum oraculis* of the first centuries A.D. were centred on fortified settlements and the vast and loose-knit *pieve* were first replaced by churches perched high on these sites and then abandoned by the faithful. It looks as if it was not until well into the tenth century that the parish network emerged and probably still later beyond the Rhine and the Danube, where huge parishes with uncertain boundaries are documented about 1150. On the other hand, the interchangeable use of *villa* and *parrochia* in the Auvergne, Poitou and Anjou around 1000 or slightly earlier provides a datable point of reference.

The emergence of the parish with its attendant patron – one or more of the apostles (Peter and Paul were particularly popular), Stephen the first martyr, John the Baptist, the Virgin Mary or some locally venerated evangelist, such as St Martin in Gaul – established a cardinal bond amongst the villagers: their loyalty to St Peter or St Martin far outstripped that owed to a secular lord nearby. The study of *nébuleuses* (groups of villages with the same patron) is still in its very earliest stages, but will undoubtedly demonstrate that such ties went far beyond the narrow confines of a parish. Attendance at services and indeed at the sacraments (with the exception of baptism) may have been extremely poor, but communal or parish processions clearly established spiritual ties within the village community.

The mechanisms for peace-keeping fall into the same category. It has already been observed that their slow diffusion in the course of the first half of the eleventh century may have been a significant influence on the establishment of territorially defined lordships, but to emphasize this role (increasingly illuminated by contemporary research) is to present these institutions as essentially negative from the peasant viewpoint. In fact, the village peace was a collective operation, and not only because it was sworn by all the villagers, as in northern France between 1035 and 1115, when the term *pax rusticorum* referred simultaneously to the group of countrymen and their land as well as the oath they swore. The concept developed further in the twelfth century with the selection of certain individuals (called variously *jurés, paziers* and *amici* in Picardy, Languedoc and the Ile-de-France) specifically charged with responsibility for village security and communal peace. Since the mid-twelfth century this peace was manifestly human rather than divine and the Church was naturally slow to become involved: it was as late as 1200 or 1215 in Anjou, Italy, Normandy or the Ile-de-France before oaths of this kind were admissible in synods or diocesan ordinances. In practice the clergy had grounds for ignoring them: in the very early stages of the movement the bishops (with the exception of some with a strong monastic background) had attempted to manipulate the peasantry against the military aristocracy, whose strength was increasing rapidly at this period; they authorized assemblies of armed villagers bearing the banners and emblems (*vexilla et signa*) of their parish, which were solemnly handed to them after being blessed by the priest. Several deplorable incidents in which the peasantry demonstrated that they were only too ready to bear arms against their masters (such as that in Berry in 1038) made the Church realize that its own interests lay with secular lordship. These movements were crushed (I shall discuss this in a different context) and one consequence was an almost exclusive emphasis on protection in oaths of peace, on defence rather than attack. When new village militias were formed in the Velay around 1175 – such as the 'hooded' brotherhoods (*encapuchonnés*), so-called because of the hoods they wore, claiming as their goal the establishment of a God-given order – they were kept within strict bounds and subject to a relatively high levy to ensure that the numbers were not swollen with social outcasts whose poverty might lead them to take up arms for their own ends.

Village fraternities undoubtedly came into being at the same period and with similar aims. However, this can be no more than a hypothesis, as their origins are shrouded in obscurity: they only appear to be fully developed in the eleventh century in Savoy, the Auvergne and Provence, perhaps slightly earlier in England and Italy and at a later date in other areas. It has been calculated that they existed in 40 per cent of parishes in the thirteenth century. They were certainly devotional groups at the outset, placing themselves under the patronage of Corpus Christi, the Holy Saviour, the Holy Spirit or the Passion – dedications which demonstrated that this association was distinct from that of the parish. Their role was to provide mutual assistance: to ensure decent burial for its members and some basic instruction for their daughters. But since membership was by payment, this common fund – in effect an embryonic collective – could acquire lands, stock and implements. An administration consequently developed and there was a predictable shift in direction: because they were the most solvent and financially reliable, the richest men were made responsible for the safe-keeping and loan of money and implements. They rapidly acquired control over the poorer members and in their hands the confraternities became a means of social pressure in the thirteenth century. Since the administration of the *dos* (parish lands used to feed the hungry) required constant supervision, it also became necessary to create a body of churchwardens (*matricularii*), responsible for the fabric, that is for all aspects of the maintenance of the church and its possessions. Not surprisingly, the richest members of the confraternity seized on these positions as well.

The way in which all spiritual power was gradually placed in the hands of the rich appears at first sight to place an intolerable burden on the very poor. But we must not forget that in the Middle Ages means had been found to counter-balance excessive power. The priest played no part in this: he could only be the lord's agent or the more or less conscious representative of the most powerful members of the community, but there were other men of God who could proffer assistance and comfort. There has been virtually no consideration of anything other than the religious role of hermits, embodiments of a particular type of faith often hostile to that which was preached by the established Church. Little attention has been paid to their role as craftsmen outside the village, practising the trade of potter, maker of clogs or wickerwork; even less to that of counsellor, comforter, fortune-teller and healer, for it was to one of these holy men that the poor and the sick, the fearful and those crossed in love took their problems. Sometimes they emerged as threatening prophets whose influence stretched as far as the castle. The eleventh century teemed with such hermits, found as often in the forests of Brittany as in the Mediterranean *maquis*, and they were at the forefront of numerous rural uprisings. These men were both a consolation and a threat: sanctified by the simplicity of their life, in their penury they constituted both a warning and a counter-weight to the powerful.

The bond of law

A hermit alone does not make a community; by no means all were admitted to the confraternity and his presence tended to weaken it. Other, more formal and concrete elements must have developed based upon the Christian faith. Settlement was more than the cessation of an itinerant existence; it was also the positive possession of the soil: natural or man-made boundaries were established and marked by boundary-stones or crosses, ratified if necessary by an agreement between two masters – in writing, even, in areas where the *convenientia* operated. Henceforth places or rights were defined in terms of their boundaries (*in finibus, infra cruces*) and these areas were distinct and unquestionable except in admittedly frequent cases of attempted fraud and boundary disputes. Nevertheless, there was a perfect understanding within the community of the extent of a property or a jurisdiction, contrary to what is often believed.

The majority of the village were affected by these concepts since they lived in a house and owned land. As I have already mentioned, settlers, travellers and vagrants were excluded. In a new village a specific period had to elapse (usually one year, sometimes as long as three) before a new arrival could become a full member of the community; and the individual who owned no property might easily be excluded from the community, as was frequently the case in towns, but also occurred in Hainault and the Mâconnais. Even if the settlement was not in possession of any known or written privileges, even marginal portions of the developed area were marked out on the ground: a palisade (*Etter*) or hedge (*cingulum, sanglas*) separated the village where the peasants lived – called the *distretto* or *détroit* from the Latin *districtus* – from the land they cultivated. This was everywhere the case, although there were obviously variations between, for example, the Scandinavian *byl*, with settlements scattered over a wide area, and the Italian *borgho* perched on a rock. I have already said that selected villagers – probably chosen from amongst the richest – were responsible for the maintenance of order within the community; others, called *messiers*, guarded the sheaves of corn left for the lord on the fields from thieves and animals; yet others were the community's spokesmen and advocates – these would be men who could express themselves well, but were also of sufficient standing in the community for the lord to give them a reasonable answer, such as the priest, blacksmith or churchwardens. It was not surprising if defence of their own interests was their prime concern.

Further problems stemmed from the existence of a mayor, a *rector* or a *Schultheiss* at the head of many rural communities and the absence of any administration similar to that found in towns. When the lord had to levy a tax, raise an army or hold his manorial court, it was very much in his interests to have one man in the village community who was both a spy and an intermediary. This individual was chosen by the lord and he might even hold the office as a kind of inheritable fief. But he was often chosen from amongst the villagers and the position gradually slipped out of seigneurial hands. There is no proof of continuity between the mayors selected by the lord, who were almost universal about 1120, and those chosen by the peasants themselves in privileged villages at a later date; but the advantages enjoyed by the former, when they are last mentioned, are very similar to those conferred on the village officials who succeeded him.

In the late classical and Byzantine periods the intervention of the state in rural communities was largely experienced through the levying of men or taxes. To ensure that it would continue to be able to obtain both, the state had to ensure that the area of land in cultivation was not reduced. This was why land which had been temporarily or completely abandoned (*adjectio sterilium*) was given by the authorities to neighbours or relatives, since this appeared the best way of maintaining the condition of the land. There is clear evidence of the disappearance of concepts of the state and central authority in the West: this was most marked in the case of taxation but was also to a certain extent true of military organization. The decline of practices so clearly alien to modes of exploitation of the early Middle Ages should not surprise us. However, it is striking that very similar notions reappear in the first charters of privileges granted to villages, from the eleventh century in Spain, for example, and in the twelfth century in northern France: take, for instance, the obligation to ensure that a piece of land did not remain in escheat for more than three years, or to admit a stranger's claim only when every possibility of inheritance by a blood relation had been thoroughly explored and, if necessary, to set a very high rate of taxation on property transfer. Such measures were naturally affected by family considerations – notably the *retrait lignager* which has already been discussed; but they also re-established the principle of the integrity of the land transferred. Finally, although its effects were only experienced at a relatively late date, the lordship itself had a part in establishing a juridical bond between the men of the community: they shared obligations to do labour service clearing ditches or keeping watch in the woods; they had to queue together at the mill, use the same measure (their master's) and present themselves as a group in the army or lawcourt – all of which could not fail to re-enforce concepts of village unity. Nevertheless, even here part of the population already felt themselves excluded, namely the unfree and recent settlers who were debarred from participation in such activities, reserved for residents and free peasants. Although these obligations were a heavy burden for some, it is clear that the richest villagers benefitted from a consensus between the lord and themselves and that the situation was one which they had an interest in maintaining. Henceforth, therefore, the agreements made were essentially conservative and the peasants themselves played an important part in formulating them.

Forms of celebration

Anthropologists and now even historians have based their research into the most important forms of group activity on the festivities of ancient societies, to ascertain both the structure of non-family relationships, practices and religious rites that may illumine aspects of collective behaviour. The Middle Ages offers a rich field of study: its interpretation, however, is made difficult by the subsequent accretion of more recent practices which are not easy to distinguish from ancient customs. Moreover, the effect across the centuries of changes in attitudes on peasant folklore has long been underestimated; much material of this kind is disappearing, almost by the minute, under the pressure of contemporary cultural uniformity. It is not yet too late, however: a whole series of characteristics typical of village festivities has been isolated, and although it would be impossible to date any one of these as protohistoric rather than to the fifteenth century, their unifying role in village society is unquestionable.

Agrarian rites were in all probability the oldest; beneath a veneer of Christianity many of their features have a very early origin; others – by the reverse process – were apparently determined by official liturgical practice and tended to re-enforce their basic Christian significance. It would be pointless to attempt a comprehensive survey, since these practices were not universal, nor did they take the same form everywhere. I shall therefore confine my remarks to celebrations which followed the cycle of work in the fields. The winter solstice marked by Christmas festivities was the beginning of the long period when the land was dormant: men were replete with pork because this was when the pigs were killed before the long 'hungry' season, rather than because of the birth of the baby king. Mid-Lent (when empty granaries dictated ritual fasting) was marked by dances, tumbling, comic incident and jokes involving masked men reminiscent of the inversion of social roles typical of the Saturnalia. As for *Brandons* (the festival of torches on the first Sunday in Lent), which they tried to combine with Palm Sunday, this torchlight procession beneath the bare trees was surely also a prudent exercise in rodent control? Finally, there was the celebration of spring, with the sacrificial lamb of the

Christian church and the offerings of eggs and flowers that marked the new year in many regions: Easter in France or Italy had more affinity with the deliverance of the Jewish people than the resurrection of Christ. Everywhere May was the most festive month, for this was the time when new trees were planted, as the animals reached the woods and their pasture, when campaigns began, garlands of flowers were fixed to the doors of girls about to get married and when ardour was kindled anew, with the approach of the hay harvest, bringing with it the promise of the land's renewed fertility for which they had all hoped. Then from late June to the end of September came the time of increasing fertility: the feast of St John the Baptist coincided with the midsummer fires which men continued to jump over in a purification ritual, dances round the animals to protect them from evil spirits, round-dances and pairing on the threshing-floor once the harvest had been brought in, and finally the feast of fools when sexual desire was given free rein, with the externalization of violence, mockery and make-believe, as they had done in the ancient world at celebrations in which wine and sex reigned triumphant.

Christian influence and the extent to which it had merged with much older ceremonies is probably best judged in the context of local celebrations, the feast-days of patron saints which may, moreover, simply have been substituted for pagan festivities. It has been estimated that, including Sundays, the medieval peasant only worked 250 or 270 days a year; and each patronal festival was an occasion for drinking (*potaciones*) – a custom also adopted by the fraternities since, as at all periods, drinking together was one of the best ways of celebrating. It should be added that the churching of women after childbirth was – once the ecclesiastical service of purification was over – the occasion of much rejoicing and drinking together at the husband's expense. It has been demonstrated without difficulty that in a village of 2–300 there would be 70–75 pregnant women a year; taking account of churchings and regular feasts the inhabitants would celebrate every other day on average.

We know even less of the significance and origin of the collective games which today constitute one of the most substantial pillars of community life in towns and elsewhere. The medieval West did not indulge in the highly formalized public games of earlier periods, when the potential hostility between two towns or two peoples was absorbed in a judicious sporting rivalry, either with teams of amateurs, as in ancient Greece, or the professionals of the Roman and Byzantine circus. But it is clear that in the Italian towns (and much of northern France and Flanders) in the fourteenth and fifteenth centuries, games in the form of jousts, tournaments or hand-to-hand fighting between teams from two clans, two families or two districts provided an outlet for rivalries which may have been political in an urban context but undoubtedly had a social basis in the country. We know very little about these activities: *soule*, which seems to have been more like cricket than modern soccer or rugby is the only rural team game documented from this period. I think it very likely that the rustic dances, or singing and music competitions, which are depicted in so many manuscript illuminations might become vehicles for rivalry between the sexes, for family feuds and the settling of old scores: subsequent letters of remission carry frequent references to brawls that ended in a man's death.

By no means every aspect of the new social groupings within the village was advantageous. This is evident in their games, but still more apparent in some of the beliefs which trapped the villagers in fear and superstition – not so much in their fear of spirits returning from the dead (who were perceived as souls in torment to whom one should listen attentively), but of superstitious practices which they saw as the result of the occult knowledge of some wizard; or even the action of elusive and malevolent beings, such as the creatures of the other world who trampled the crops, or the goblins who led travellers across the marsh into a misery of confusion, or sorcerers said to be hidden in the depths of the wood or incarnate in some village woman. For these beliefs were by no means confined to the female population: rites that propitiated or conjured, involving a combination of bloodshed, grains of wheat, exorcisms and other rituals were denounced and actively opposed by the Church from the councils of the eighth century to the accounts of Dominicans weary from this struggle, such as Etienne de Bourbon or Hugues de Romans in the thirteenth century. Only after Voltaire could the subject be laughed at – and yet even now who has not flown in the face of reason and experienced the terror emanating from the depth of a forest at night, or the profound mystery of a spring – to say nothing of the very real dangers of the ravening wolf or a sheet of lightning?

The neighbourhood provided comfort and also complicity, a context in which both the moral and intellectual characteristics of the sexes were particularly apparent. Here, neighbourhood was not synonymous with proximity, which was more likely to be a source of jealousy and conflict, but of circumstantial relationships – those of the women at the mill or the market, as they did the washing or de-loused each other; the men at the forge or the inn, or at their assemblies round the elm. The village was criss-crossed by a network of meeting-places, where news was exchanged, recriminations expressed and plans were laid, at the well, by the rubbish heaps, on the common, at the graveyard and in the still-room, at the mill or the smithy. The only rival to these nerve-centres of the community was the hearth round which the villagers had gathered ever since the household fire had moved inside the building, where the old men – and others – gathered to tell stories; but if a professional minstrel or a wandering player (*diseur, joven*) appeared, the villagers might gather in the larger room (*salle*) of one of the village's richest inhabitants.

The rhythm of village life was slow, its evolution uncertain and there were set-backs and periods of regression. These pauses and changes in pace are familiar to every anthropologist. Many elements of the community were only added at a relatively late date and we are not yet in a position to say whether they were all in place when the boldest and richest (inevitably synonymous) finally became aware of their individual roles. They realized they had some control over their destinies and decided to go up to the castle and talk seriously to their master.

Realization

The emancipation of the medieval village is a well-worn subject; it features in even the most conservative textbooks, whilst Marx makes it a crucial factor in the history of individual freedom. The only real problem it poses is the distinctiveness of rural, as compared with urban liberties and I have already stressed that it seems clear that the two phenomena have no more than a few copied texts in common. As we have seen, village emancipation had its roots in protohistory; it was developed in and through the seigneurial system which formed the basis of the established order. By contrast urban development was sudden, violent and hostile to this order, even rebellious. Moreover, throughout Europe, towns that had won freedom for themselves generally suppressed emancipation in the villages around them. I hope it will therefore be accepted that there is not even a synchronic connection between the two movements.

Another highly significant feature instantly highlights the difference between them. While the urban communes were concerned with political and judicial issues, village demands were motivated by economic factors. When the seigneurial system was established at the beginning of the eleventh century there were clearly social and economic factors in peasant resistance: the Norman revolt of 996 has already been mentioned; other instances include the refusal of the Lombard and Angevin peasants to perform labour services and their insistent demands for common land in 1030 and 1050 – actions that were not without cruel reprisals in areas such as the Loire Valley. There was also dissatisfaction when the aristocracy first appropriated forest-land on a large scale, with similar consequences; there were risings over the demarcation of boundaries of common land called *épaux* in Maine and against the English kings' frequent practice of seizing vacant lands. Both resulted in loss of life and it is possible that the killing of lords in Cambrésis and the Boulonnais – and even the death of William Rufus in 1100 – were connected with this discontent. The first half of the eleventh century was characterized by supposedly 'heretical' movements that may have been linked with this first wave of peasant resistance. Wandering preachers – whether, like Robert d'Arbrissel, accepted by the establishment or condemned by it, like Pierre de Bruys – were followed by a crowd of women, artisans and young people (*juvenes*) who made their homes in the forests like these hermits, or even with them. Did this represent the collapse of part of the family structure, rejection of seigneurial tutelage or withdrawal from an oppressed village unit? Whatever the entrenched opponents of social history may think, it is striking that the religious revivals of this period all started in the countryside: Vertus (northern Italy), Cambrésis, Monforte and Maine all provide examples and we have already discussed the way the peasant militia hoped to take advantage of the peace movement. Every episode teaches the same lesson, that it was impossible for town- and country-dwellers to agree over their aims, and shared goals were out of the question. Rural movements were speedily engulfed in urban uprisings: this happened in the Patarene revolt in Milan (1057–75) and it was the same at Le Mans 20 years later.

This was so much the case that from this point onwards – and especially during the increased stability of the twelfth century – peasant opposition became much less overt and less easy to trace in documentary sources: they might deliver the lord green wood that was not fit for use or offer him wretched lodgings, send children or the sick to perform labour services, deliberately skimp their duties or delay payments; sometimes the action may have been violent, with mills burnt, tools destroyed or the provost's daughter raped. We have no evidence of such disruption and it is unlikely that any will be found, but in 1117 the abbot of Marmoutier declared that he would rather go without labour dues than see them used as a vehicle for deliberate sabotage. Moreover, the period before 1140 or 1160 was one when the lord's priority was to preserve his judicial authority and his force of arms: at that moment the need for liquid capital represented the sum of his economic concerns. These were his reasons for preferring commutation of labour services for money rent just at the time when, for the peasants, these also provided the guarantees required to sustain their burgeoning economy.

Rural demands gave a fairly clear priority to fixing the rate of tallage because it typified what most concerned the villein, namely the irregularity rather than the level of these payments. Almost every locality had different labour dues and the next step was to fix them at a specific level, sometimes with the option of buying off this obligation with a lump-sum payment. Commutation was characterized above all by a graduated scale of payments. When agreements concerning such practices were put in writing, it is easy to see (at least when it is not a question of modifications as a result of growing pressure from the peasant elite, which was a factor throughout the thirteenth century) that such demands came from the richest members of the community, for the rate was proportionate to an individual's wealth, or rather the amount of equipment he owned, up to a certain level (say, four horses and two ploughs), when it remained constant. Concessions of common rights were linked still more closely to the requirements of the food supply, this time notably of the poorest: this was why it was increasingly the practice, especially as the twelfth century progressed, for the lord to fix the level of repurchase at a fairly low level. If the sum required was too high for the most impoverished they were allowed to substitute an additional labour service, a turn of duty at the castle, or watching over the lord's flock: there are examples of this practice from Catalonia to the *contado* of Verona and from Mâcon to Ratisbon.

Apart from concessions made by the lord, which were generally granted at least to all free men, the peasants were linked by other forms of common economic interest, particularly when concerted action was essential for the maintenance of their day-to-day existence. First among these was undoubtedly protection from natural disasters, such as the fear of forest fires which led to the building of watch-towers and the organization of guards in both Scandinavia and the Mediterranean coasts; there was also the fear of high tides at the equinox breaking the dykes, flooding low-lying fields, which prompted the formation of *Wateringen*, teams to watch over the dykes. But it was the complications of large-scale pastoral activity that necessitated more than a communal guard and combined action when the flocks were moved. The route they would travel and the summer pastures had to be supervised, a communal fund established for the payment of the taxes demanded by the lords of mountainous areas for crossing their land and for the use of passes, or even on the mountain pasture itself – the *escarterons* of the Briançonnais, the *fruitières* of the Jura and the Castilian Mesta are well-known examples. Thus in the Alps and the Pyrenees the common interest of several valleys could lead to the formation of vast territorial units virtually outside all seigneurial control: a sense of identity remains in those areas today and this economic cohesion might give rise to political unity, as the Swiss were to demonstrate forcibly in the fourteenth century.

The problems raised by the constitution of common lands, to which I have already referred, were one result of this awareness of a shared economic interest. The terms used to describe these areas were vague (*communia, terra communis, terra francorum*) and they communicated nothing about their nature, origin or status. Were they the property of the local confraternity? Were they plots acquired by the village as a whole to be used as shared pasture? Or were their origins in the simple green (*pratellum*) at the centre of the village? The fact that these lands were divided amongst the richest villagers at the end of the thirteenth century lends support to the first theory, all the more so since the lord often presided over this development and received a share for himself. The relative failure of this form of communal activity can of course be seen as indicative of its weakness and a testimony to the villagers' disagreements from at least as early as the thirteenth century. It is perhaps wiser to concede that by this date 'property' was seen even (perhaps especially) amongst tenants as a matter for the individual and that contemporary attitudes did not favour the collective property-holding known as 'primitive communism' in the context of itinerant societies of the classical period. Henceforth when rights to neighbouring woodland were available there was only a very limited interest in communal action which undoubtedly suffered more from indifference than from avarice.

The path to self-management

The key economic advances in rural society took place between 1050–60 and 1120–40. Outside these periods there was greater resistance by the lords. Progress in the form of markets, a quicker rate of currency circulation and price increases undoubtedly did nothing to check the lords' need for liquid capital, but they clearly realized the economic advantages of more profitable and better-managed estates. They were therefore less favourably disposed towards the demands made by their men. On the other hand, however, a lord's privileged rights of justice over his tenants tended to become devalued, in the first place because the peasants (by contrast with town-dwellers) did not seem to want any general control over the system, in particular over capital crimes, and also because the threat of royal or princely competition forced the lords to compromise in this field.

By contrast they continued to place heavy emphasis on their military prerogatives: there was no question of letting peasants bear arms without formal permission, or to keep them afterwards, nor of dispensing with billeting rights and requisitioning for the seigneurial levy. With the exception of the few cases documented from the eleventh century (such as the risings at Bourges or Le Mans already mentioned), the rare instances of rural insurrection – around 1120 or 1150 in Picardy and the area round Bray, or 1170–75 in the Velay – ended badly for the villagers; the leagues assembled around Laon were forcibly suppressed. No concessions were ever made in this area.

Agreement was reached more easily on judicial matters. In the first place the lord delegated responsibility for a whole range of issues, especially if he had concerns further afield; he was only interested in instances of homicide and, obviously, feudal cases. In Germany, the formal separation of territorial law from feudal law (*Landgerichte* from *Lehngerichte*) occurred at a very early date. Moreover, because of the development of a common law based on local legal customs, there was a continual tendency to leave these matters to the older inhabitants rather than professional lawyers, even in areas with a written legal code. Finally, many straightforward property transactions (such as the straightforward seisin of a piece of land or the levying of a tax on its sale) were entrusted either to the lord's commissioners (responsible for establishing what local custom in such matters was and ensuring that justice was then done); or to advocates who put the case for fellow-villagers, or even newcomers, before the *scabini* or *sculteti* – deceptively archaic terms, since these tribunals had a very real role in village life.

In this way high and low manorial justice evolved, encompassing property transactions, the *cognitio fundi* (sworn inquest) and the maintenance of law and order. Since, moreover, these seigneurial commissioners and their executive arm, the serjeants or *prévots*, were always in contact with the villagers (indeed were chosen from amongst them), such local and informal justice was

quickly perceived as the personal affair of the local inhabitants
and the entire spectrum of judicial authority, from complicity to
negligence, passed beneath their eyes and through their hands.
In serious cases (when there was bloodshed, disturbance of the
peace or some threat to the established order) the lord made an
appearance in all the splendour of his regalian power, glad that
he had not delegated his authority to a lieutenant. Otherwise
such matters as the levying of fines and their expenditure on
items such as the repair of prison locks or the serjeant's pay were
decided entirely at village level. This development doubtless
explains the ease with which the lords relinquished control to the
local community of those aspects of low justice that brought
them very little financial return. The villagers accepted these
opportunities with enthusiasm, for it seemed vital to them to
settle their own conflicts at this level: all the custumals drawn up
in the thirteenth century enumerate lists of 'cases' (cas) with a
touching concern for comprehensiveness, together with the
relevant fines and wide-ranging references to other jurisdictions
for such matters as were inevitably omitted from the list. As for
the rest, it was a public matter and medieval attitudes were far
too conservative to confuse stability with freedom.

But this organization and the sentences passed required
methods that were not mere reflections of the lord's interests. We
may therefore say that the judicial system was the basis of village
administration; moreover, the terms employed for the 'notables'
responsible for the initial inquiry, for passing sentence and
finally ensuring that it was carried out were taken from the realm
of justice: the échevins of northern France, syndics or consuls in
the south, gastaldi in northern Italy, jurados in Spain and sculteti
in Germany – only the rachimburgi were missing from what
would otherwise have been a full-scale Renaissance of 'Carolingian' legal terminology, and it is the use of identical terms that has
led some historians to look for continuity between the eighth and
the twelfth centuries. This team of six or eight men was normally
headed by the mayor (maire) to whom I have already referred and
who in this context found or rediscovered his eminent position.
Clearly it would be desirable to know more. These men were élus
(elected), but the word only signifies 'chosen'. By whom? The
lord? The leading inhabitants who took the initiative at a docile

assembly of the rest of the village? If so, how? How long did the appointment last? We know nothing of these matters, but it is quite possible that if we did – as we do in urban contexts – we should see only the pressure exerted by the wealthy (as in every period) on supposedly 'democratic' processes to ensure that power remained in the same hands.

In order to understand the final, crowning step of the movement – the written expression of privileges and custom – I think it is vital to realize that there was a profound shift of social attitudes in the twelfth-century West. What Georges Duby has characterized as 'the great century of progress' was not merely a period of economic and territorial expansion, combined with a growth in the money supply, but also saw a vigorous development of initiatives which translated these achievements into collective attitudes. This is not the place for a discussion of the innovations in romanesque art, improvements in education or the new status of legal studies. But respect for established custom went hand-in-hand with cultural progress: this was only to be expected in regions with written customs: here even the humblest were used to announcements of court sittings and *convenientiae*. In the north, however, it was more of a novelty to have recourse to a written corpus, rather than calling the old men together with the witnesses, putting on oath those who had to initiate the proceedings. Soon there was almost total reliance on written precedent, as in the south. The earliest surviving examples seem to be somewhat late, namely the Assizes of Count Geoffrey of Brittany, the Customs of Normandy of Ranulf Glanville dating from before 1185, but it was only at the beginning of the thirteenth century that this became common practice in northern and eastern France and reached its apogee in the time of Louis IX, the Emperor Frederick II and Henry III of England. There was always an interval of several decades before a lawyer crystallized an established practice on parchment, and it was only when the permanence of the written word had been fully understood that village charters appeared. At the same time all recollection of the old tenth- and eleventh-century lists of rents and services (*censiers*) and even the Carolingian estate surveys polyptichs was lost: until this juncture these documents had been the supposed terms of reference in the absence of any other sound legal basis.

At the same time, the profit motive became widespread amongst all classes of rural society, perhaps because this was an integral part of their dealings, or because there was greater opportunity for profit and a higher profit margin. There are dozens of examples of conflict between lords over mills, fish ponds, horses and the like and of clashes between lord and peasants over such issues as an oak tree felled in secret, boundary stones moved at night and crops stolen at harvest from the individual responsible for collecting the lord's share. The medieval mind is often held to be quintessentially litigious – as if this characteristic were entirely lacking in other periods – and the historian has to assume something of the same attitude better to understand, or rather, to guess at the negotiations that undoubtedly preceded the formulation of a document embodying the resultant compromise. In this context the preambles of charters granting customs deserve more attention than they usually receive, for the reasons given by the lord for his assent – it was almost invariably the lord who issued these documents – were not stereotyped formulae (with the exception of a clause of protest over the encroachment on his rights that had already occurred), but the results of demands formulated by the peasants, agreements satisfactory to all parties, or even because of pressure from another authority, perhaps a bishop or count, or alternatively because the villagers had paid a sum of money to secure agreement. We seldom learn the real origin of any initiative, for most texts give the impression of a division of advantages with benefits of some kind to each party involved, but it has been calculated that some 20 per cent were fairly clearly imposed on a reluctant lord. There has been very little examination of the question of 'policy' adopted by contemporary powers on this issue, although it has been repeated for more than a century that the Capetians encouraged rural communities (*communes*). My own research into this question in Picardy indicates that resistance came from the regular clergy who, lacking both the military strength of the laity and the political power of the bishops, were left virtually no demesne land once the concessions had been made. Opposition was also strong amongst the lesser landed nobility whose territories lay away from major trade routes and for whom negotiable concessions consequently held little attraction. Both groups had to give way: the monks because their tenants threatened to go to neighbouring villages where they could enjoy the rights they demanded, and the minor lords, as in Lorraine or Anjou, because (apart from the same threats from their tenants) they were also subjected to pressure from counts and castellans, whose major concern was to avoid a repetition of the unrest of the eleventh century in the areas under their jurisdiction and to maintain the position of the dominant classes in the established order.

But the reader must bear in mind the enormous degree of local variation and beware of the danger of over-generalizing from this sketch of regional characteristics.

The outward appearance of rural communities

It is important to stress what really applies to the whole of this chapter, that is the complete absence of parallels between urban and rural development at this period in the same region. This is true on feudal, economic and demographic levels and such a universal contradiction appears quite insoluble.

Logically, one would expect rural society to be most developed in the southern Mediterranean – and, in Italy at least, at an early date – where there were many old and flourishing towns with written customs and well-established legal and municipal traditions. In fact the opposite is true: Spain, where the towns had long been inert because of the divisions within the peninsula, saw the earliest as well as the fullest rural developments. The Spanish *fueros* (customs) – *fors* in the Basque region, the Béarnais and the southern part of Gascony – were established at a very early date: 1070 in Jaca, 1077 in Oloron, 1117 in Morlaas and 1125 in Teruel, to mention only a few examples that frequently served as a model for other places. Here Visigothic law (*lex gothica*) was invoked to give villages a greater degree of autonomy and it is not yet clear whether the movement was considerably older than this. Spanish village revival combined simultaneously a very

active role for the *sagreres*, or devotional guilds, for the foreigners
who were always referred to as *francos* and lived in the *barrio*
(suburbs populated by immigrant fighting men and merchants
who had to be regulated) and for the 'brothers' (*paciarii*)
responsible for preserving order in settlements that were often on
constant alert on the Islamic frontier. As a result the *jurados* who
controlled the villages had total jurisdiction over them and over
the *aldea*, or surrounding countryside; moreover, the peasants
were a fighting force and I have already referred to the village
cavalry which would have caused an outcry further north.

Of course, you will say, this was a region often at war, where it
was imperative that the needs and requirements both of the
Christian communities and of those administered through
conquest were quickly and comprehensively provided for. On
the other side of the Pyrenees everything was different: in
Languedoc and especially in Italy the network of towns was
much denser and their control over the *contado* or surrounding
countryside probably also much tighter. Moreover, the Church
had a firm hold, too: laicized or not, the monasteries and the
bishops had built up between them a solid web of well-defended
political and economic immunities. Here village development
atrophied: even in the Po valley, which saw the birth of the
Patarene revolt in the eleventh century, the authority of the
castle-holding lords – the *capitanei* – remained firm and
elsewhere imperial power was upheld. The forces of feudalism
were ranged against the towns, but rural areas only benefitted
from a minimal degree of emancipation, and tardily at that – in
the second half of the twelfth century in Provence and
Languedoc and as late as the mid-thirteenth in the valleys of the
Rhône and in Lombardy, where the somewhat artificial movement of the *statuti* was inspired by Frederick II with the primary
aim of providing opposition to the towns and the Papacy. The
most emancipated communities were controlled by *veridici
homines* (*syndics* in the Languedoc) who might be lawyers and
were invariably eminent individuals; sometimes there was a
mayor, but the Italian term *gastaldo* for this individual suggests
that he was nominated by a count or other local secular power.
There is occasional evidence of the survival of the entirely urban

concept of a general assembly of free men (the Lombard *arengo*), as in the charter of Bassano in 1170, but its role seems to have been reduced to little more than registration.

Even this limited degree of autonomy was exceptional on the Atlantic seaboard of north-west Europe. The striking feature here is the juxtaposition of extremely disparate situations. Overall, the region was colourless: it corresponded to the Plantagenet dominions together with Berry and the Auvergne. It was not until well into the thirteenth century that they were affected to any extent by the great overland trade routes; towns were scattered and had no real liberties – and this was as true of London as of Bordeaux or Rouen, all towns on which rulers kept a strong grip. As a result rural developments in these areas have an isolated and occasional character: they were the result of seigneurial initiatives with a specific end in view – the *sauvetés* of Aquitaine enabled new areas to be settled, the *bastides* contributed to the defence of a threatened area, while the Gascon *castelnaux* or the Norman *bourgages* acted as an assembly-point for scattered peasant settlements. These villages were often redesigned on a geometrical plan and granted their own customs, but in the great majority of instances the castle continued to be the source of local power. The impression is rather that these developments were designed to benefit the artisan community who were undoubtedly very active and probably a driving force. But since there are obviously enormous differences between Yorkshire and the Gers (south-west France) one is forced to conclude that the opposition of the Angevin rulers played a considerable role, since they were the only cohesive factor across this vast region.

Next we come to the old kingdom of the Franks which was to be the cradle of peasant emancipation, covering the Low Countries, Lotharingia and the Paris basin – an area that merits study all the more because, like Italy, it was also a hotbed of urban emancipation. But in this case the developments in town and countryside occurred simultaneously in the same context and it was this (as I have already stressed) that resulted in the confusions that still abound amongst historians who fix their attention on Flanders to the exclusion of surrounding areas. The region is large and by no means uniform: serfdom continued in the south and east, in the north urban documents were re-used in a rural context; elsewhere, further east, agreements were reached with lay-protectors or the Church. But other identical characteristics are to be found everywhere: a written document was drawn up (of which often the confirmation alone survives) with details of customs and privileges (Flemish *keure*) and lengthy, detailed legal reports even claiming to anticipate all eventualities with reference to other, more explicit texts. These statements were the product of compromise and were, moreover, revisable at regular bipartite meetings, frequently attested in the thirteenth century; most reveal a readiness to agree – originating no doubt in common economic interest, but also explaining the support of princes, counts and castellans, who all found it possible to make concessions without feeling threatened. Moreover, traditions were long established here, it was a wealthy region with demographic pressure at its greatest. No attempt at urbanization was required: in an area where charters from the nearest town were taken word for word (in Picardy this occurred 14 times with Amiens, 7 with Cambrai and 6 with Saint-Pol, to cite just a few examples) to such an extent that villagers and their cottages were referred to as the *bourgeois* and the *commune*, the process is best seen as a convenience. Various degrees of development were attained: taxes, generous rights of common pasturage and the repurchase of labour dues; but *échevins*, a mayor and well-developed proprietary law and automatic enfranchisement were also widespread. The clarity of their charters led to imitators: the charters of privileges of Lorris-en-Gâtinais (a confirmation dating from 1155 at least), of Prisches in Hainault (1158) and above all of Beaumont-en-Argonne which spawned almost 500 identical texts in Lorraine, Champagne and the Ardennes; but others, such as Oppy (1162), Liverdun (1177), Esne (1193) were also copied on a large scale. As a whole, this movement started around 1140–50, appreciably later than in Spain, but continued in the form of revisions and re-endorsements until about 1260 in Picardy, 1270 in Champagne and the Ile-de-France, 1300 in Luxembourg and 1321 in the Liège area. On the other hand, although we may reasonably assert that on average every other village was endowed with these considerable privileges (200 definite examples are recorded in Picardy, 300 in Lorraine and

150 in Luxembourg), the level of political autonomy that would have enabled the formation of village leagues was never attained. They were clearly attempted in this privileged region: in about 1174 groupings of wine-producing villages near Laon, towards Anizy and La Neuville-Le-Roy, possibly armed, were identified and destroyed by the nobility with royal support; a similar endeavour in Ponthieu between 1219 and 1235 proved scarcely more effective. The formation of village leagues seems to have been an impassable threshold.

The Empire offers a close parallel. This was undoubtedly because it was so important to bring new land into cultivation; the majority of newly founded villages in Silesia, Lusatia and even in the German heartland, in Thuringia or the Rhine Palatinate received generous enfranchisements, with a mayor or *Schultheiss* and *sculteti* playing the part of *échevins*. They also had their own legal code, the *Landrecht*, as did towns in other areas. The two essential differences seem to have been the fact that for a long while these grants were purely verbal – the majority of the *Weistümer* (collections of judicial sentences) only acquired their final form in the thirteenth century – and that the movement seems to have begun at a considerably later date and also continued well into the fourteenth century.

I trust that this survey will at least have enabled the reader to appreciate what I have persistently reiterated – that although it is possible to isolate specifically 'peasant' characteristics from the mass of European Christendom, the movement as a whole varied in both extent and pace; probably nothing demonstrates this better than the changing face of rural conservatism.

Concessions once made to the peasantry could not be withdrawn. The peasantry clung to them when circumstances seemed particularly threatening and found in them a source of strength. I think it is impossible to understand the character of rural revolt in the fourteenth century without being aware of the great variations in development that we have just considered. When the 'breakdown' of seigneurial society became apparent around 1315–30 it hardly impinged on the peasant, or rather he was affected only by the slump in agricultural prices which undermined the profits of even large-scale producers and consequently eroded the hitherto stable agreement of workers with their employer. The lord himself could no longer increase his dues and taxes to compensate for losses and a higher level of expenditure: in other words he could no longer fulfil his role as protector, patron or judge – how could he possibly ask for more from the peasants or, worse still, take back the privileges his ancestors had granted them? And so it was the most affluent who enjoyed the greatest freedom, who were the first to revolt: contemporaries were especially appalled by the Jacquerie of 1358 because the regions where it occurred, and the men who participated, were precisely those whom they believed most satisfied with their lot. For the same reasons much less attention was paid to the sudden uprisings of the Tuchins in Languedoc after 1360, hiding in the woods, half-starved and poverty-stricken, although the effects of this movement were to be more profound and longer lasting. No-one was interested in a retarded and impotent peasantry.

Conclusion

In the mid-thirteenth century wandering bands of *pastoureaux* led by the visionary 'Master of Hungary' disturbed both secular and ecclesiastical authorities. With the approach of the Papal jubilee of 1300 there were several outbursts of millenarianism; these were also provoked by various wandering preachers in the countryside, especially in Italy. Even so, the countryside hardly ever witnessed the brief, impassioned outbursts that regularly shook the towns after 1280 or 1285 and continued uninterrupted into the fourteenth century. Keen observers, however, could and should have been able to detect the first signs of social disintegration, some of whose features we have just considered: the first decades of the fourteenth century were universally difficult, particularly after the return of famine in 1315 and 1316, and resounded with protests from the French aristocracy which threatened to overwhelm the royal administrative machine. The time came when social unrest reached village level; the great Flemish uprising of 1325–27 was like a dress rehearsal for the Jacquerie, although its rural character was blurred by the characteristic Flemish involvement of the towns. However, their chief was a village leader, Nicolas Zannequin, just like those of the Jacquerie. Admittedly, these *Karls*, as they were called, were brought rudely to their senses by the Valois army and kept in check until the uprising of 1358. Elsewhere the fire continued to smoulder – amongst both the visionary Flagellants who travelled through Lorraine, Alsace and the Rhineland and also the very poorest peasants who in around 1336–39 fled the villages and turned to brigandage in Quercy, around Narbonne and in Béarn, biding their time for the Tuchins of 1360. My account legitimately stops short of these signs of evident breakdown and a peasant world on the verge of collapse.

These fourteenth-century disturbances give rise to several observations: firstly, that between the early twelfth and the early fourteenth centuries the countryside had experienced two centuries of relative tranquillity; secondly, that once the system of lordship was established in the 150 or so years before 1100 social and economic unity was unquestionable, even when it embraced the birth and growth of the movement that carried the seeds of its downfall. My aim has been to present the birth and flowering of this peasant culture, not to describe the crises which brought it to an end: to conclude, I will summarize some of the most distinctive features of this evolution.

The characteristic which immediately springs to mind is the weakening of what, for want of a better word, we call 'feudalism' – that is of the tacit contract between the master (who exploited his peasants but was also the embodiment of the feeble state) and the men who worked for him because of their own physical need (*necessitas*) and also because of his *nobilitas*. The re-emergence of the state was undoubtedly a primary cause of this breakdown since it removed the master's monopoly of justice and protection – in short his *raison d'être*. But, in practical terms, this development was itself only one result of the progressive retreat of the landed aristocrat: obliged to face a price increase for which they were in fact responsible, since they had themselves unleashed the mechanisms of profit and of market forces on the rural economy; impelled towards increasingly heavy expenditure on luxuries, administration, arms, accoutrements and royal taxes; forced to throw themselves into escalating wars in the hope that the resulting booty would be their salvation but which, in practice, brought them to financial ruin and, moreover, isolated and debased them in the eyes of the peasantry – not only were they unable to revoke the grants made by their forefathers, worse still, they came under increasing pressure to make still further concessions. In about 1330–1340 24 of 38 lords with landed property documented near Bar-sur-Seine had less than 10 *livres* annual revenue; in Provence the Hospitallers abandoned labour services on three-quarters of their lands; in Forez only 1 *noble* in 15 could afford to have his son knighted; in England landholders were forced to allow appeals from their courts to that of the sheriff and, similarly, in northern France to the court of the *bailli*. The return on landed capital fell dramatically: quit-rents, whose level was fixed by custom and devalued in line with currency mutations, comprised only two per cent of seigneurial returns in the Ile-de-France and four per cent seems to have been the average return on lands leased to tenant farmers. What was the solution? To fight back in the manner I have already described, with an attempt to re-establish direct controls; or enforced cultivation of the remaining land, forest included; or, again, to drive the hardest possible bargain with tenant farmers on their lands? All of these methods were tried after 1260 or 1270 but only a small minority – those who controlled weak communities with lands that were poor or stretched over a vast area – were successful: the rest, threadbare and belligerent country squires, retreated into their useless strongholds. The splitting of the nobility into two destroyed the seigneurial system because it broke the reciprocal relationship between the master and his men and because it removed from lordship its grounds for existence.

At the same time the second pillar of the system was weakening: the painfully achieved equilibrium between ploughed lands and forest, cereal crops and livestock (which was the foundation of sound nutrition and good health appropriate for contemporary needs and resources) was irreparably disturbed. This was not a question of technical problems: the late medieval agrarian 'crisis' was characterized by increased yields and innovations; nor was it even a matter of relative overpopulation – although this was undoubtedly a factor in the fragmentation of landholdings between 1270 and 1350, a point to which I shall return – but the dramatic fall in population after the Black Death should have made it possible for this balance to be re-established; in fact this never happened. It was not these factors which had such a profoundly damaging effect on the medieval eco-system, but yet again, the introduction of a market economy when domestic production only reached subsistence level. Production with a view to sale superseded the simple goal of increasing landed capital. We have already seen that there was a growing number of specialized activities: some forest that had been brought into cultivation slipped back into its original state. This was not because of any shortage of man-power or because there was no demand for new land (on the contrary, there was strong and persistent population pressure right up to the Black Death), but because the contemporaries and descendants of those who thought that 'the forests had returned to France with the armies of the English' laid great stress on the possession of forests for hunting and other sports. They had every incentive to replant former woodlands with quick-growing conifers that could be used for a variety of purposes, rather than turn it to less profitable ploughed land. Even in regions like Sologne, the Limousin and parts of Germany where there is evidence of assarting as late as 1300, it stopped everywhere in the fourteenth century. There was also pressure from rulers towards re-afforestations because they saw them as important new resources: in England about 1200 the royal 'forest' annexed open clearings in the Chilterns, on Dartmoor and in Sherwood Forest; in the Empire in about 1309 Henry VII authorized the purchase (from himself, at a very good price) of lands for re-afforestation by the citizens of Nüremberg and Frankfurt. In France a tax was levied after 1280 or 1290 on the purchase of woodland (known as the *tiers ou danger*) and the creation in 1319 of a *maîtrise des forêts* (keepership of the forests) reflects the profit anticipated from felling. At the same time livestock also appeared a secure source of revenue, since there was a general increase in demand for wool, leather and red meat: driven out from the woods, the cattle had to be provided with grazing from cultivated land, even in areas where this requirement did not – as in England – result in woodland enclosure. Viticulture had similar consequences: the return from a vineyard was considerable, for the sales of wine in a good year repaid the capital investment and in the mid-fourteenth century the area covered by vines was extended in the Jura, around Metz and in the Charente. Finally, dye-plants and legumes were substituted for cereal crops on what arable land remained, since there was a huge, guaranteed market for them in towns and as fodder for cattle and horses; in Flanders it was accepted practice to plant turnips, peas and various root-crops on fallow land by 1360, if not earlier.

Such changes in traditional rural land-use proved fatal for the mixed subsistence farming that had been practised until then and there was an inevitable reduction in the volume of foodstuffs produced. Although there were other reasons and other features of the so-called agrarian 'crisis' which developed after 1310–20, there is no doubt that the falling rate of cereal production had the most acute effect upon contemporaries. It is significant that this reduction did not involve a rise in grain prices – the *sine qua non* of 'classic' food shortages in the fourteenth and fifteenth centuries – rather it was persistent stagnation that led to the ruin of small farmers. This novel situation arose because rulers and towns instigated the importation, not only of cereals, but also of other specialized products (foodstuffs and others) which were in high demand and consequently absorbed any residual liquid capital. After 1350, moreover, there was no longer a market for wheat because of the sharp fall in population after the Black Death. This presents us with the crucial phenomenon of a split within rural society itself, but it should come as no surprise to the reader, to whom I have attempted to demonstrate that even within the village community – and above all when privileges were renewed – the leading villagers, such as craftsmen, those who owned plough beasts, or churchwardens were at pains to ensure the continuance of the privileged status they had obtained from the lord. It was they who replanted, enclosed meadows, sowed saffron or woad; it was they again who were responsible for the division of common land and, after the beginning of the Hundred Years War (possibly even earlier in Italy and Germany) it was they who were authorized to bear arms, even to make agreements (*pâtis*) with free companies or pillagers: they were termed *capitaines* in northern France, *caps d'hostau* in the south – 'cock of the walk' we would almost say. It was relatively easy for them to negotiate long-term or even hereditary leases with a hard-pressed lord: indeed a third of them did just that in Normandy around 1360. Finally, they had the opportunity of making loans and of renting out implements or draught animals to the less wealthy. Very few labourers could afford the *sou* per day which it cost to hire a horse, however, and this section of society gradually slid, first towards debt, then towards the loss of personal liberty, in the manner I have already described. Moreover, the reduction in area of the available arable land meant that they had either all to crowd together or divide their holdings into even smaller segments. Before the Black Death 70 per cent of the peasants in Normandy had less than the four crucial hectares necessary for survival. A split between rich and poor in the village characteristic of 'modern' periods was beginning to be visible.

A final factor profoundly disturbed the pattern of life in the countryside: the towns inverted for their own profit the relationship they had hitherto had with the surrounding areas. Rural areas had always been predominant in the relationship between towns and the countryside, a source of food and even inhabitants. But once the city emerged from its economic and political isolation in the thirteenth century, it adopted two attitudes which became the norm until our own day. On the one hand the old process of osmosis with the neighbouring villages was no longer acceptable, with the circulation side-by-side of raw materials and finished goods from a variety of sources: after 1275 in Italy, 1320–25 in Provence and the Meuse region, Pisa, Siena, Aix and Liège all started to control immigration from the country. Rural immigrants were packed outside the walls, sometimes for several years. Demand for these measures undoubtedly came from the urban workforce rather than from the masters of guilds or the city's oligarchy: the aim was to prevent villagers from entering the town and threatening established urban workers, since they would work for far lower wages because they had no specialized training and could be more easily exploited. In Italy and Flanders this new outlook was accompanied by raids on nearby villages to destroy their implements or objects made or used by rural craftsmen. For the masters' reaction had been to have work done in the countryside rather than the town; as a result several regions, including Brabant, Brittany, Liguria and the areas around Lyons and Toulouse found that this reduced expenditure on wages was sufficient to contain some of the effects of the economic crisis. At first sight this appears very satisfactory, but one cannot fail also to see in it the beginnings of the domestication of peasant labour for the town.

The process went a step further with the possession of village lands by townsmen. As I have already said, this trend was negligible in our period. Although there are examples around Metz, Liège, Florence and Barcelona, the city-dweller seems to have been more interested in control of the market (including country fairs at which his workshop's products were sold) than in acquiring arable land or lordship – at the most he was involved in speculative dealings with a wood here, a vineyard there and a few meadows elsewhere. When this phenomenon became more widespread it signalled the end of village autonomy.

The imperative reasons for setting the early fourteenth century as a chronological limit for this study are now even clearer. Very little then remained of the peasant world of a few centuries earlier: the structure of seigneurial society was no more than an empty shell, the basis of seigneurial production had disappeared, the village community was split in two (and the master's likewise in some areas) and the countryside was starting to become subordinate to the town. This is what leads me to reject the notion (dear to many historians) of the continuity of a hierarchically based society from the high Middle Ages to the Ancien Régime. When eleventh-century thinkers formulated their clearly defined tri-partite schema even the word *laboratores* did not correspond precisely to 'peasants'. However, the concept of a social order at least established two notions: firstly, the role of producer, which devolved entirely upon a single category, largely but not entirely rural; secondly, the nature of the 'order' assigned to this particular group in the divinely appointed scheme of things which gave a specific role to each of them. There is no evidence to suggest that these concepts were more significant in the fourteenth and fifteenth centuries than they had been earlier: quite apart from the splintering of the group of 'tillers of the soil' that took place, there was no longer – if indeed there ever had been – any sense of corporate identity amongst the peasant population, or awareness of their supposed role as the providers of food for other members of society engaged in different tasks. French peasants of the Jacquerie, or the German peasants of the Peasants' War (1525), were not motivated by any sense of social hierarchy, not even as objects to hold up to ridicule; their demand was simply recognition as a social group, as an 'estate', and to deny it the name 'class' is the merest pedantry.

The history of the peasantry from the fourteenth to the twentieth century is a chequered one, with periods of expansion followed by a decline and, naturally, it lies outside the scope of this book. Even so, I do not feel it is an exaggeration to say that the peasant's situation was not to be as stable as it was in the first two centuries of his existence until the end of the nineteenth century (at least), if not until the apogee of rural France in 1900. It is true that the medieval period was neither a dark nor a golden age and nothing demonstrates this better than the history of the village. There were many permanent achievements, not least mastery of the soil, an understanding of the weather and a balanced system of production; others (such as autonomous village administration, freedom from the heavy shackles on individual liberty and possessions, or the understanding of even very basic machinery) were only glimpsed, even though tangible progress was made in these directions. Finally, in matters such as living conditions or political involvement no significant progress was made at all. But all of these endeavours left their mark on the countryside as we know it today. They are reflected in settlement patterns, transport networks and a highly developed sense of local identity. Now intensive urbanization occurs at such a pace that a little more of this heritage is destroyed every year: the preservation of what does remain is one of our most pressing tasks.

Glossary

agrière	Form of share-cropping (q.v.)
allod	Patrimonial freeholding held by natural inheritance, not subject to a feudal superior.
ard	Simple plough with a symmetrical ploughshare that does not turn over the soil.
assart	A piece of land cleared from woodland, heath or other scrubland.
ban	Area of seigneurial jurisdiction and the services owed within it.
cadastre, *cadastro*	Land-register (twelfth to fourteenth centuries) in Italy, France and Switzerland.
castelnau	New castellated village in Gascony (twelfth to thirteenth-centuries).
censier	List of rents and services in France.
champart	Form of share-cropping (q.v.).
charivari	Popular ritual mocking individuals, often as a result of second or unpopular marriages.
complant	Form of share-cropping lease whereby land is granted specifically for mixed arboriculture in return for a proportion of the harvest.
coutumier, custumal	Collections of customary law.
demesne, *domaine*	Seigneurial land remaining in the lord's hands, originally worked by the labour services of unfree peasants (cf. *réserve*).
denshireing	Burning of cleared weeds and turf and spreading the resultant ashes on the land.
escheat	Reversion of land to the lord on failure of heirs.

état des feux, *fouage* of 1328	French survey of hearths for taxation purposes.
incastellamento	Provision of a defensive wall and, normally, a castle for a settlement in Italy and parts of southern France.
infield-outfield system	Relationship of permanently and intensively cultivated land with larger areas only intermittently cropped.
latifundia	Very large estates of the late classical period.
manse	Frankish peasant tenement and unit of taxation and service (seventh to twelfth centuries).
métayage	Form of share-cropping (q.v.).
mezzadria	Form of share-cropping (q.v.).
partible inheritance	Division of possessions among heirs, normally brothers.
plebes cum oraculis	Rural parishes and chapels not possessing full parochial powers.
podzol	An acid soil where iron and aluminium compounds are leached from the soil and redeposited at a lower level.
polyptych	Survey of the landed and movable wealth of an ecclesiastical institution in the Carolingian period.
réserve	Seigneurial demesne (q.v.) as distinct from tenanted land (seventh to twelfth centuries).
retrait *lignagier*	Relative's right to buy back alienated land, or to be preferred as a purchaser.
seisin	Freehold possession; the act of taking such possession.
share-cropping	Form of landholding whereby the tenant pays a proportion of his crop to the owner rather than a money rent.
tallage (*exactio,* *questa, queste,* *taille*)	Monetary exaction levied on the peasantry; originally arbitrary, but later regulated by custom.
villein, *vilain*	Peasant or bondman of unfree status
weekwork	Regular agricultural service throughout the year in England (as opposed to boonworks, performed at specific periods, e.g. ploughing, harvesting, haymaking etc.).

Select Bibliography

General surveys

a)

Cipolla, C.M. (ed), *The Fontana economic history of Europe*, vol. 1: *The Middle Ages*, London/Glasgow, 1972.

Duby, G., *The early growth of the European economy: warriors and peasants from the 7th to the 12th century*, tr. H.B. Clarke, London, 1974.

Duby, G., *Hommes et structures du Moyen Age*, Paris, 1973 (partially tr. C. Postan as *The chivalrous society*, London, 1977).

Fossier, R., *Enfance de l'Europe x^e-xiie siècles; aspects économiques et sociaux*, 2 vols., Paris, 1982.

Fossier, R. (ed), *The Cambridge Illustrated History of the Middle Ages*, tr. S. H. Tenison, vol. 3: Cambridge, 1986; vol. 1: forthcoming; vol. 2: in preparation.

Genicot, L., *Le XIIIe siècle européen*, Paris, 1968.

Heers, J., *L'Occident aux xive et xve siècles: aspects économiques et sociaux*, 4th edn, Paris, 1973.

Le Goff, J., *La civilisation de l'Occident médiéval*, Paris, 1964.

b)

Abel, W., *Agricultural fluctuations in Europe*, tr. O. Oridish, London, 1980.

The Cambridge economic history of Europe, vol. 1: *The agrarian life of the Middle Ages*, 2nd edn, Cambridge, 1966.

Duby, G., *Rural economy and country life in the medieval West*, tr. C. Postan, London, 1968.

Fossier, R., and Higounet, C., Sources et problématique de l'histoire des campagnes, in *Tendances, perspectives et méthodes de l'histoire* *médiévale. Actes du C^e Congrès des sociétés savantes, Paris, 1975*, I, Comité des Travaux Historiques et Scientifiques, Paris, 1977.

Fourquin, G., *Le paysan d'Occident au Moyen Age*, Paris, 1972.

Hodgett, G.A.J., *A social and economic history of medieval Europe*, London, 1972.

Le Mené, M., *L'économie médiévale*, Paris, 1977.

Lewis, A.R., The closing of the mediaeval frontier 1250–1350, *Spec.*,

Postan, M., *The medieval economy and society. An economic history of Britain in the Middle Ages*, London, 1972.

Pounds, N.J.G., *An economic history of medieval Europe*, New York, 1974.

Slicher van Bath, B.H., *The agrarian history of western Europe, A.D. 500–1850*, 2nd edn, tr. O. Ordish, London, 1963.

Thrupp, S.L. (ed), *Change in medieval society. Europe North of the Alps 1050–1500*, New York, 1964.

Society and the economy in different countries

a)

Cipolla, C.M. (ed), *Storia dell'economia italiana*, Turin, 1959.

Fiumi, E., Sui rapporti economici tra città e contado nell'età communale, *Archivio storico italiano*, 114, 1956.

Jones, P.J., Per la storia agraria italiana nel Medio Evo: lineamenti e problemi, *Rivista storica italiana*, 76, 1964.

Leicht, P.S., *Operai, artigani, agricoltari in Italia dal secolo vi al xvi*, Milan, 1946.

Luzzatto, G., *An economic history of Italy: from the fall of the Roman Empire to the beginning of the sixteenth century*, tr. P.J. Jones, London, 1961.

b)

Gautier Dalché, J., *Economie et société dans les pays de la couronne de Castille*, London, 1982.

Jackson, G., *The making of medieval Spain*, London, 1972.

Marques, A.H.R. de O., *A sociedade medieval portuguesa*, 2nd edn, Lisbon, 1971.

Valdeavallano, L.G. de, *Historia de Espana*, vol. I: *Desde los origines hasta la baja edad media*, 5th edn, Madrid, 1973.

Vicens-Vives, J., *An economic history of Spain*, tr. F. M. López-Morillas, Princeton, 1969.

c)

Bloch, M., *French rural history. An essay on its basic characteristics*, tr. J. Sondheimer, London, 1966.

Duby, G. (ed), *Histoire de la France rurale*, vol. I: *La formation des campagnes des origines au xive siècle*, Paris, 1973.

d)

Aston, T.H., The English manor, *PP*, 10, 1956.

Bolton, J.L., *The medieval English economy, 1150–1500*, London/ Totowa, N.J., 1980.

Homans, G.C., *English villagers in the thirteenth century*, rev. edn, New York, 1960.

John, E., English feudalism and the structure of Anglo-Saxon society, *Bulletin of the John Rylands Library*, 46, 1963.

Miller, E. and Hatcher, J., *Mediaeval England. Rural society and economic change, 1086–1348*, London/New York, 1978.

Stenton, D.M., *English society in the early Middle Ages, 1086–1307*, 4th edn, Harmondsworth, 1965.

e)

Droege, G., *Deutsche Wirtschaftsgeschichte*, Frankfurt, 1974.

Franz, G., *Deutsche Agrargeschichte*, Stuttgart, 1967.

Franz, G., *Geschichte des deutschen Bauernstandes vom frühen Mittelalter bis zum 19. Jarhundert*, 2nd edn, Stuttgart, 1976.

Lütge, F., *Deutsche Sozial- und Wirtschaftsgeschichte*, 3rd edn, Berlin, 1966.

f)

Beech, G.T., *A rural society in medieval France. The Gâtine of Poitou in the eleventh and twelfth centuries*, Baltimore, 1964.

Bonnassie, P., *La Catalogne du milieu du xe siècle à la fin du xive siècle. Croissance et mutations d'une société*, 2 vols, Toulouse, 1975–6.

Chédeville, A., *Chartres et ses campagnes, xie-xiiie siécles*, Paris, 1973.

Deléage, A., *La vie rurale en Bourgogne jusqu'au début du onzième siècle*, 2 vols, Mâcon, 1942.

Devailly, G., *Le Berry, du xe siècle au milieu du xiiie. Etude politique, réligieuse, sociale et économique*, The Hague/Paris, 1973.

Duby, G., *La société aux xie et xiie siècles dans la région mâconnaise*, Paris, 1971.

Fossier, R., *La terre et les hommes en Picardie, jusqu'à la fin du xiiie siècle*, 2 vols, Paris/Louvain, 1968.

Fournier, G., *Le peuplement rural en Basse Auvergne durant le Haut Moyen Age*, Paris, 1962.

Genicot, L., *L'économie rurale namuroise au bas moyen âge, 1199–1429*, 2 vols, Louvain, 1943–82.

Harley, J.B., Population trends and agricultural developments from the Warwickshire Hundred Rolls of 1279, *Econ. H. R.*, 2nd ser., 11, 1959.

Harvey, B., *Westminster Abbey and its estates in the Middle Ages*, Oxford, 1977.

Harvey, P.D.A., *A medieval Oxfordshire village. Cuxham 1240–1400*, Oxford, 1965.

Hatcher, J., *Rural economy and society in the Duchy of Cornwall, 1300–1500*, Cambridge, 1970.

Higounet, C., *Le comté de Comminges de ses origines à son annexion à la couronne*, Toulouse/Paris, 1949.

Hilton, R.H., *A medieval society. The West Midlands at the end of the thirteenth century*, reissue, Cambridge, 1983.

King, E., *Peterborough abbey, 1086–1310. A study in the land market*, Cambridge, 1973.

Lennard, R.V., The demesnes of Glastonbury Abbey in the eleventh and twelfth centuries, *Econ. H.R.*, 2nd ser., 8, 1956.

Miller, E., *The abbey and bishopric of Ely. The social history of an ecclesiastical estate from the tenth century to the early fourteenth century*, Cambridge, 1951.

Perrin, C.E., *Recherches sur la seigneurie rurale en Lorraine d'après les plus anciens censiers, ixe-xiie siècle*, Paris, 1935.

Plaisse, A., *La baronie du Neubourg. Essai d'histoire agraire, économique et sociale*, Paris, 1961.

Poly, J.P., *La Provence et la société féodale, 879–1166*, Paris, 1976.

Postan, M.M., Glastonbury estates in the 12th century, *Econ. H.R.*, 2nd ser., 5, 1953; 9, 1956.

Raftis, J.A., *The estates of Ramsey abbey. A study in economic growth and organization*, Toronto, 1957.

Searle, E., *Lordship and community. Battle Abbey and its banlieu, 1066–1538*, Toronto, 1974.

Sivéry, G., *Les structures agraires et la vie rurale dans le Hainaut (de la fin du xiiie siècle au début du xvie siècle)*, Lille, 1973.

Stiennon, J., *Etude sur le chartrier et le domaine de l'abbaye de Saint-Jacques de Liège, 1015–1209*, Paris, 1951.

Titow, J.Z., *Winchester yields. A study in medieval agricultural productivity*, Cambridge, 1972.

Verhulst, A.E., *De Sint-Baafsabdij te Gent en haar grondbezit, viie-xive eeuw*, Brussels, 1958.

Verriest, L. (ed), *Corpus des records de coutumes et des lois de chefs-lieux de l'ancien comté de Hainaut*, Mons/Frameries, 1946.

Daily life and the countryside

a)

Alexandre, P., *Le climat au Moyen Age en Belgique et dans les régions voisines*, Liège/Louvain, 1976.

Le Roy Ladurie, E., *Times of feast, times of famine. A history of climate since the year 1000*, tr. B. Bray, London, 1972.

b)

Bradford, J., *Ancient landscapes: studies in field archaeology*, London, 1957.

Chaumeil, L., L'origine du bocage en Bretagne, in *Hommage à Lucien Febvre. Eventail d'histoire vivante*, 2 vols, Paris, 1953.

Clarke, H., *The archaeology of medieval England*, Oxford/London, 1984.

Faucher, D., L'assolement triennal en France, *Et. rurales*, 1, 1961.

Hoskins, W.G., *The making of the English landscape*, London, 1977.

Meynier, A., *Les paysages agraires*, Paris, 1958.

Orwin, C.S. and C.S., *The Open Fields*, 3rd edn, Oxford, 1967.

Le paysage rural: réalités et représentations. Actes du X^{éme} congrès des historiens médiévistes de l'enseignment supérieur public, Lille-Villeneuve d'Ascq, 18–19 mai, 1979 in *Revue du Nord*, 62, 1980.

Roberts, B.K. and Glassock, R.E. (eds), *Villages, fields and frontiers. Studies in rural settlement in the medieval and early modern periods*, British Archaeological Reports, International series 185, Oxford, 1983.

Sereni, E., *Storia del paesaggio agrario italiano*, Bari, 1961.

Soyer, J., *La conservation de la forme circulaire dans le parcellaire français*, Paris, 1970.

Verhulst, A., *Histoire du paysage rural en Flandre de l'époque romaine au xviiie siècle*, Brussels, 1966.

c)

Braunstein, P., Le fer et la production de fer en Europe de 500 à 1500, *Ann.*, 27, 1972.

Carus-Wilson, E.M., An industrial revolution of the thirteenth century, *Econ. H.R.*, 1st ser., 11, 1941.

Dion, R., *Histoire de la vigne et du vin en France, des origines au XIXe siècle*, Paris, 1959.

Gille, B., *Histoire des techniques, techniques et civilisations, technique et sciences*, [Paris], 1978.

Gille, B., Recherches sur les instruments de labour au Moyen Age, *BEC*, 120, 1962.

Grand, R., *L'agriculture au Moyen Age*, Paris, 1950.

Halpérin, J., Les transformations économiques aux xiie et xiiie siècles, *RHES*, 28, 1950.

Haudricourt, A.G. and Delamarre, J. B., *L'homme et la charrue à travers le monde*, 4th edn, Paris, 1955.

Joris, A. and Herbillon, J., Les moulins à guède en Hesbaye au Moyen Age, *RBPH*, 42, 1964.

Langdon, J., *Horses, oxen and technological innovation. The use of draught animals in English farming from 1066–1500*, Cambridge, 1986.

Lerche, G. and Steensberg, A., *Agricultural tools and field shapes*, Copenhagen, 1980.

Singer, C., Holmyard, E.J., Hall, A.R. and Williams, T.I. (eds), *A history of technology*, vol. 2: *The Mediterranean civilizations and the Middle Ages c.700 B.C. to c.A.D. 1500*, Oxford, 1956.

Slicher van Bath, B.H., *Yield ratios, 810–1820*, Wageningen, 1963.

Sprandel, R., Le production de fer au Moyen Age, *Ann.*, 24, 1969.

Stenton, F.M., The road system of medieval England, *Econ. H.R.*, 1st ser., 7, 1936.

Le vin au moyen âge. Production et producteurs. Actes du IIe, congrès des historiens médiévistes de l'enseignement supérieur public, Grenoble, 4–6 juin 1971, Grenoble, 1978.

White, L., Jr., *Mediaeval technology and social change*, Oxford, 1962.

Population and social groups

a)
Baratier, E., *La démographie provençale du xiiie au xvie siècle*, Paris, 1961.

Carpentier, E. and Glénisson, J., Bilans et méthodes: la démographie française au xive siècle, *Ann.*, 17, 1962.

La démographie médiévale. Sources et méthodes. Actes du Ier congrès des historiens médiévistes de l'enseignement supérieur public, Nice, 15–16 mai, 1970, Nice, 1972.

Fossier, R., La démographie médiévale: problèmes de méthode (xe-xiiie siècles), *Annales de démographie historique*, 1975.

Genicot, L., Sur les témoignages d'accroissement de la population en Occident du xie au xiiie siècle, *Cahiers d'histoire mondiale*, 1, 1953.

Lot, F., L'état des paroisses et des feux de 1328, *BEC*, 90, 1929.

Russell, J.C., *Late ancient and medieval population*, Philadelphia, 1958.

Titow, J.Z., Some evidence of the thirteenth century population increase, *Econ. H.R.*, 2nd ser., 14, 1961.

Villages désertés et histoire économique, xie-xviiie siècles, (Ecole pratique des hautes études), Paris, 1965.

b)

Coleman, E.R., Mediaeval marriage characteristics: a neglected factor in the history of medieval serfdom, *Journal of Interdisciplinary Hist.*, 2, 1971.

Delort, R., *Le Moyen Age. Histoire illustrée de la vie quotidienne*, Lausanne, 1972.

Famille et parenté dans l'Occident médiéval. Actes du colloque de Paris, 6–8 juin 1974, Rome, 1977.

La Femme dans les civilisations des xe-xiiie siècles. Actes du colloque tenue à Poitiers les 23–25 septembre 1976, Centre d'Etudes supérieures de civilisation médiévale, Poitiers, 1977.

Gaudemet, J., *Les communautés familiales*, Paris, 1963.

Goody, J., Thirsk, J. and Thompson, E.P. (eds), *Family and inheritance. Rural society in Western Europe, 1200–1800*, Cambridge, 1976.

Herlihy, D., Land, family and women in Continential Europe from 701 to 1200, *Traditio*, 18, 1962.

La Femme in *RSJB*, 12, 1962.

Krause, J., The mediaeval household: large or small?, *Econ. H.R.*, 9, 1956–7.

Painter, S., The family and the feudal system in twelfth-century England, *Spec.*, 35, 1960.

Power, E., *Medieval women*, ed. M.M. Postan, Cambridge, 1975.

Village, house and land holding

a)

L'archéologie du village médiéval, Publications du centre belge d'histoire rurale, 6, Louvain/Ghent, 1967.

Boüard, M. de, *Manuel d'archéologie médiévale*, Paris, 1975.

Chapelot, J. and Fossier, R., *The village and house in the Middle Ages*, tr. H. Cleere, London, 1985.

La construction au moyen âge. Histoire et archéologie. Actes du IIIe congrès des historiens médiévistes de l'enseignement supérieur public, Besançon 2–4 juin 1972, Besançon, 1973.

Cunliffe, B., Chalton, Hants: the evolution of a landscape, *Antiquaries Journal*, 53, 1973.

Demians d'Archimbaud, G., *Les fouilles de Rougiers. Contribution à l'archéologie de l'habitat rural méditerranée*, Paris, 1980.

Géographie historique du village et de la maison rurale. Actes du colloque de Bazas, 19–21 octobre 1978, Paris, 1979.

Wood, M., *The English mediaeval house*, London, 1965.
b)
Beresford, M. and Hurst, J.G., *Deserted medieval villages*, 2nd edn, London, 1971.
Bonenfant, P., La fondation des 'villes neuves' en Brabant au Moyen Age, *Vierteljahrschrift für Sozial- und Wirtschaftsgeschichte*, 49, 1962.
Boussard, J., Hypothèses sur la formation des bourgs et des communes en Normandie, *Annales de Normandie*, 8, 1958.
Cursente, B., *Les castelnaux de la Gascogne médiévale: Gascogne gersoise*, Bordeaux, 1980.
Duparc, P., Le cimetière, séjour des vivants (xie-xiie siècle), *BPH*, *1964*, 1967.
Fixot, M., *Les fortifications de terre et les origines féodales dans le Cinglais*, Caen, 1968.
Fournier, G., *Le château dans la France médiévale*, Paris, 1978.
Higounet, C., *Paysages et villages neufs du Moyen Age, Recueil d'articles*, Bordeaux, 1975.
Musset, L., Le cimetière dans la vie paroissale en basse Normandie (xie-xiie siècles), in *Cahiers Léopold Delisle*, Société Parisienne d'histoire et d'archéologie normandes, 1963.
Musset, L., Peuplement en bourgage et bourgs ruraux en Normandie du xe au xiiie siècle, *Cahiers de civilisation médiévale*, 9, 1966.
Musset, L., Une transformation du régime seigneurial: l'essor des bourgs ruraux normands, *TR*, 71, 1948.
Ourliac, P., Les villages de la région toulousaine au xiie siècle, *Annales*, 4, 1949.
Sawyer, P.H. (ed), *English medieval settlement*, London, 1979.
Settia, A.A., Incastellamento e decastellamento nell'Italia padana fra x e xi secolo, *Bollettino Storico-Bibliografico Subalpino*, 74, 1976.
c)
Antonetti, G., Le partage des forêts usagères ou communales entre les seigneurs et les communautés d'habitants, *RHDFE*, 1963.
Boutruche, R., *Une société provinciale en lutte contre le régime féodal: l'alleu en Bordelais et Bazadais du xie au xviiie s.*, Paris, 1947.
Caenegem, R.C. van, *The birth of the English common law*, Cambridge, 1973.
Castaing-Sicard, M., *Les contrats dans le très ancien droit toulousain xe-xiiie siècle*, Toulouse, 1959.
Droege, G., *Landrecht und Lehnrecht im hohen Mittelalter*, Bonn, 1969.
Fontette, F. de, *Recherches sur la pratique de la vente immobilière dans la région parisienne au Moyen Age*, Paris, 1957.

Fourquin, G., Les débuts du fermage: l'exemple de Saint Denis, *Et. rurales*, 22–4, 1966.

Harvey, P.D.A. (ed), *The peasant land market in medieval England*, Oxford, 1984.

Imberciadori, I., *Mezzadria classica toscana, con documentazione ined. dal ix al xiv secolo*, Florence, 1951.

Le domaine, in *RSJB*, 4 (1949).

La tenure, in *RSJB*, 3 (1938).

Ourliac, P., La convenientia, in *Etudes d'histoire du droit privé offertes à Pierre Petot*, [Paris], 1959.

Rackham, O., *Ancient woodland. Its history, vegetation and uses in England*, London, 1980.

Saint-Jacob, P. de, Etudes sur l'ancienne communauté rurale en Bourgogne, *Annales de Bourgogne*, 13, 1941; 15, 1943; 18, 1946; 25, 1953.

Sée, H., Les droits d'usage et les biens communaux, *Revue internationale de sociologie*, 6, 1898.

Human groups: status, movements and communities

a)

Boussard, J., Serfs et 'colliberti' (xie-xiie siècles), *BEC*, 107, 1947–8.

Boutruche, R., *Seigneurie et féodalité*, 2 vols, Paris, 1968–70.

Cam, H.M., The evolution of the medieval English franchise, *Spec.*, 32, 1957.

Chomel, V., 'Francs' et 'rustiques' dans la seigneurie dauphinoise au temps des affranchissements, *BPH, 1965*, 1968.

David, M., Les 'laboratores' jusqu'au renouveau économique des xie et xiie siècles, *Etudes d'histoire du droit privé offertes à Pierre Petot*, [Paris], 1959.

David, M., Les 'laboratores' du renouveau économique du xiie siècle à la fin du xive siècle, *RHDFE*, 1959.

Duparc, P., La commendise ou commende personnelle, *BEC*, 119, 1961.

Estey, F.N., The Scabini and the local courts, *Spec.*, 26, 1951.

Fourquin, G., *Lordship and feudalism in the Middle Ages*, tr. I. and A.L. Lytton Sells, London, 1976.

Hilton, R.H., Freedom and villeinage in England, *PP*, 31, 1965.

Hilton, R.H., *The decline of serfdom in medieval England*, 2nd edn, London, 1986.

Hyams, P.R., *King, lords and peasants in medieval England. The common law of villeinage in the 12th and 13th centuries*, Oxford, 1980.

Kieft, C. van de, Les *Colliberti* et l'évolution du servage dans la France centrale et occidentale (xe-xiie siècle), *TR*, 32, 1964.

Koch, A.C., L'origine de la haute et de la moyenne justice dans l'Ouest et le Nord de la France, *TR*, 21, 1953.

Kosminsky, E.A., The evolution of feudal rent in England from the XIth to the XVth centuries, *PP*, 7, 1955.

Mousnier, R., *Problèmes de stratification sociale*, Paris, 1978.

Ourliac, P., Le servage à Toulouse aux xiie et xiii siècles, *Economies et sociétés au moyen âge. Mélanges offerts à Edouard Perroy*, Paris, 1973.

Perrin, C.-E., Le servage en France et en Allemagne, in *Relazioni del X congresso internazionale di scienze storiche*, III, Florence, 1955.

Petot, P., Les fluctuations numériques de la classe servile en France du xie au xive siècles, in *Relazioni del X congresso internazionale di scienze storiche*, III, Florence, 1955.

Le Servage in *RSJB*, 2, 2nd edn, revd Brussels, 1959.

Verlinden, C., *L'esclavage dans l'Europe médiévale, vol. 1: Peninsule Ibérique-France* (Ghent, 1955).

b)

Dobson, R.B. (ed), *The Peasants' Revolt of 1381*, 2nd edn, London, 1983.

Duby, G., Les laïcs et la Paix de Dieu, in *Atti IV settimana La Mendola, 1966*, Milan, 1969.

Duby, G., Les pauvres des campagnes dans l'Occident médiéval jusqu'au xiiie siècle, *Revue historique de l'église de France*, 52, 1966.

Fossier, R., Les mouvements populaires en Occident au xie siècle, *Comptes rendus de l'Académie des Inscriptions et Belles Lettres*, 1971.

Fossier, R., Remarques sur l'étude des 'commotions' sociales aux xie et xiie siècles, *Cahiers de civilisation médiévale*, 16, 1973.

Fourquin, G., *Les soulèvements populaires au Moyen Age*, Paris, 1972.

Hilton, R.H., *Bondmen made free: medieval peasant movements and the English rising of 1381*, London, 1973.

Le Goff, J. (ed), *Hérésies et sociétés dans l'Europe préindustrielle (xie-xviiie s.). Communications et débats du colloque de Royaumont*, Paris, 1968.

Mollat, M. and Wolff, P., *The popular revolutions of the late Middle Ages*, tr. A.L. Lytton-Sells, London, 1973.

Musy, J., Mouvements populaires et hérésies au xie siècle en France, *RH*, 253, 1975.

c)

Arvizu, F. de, Les fors espagnols au Moyen Age: problèmes et bibliographies, *RHDFE*, 1979.

Ault, W.A., The village church and the village community in mediaeval England, *Spec.*, 45, 1970.

Bader, K.S., *Studien zur Geschichte des mittelalterlichen Dorfes*, vol. 1:

Das mittelalterliche Dorf als Friedens- und Rechtsbereich (Weimar, 1957); vol. 2: *Dorfgenossenschaft und Dorfgemeinde* (Cologne/Graz, 1962).

Bosl, K., *Die Gesellschaft in der Geschichte des Mittelalters*, 2nd edn, Göttingen, 1969.

Boulet, M., La loi de Daours (1239), *Revue du Nord*, 31, 1949.

Colin, H., La charte de Beaumont-en-Argonne (1182), *Revue historique ardennaise*, 12, 1977.

Les communautés villageoises en Europe occidentale, du moyen âge au temps modernes, 4e journées de Flaran, 8–10 septembre 1982, Flaran IV, Auch, 1984.

Dubled, H., La communauté de village en Alsace au xiiie siècle, *RHES*, 41, 1963.

Du Boulay, F.R.H., *The lordship of Canterbury. An essay on medieval society*, London, 1966.

Duparc, P., Confréries du Saint-Esprit et communautés d'habitants au moyen âge, *RHDFE*, 1958.

Font-Rius, J.-M., Chartes de peuplement et chartes de franchises de la Catalogne, in *XXXIXe Congrès de la Fédération Languedoc-Roussillon, 1966*, Montpellier, 1967.

Fossier, R., *Chartes de coutume en Picardie xi–xiiie siècles*, Paris, 1974.

Le Bras, G., Les confréries chrétiennes, Problèmes et propositions, *RHDFE*, 19–20, 1940–1.

Libertés urbaines et rurales du xie au xive siècle: colloque international 4–6 septembre, 1966, Centre Pro Civitate, Spa, 1968.

Mariotte-Löber, R., *Villes et seigneurie: les chartes de franchise des comtes de Savoie fin xiiie siècle-1343*, Annecy, 1973.

Perrin, C.-E., *Catalogue des chartes de franchise de la Lorraine antérieures à 1350*, Metz, 1924.

Perrin, C.-E., Les chartes de franchise de la France: état des recherches: Le Dauphiné et la Savoie, *RH*, 231, 1964.

Reynolds, S., *Kingdoms and communities in Western Europe, 900–1300*, Oxford, 1984.

Santini, G., '*I communi di pieve*' nel medioevo italiano, Milan, 1964.

Semousous, J., Chartes de coutume et de franchise d'entre Cher et Sioule du xiiie au xviiie siècles, *Revue d'Auvergne*, 1956.

Toulgouat, P., *Voisinage et solidarités dans l'Europe du moyen âge: 'lou besi de Gascogne'*, Paris, 1981.

Vaillant, P., *Les libertés des communautés dauphinoises des origines au 5 janvier 1355*, Annecy, 1951.

Verriest, L., La fameuse charte-loi de Prisches, *RBPH*, 2, 1923.

Walraet, M., Les chartes-lois de Prisches (1158) et de Beaumont-en-Argonne (1182). Une contribution à l'étude de l'affranchissement des classes rurales du xiie s., *RBPH*, 23, 1944.

Index

Mâconnais, 34, 107, 127, 155, 166
Main, river, 64
Maine, 64, 107, 110, 172, 173
markets, 6, 148–50, 171, 175
Marmoutier, abbot of, 173
marriage, 19–23, 38, 47, 73, 78
  taxes on, 136, 154, 155, 157
mayor, of village, 166, 177, 184
Merton, Statute of, 116
Metz, 98, 189, 192
Meuse, valley of, 8, 157, 191
Middelburg, 87
Middlesex, 15
Milan, 173
mill, 32, 66, 99–100, 136, 138–9,
  147, 167, 171
monasteries, estate management by,
  16, 56–7, 81, 100, 111–12, 115,
  117, 119, 133, 140, 145, 151
Monforte, 173
Montaillou, 39, 60, 65
Morlasas, 180
mortality, 10–11, 16–17, 83–4

Namur, Namurois, 10, 39, 144
Naples, 141
Narbonne, 187
Norfolk, 63
Normandy, 15, 25, 45, 54, 55, 57,
  64, 116, 124, 143, 157, 163,
  182, 190, 191
  Norman revolt (996), 45–6, 172
  see also invasions
Nüremberg, 189

Odoorn, 57, 67
Oisans, 15, 69
Oloron, 180
Oppy, 183
osteology, 3, 4, 82–3, 117
Oxfordshire, 58, 63, 71, 87, 131

palaeobotany, 3, 16, 87
Palladius, 97, 99
Papacy, 181
Paris, region, 13, 182
parish, 14, 51, 53, 54, 63, 162, 164

parochial system, establishment of,
  14, 53–4, 162
partible inheritance, 35, 36, 132,
  146
  see also inheritance customs
Patarene revolt, 173, 181
peasant house, 6
  plans and types of, 60–1, 63,
  68–70, 71–2, 74
  subdivision of, 8, 21, 73
peasant landholdings
  fragmentation of, 15, 34, 36, 122,
  133, 142, 146, 188, 191
  size of, 143, 146, 148
  vacant, 167, 189
peasantry
  attitudes to lord of, 45–6, 110,
  131–2, 134, 136, 138–9, 142,
  146, 149, 163, 166–7, 172, 173,
  179, 188
  condition of, 23, 44, 82–5, 113,
  147–8, 154–5, 174, 179, 184–7
  divisions within, 8, 74, 100, 139,
  141, 146, 150, 164, 166–7, 174,
  175, 177–8, 190–1
Pen er Malo, 69
Perche, 74, 123
Périgord, 72
personal names, significance of,
  28–9
Picardy, 15, 16, 34, 39, 46, 57, 61,
  62, 64, 98, 100, 102, 104, 107,
  108, 110, 114, 115, 116, 127,
  143, 146, 148, 155, 157, 163,
  176, 179, 183
Piedmont, 55, 107
Pisa, 191
Pisan, Christine de, 32
place names, evidence of, 50, 63, 94,
  107
plough, 94, 97–9, 118
Po, valley of, 8, 45, 106, 181
Poitou, 35, 54, 61, 99, 103, 106,
  107, 109, 117, 127, 149, 162
Poland, 10, 37, 48, 53, 67, 98
polyptychs, 13, 50, 115, 142, 178
Ponthieu, 184